SPYWORLD

Inside the Canadian and American Intelligence Establishments

Mike Frost

as told to

Michel Gratton

Doubleday Canada Limited

Canadian Cataloguing in Publication Data applied for
ISBN 0-385-25494-6

Jacket design by Amy King
Front jacket photographs by Comstock
Back jacket and all inside photographs by Danny Frost
Printed on acid-free paper
Printed and bound in the U.S.A.

Published in Canada by
Doubleday Canada Limited
105 Bond Street
Toronto, Ontario
M5B 1Y3

ACKNOWLEDGEMENTS

My deepest gratitude to all the people whose path I have crossed and without whom this book would not exist. Especially to Carole, Tony, Danny and David, for their love, support and encouragement; Marguerite, for being the best sister any brother could have; Michel for listening, for being a master at expressing my thoughts and feelings, and for his shrewd political antennas; my agent, for believing it could be done; John Pearce, for accomplishing the impossible.

Mike Frost

Thanks a million to Mike Frost, mostly for the trust he put in me, but also for telling me so courageously and frankly one of the greatest stories I've heard. And to his wife, Carole, and son Danny, who contributed more than they think to helping me achieve this. As usual, thanks to my agent, who provided great support at a crucial time in the writing of this book. The same goes for John Pearce and Doubleday Canada, who took the gamble. Others, who contributed a great deal and deserve our gratitude also, will have to remain anonymous. But Mike and I are in their debt.

Michel Gratton

CONTENTS

The following names of CSE, NSA, CIA or External Affairs employees are all pseudonyms: Steven Blackburn, Frank Bowman, Charles Clark, Mary Cook, Alan Foley, Tom Murray, Patrick O'Brien, Guy Rankin, Richard Robson, Greg Smythe, Victor Szakowski, Lloyd Taylor, Peter Vaughn, Sharon West.

PREFACE

MANY OF YOU WILL ASK WHY.

Why did I decide to co-operate fully in writing this book when so much of the information I divulge may seem harmful to the employer I gave my body and soul to for almost twenty years of my life?

Some of you may have the reflex to brand me as unpatriotic. I understand that. There are many people who would rather not know what is revealed here and believe that to expose it is damaging to Canada.

Let me make one thing clear. Nothing matters more to me, with the exception of my family, than the welfare of my beloved country, Canada. It may not change your opinion, but I assure you that is my belief.

After years of holding secrets within myself that I couldn't discuss except with a handful of people, after all that time of doing what I felt to be my duty for my country with very few Canadians knowing about it, I have come to believe that the people have a right to know what is really going on when it comes to the Canadian government and international espionage.

We can no longer hide our heads in the sand and pretend that we are bystanders, not part of the game. We cannot be hypocritical any more about our tame and "neutral" nature. Because when it comes to the gathering of intelligence, we are neither tame nor "neutral". In fact, we have become pretty good and aggressive at it. Indeed, I feel proud that I was part of the team that brought us into the "big leagues" of the espionage-intercept world.

I have also become fully aware of my former employer's formidable potential for abuse and invasion of private lives. I did it myself, against my natural instincts, but again, out of "duty".

I hope it is well understood that this all started and went on during the days of the "Cold War". It was easy to hide behind "national security" when the Soviet nuclear threat was upon us. Nuclear threat is still a valid concern, but surely things have changed to a point where government agencies like my former employer, the Communications Security Establishment (CSE), should no longer be totally unaccountable, not only to the people but to the elected Parliament of their country. There is simply too much power behind those secretive walls at CSE's Heron Road headquarters not to curb it in some way.

Such transformations have already taken place in the United States where the National Security Agency has become more open, but perhaps more so in Britain where the Goverment Communications Headquarters has now been forced into greater transparency. The head of MI5, Stella Rimmington, much as she seemed uncomfortable in the role, even had to give a press briefing recently.

I believe this has to take place in Canada too. I believe the Auditor-General should give the taxpayers at least a vague idea about how, where and for what purpose their money is being spent. And that can only come if our Parliament also gets to oversee CSE's budget, instead of letting the Defence Department fudge it.

In a perfect world, CSE would not be necessary. Unfortunately it is. But its methods and, surely, the reporting of its activities must be revised.

I hope this book will help explain why. It will also tell you where a lot of your tax dollars are going, and help you decide whether it is worth it or not.

I have provided a lot of information in this book that no doubt will send shockwaves through CSE and probably the entire Canadian government — not to mention foreign countries. But, in doing so, and in selecting what information to give, I have been careful not to threaten national security or endanger the lives of agents who are still in the field at the present moment.

These concerns were paramount to me, since I have great respect for those who gave me the opportunity to have an exciting and challenging career, just as much as I care for those men and women who are still there pursuing their calling with the firm belief that Canada will be grateful. This is perhaps another reason for writing this book: my sincere hope that our government and the higher authorities within CSE will recognize a little more how high the price can be for performing the duties required of its employees. Maybe some good will come of this, some beneficial changes in procedure.

Finally, another reason for this book was my love and concern for my family, my wife Carole, and my three sons, Tony, Danny and David. They never had a father or husband like other families had. Maybe this book will go some way to fill the void in their hearts and answer the questions they were never able to ask.

Mike Frost

"THERE IS A SERIOUS moral issue involved in a government employing a secret agency whose *modus operandi* requires it necessarily to break the laws of other nations. It may be argued that the existence of an agency with such a mandate brings with it a risk of influencing the practices of a country's security intelligence agency. Lawbreaking can become contagious both within a country's 'intelligence community' and amongst those senior officials of government and the national political leaders who are responsible for directing the intelligence community. Were this to happen in Canada it could seriously undermine reforms which we hope will be put in place to guard against illegality and impropriety in the activities of the security intelligence agency and the RCMP. On the other hand, it may be argued that so long as this risk is recognized, and the proper controls are in effect, the risk of such influence and contagion can be minimized."

Commission of Inquiry Concerning Certain Activities of the Royal Canadian Mounted Police (The McDonald Commission.) Second Report: "Freedom and Security under the Law," August 1981.

PROLOGUE

IT WAS AN UNUSUAL LETTER. Everything about it was unusual.

First, there was the line, or rather the warning: "If anybody ever asks me if I wrote this letter, I'll deny it. If anybody ever asks you if you received this letter, please deny it." It was one thing to have someone issue such a veiled threat verbally, but it was totally strange, if not absurd, to put it in writing.

But then in 1971 Mike Frost's whole world was on the verge of the unreal. How else could it be in the Arctic's windswept frozen desert, performing a tedious job he had been trained to believe was vital to the security, even the survival, of the free world? He was in Alert, Ellesmere Island, 600 miles from the North Pole, the closest military listening post to a U.S.S.R. that was poised to strike just beyond the frigidly white horizon. The Arctic was the gateway to an invasion of North America and, in the Cold War days of the sixties and seventies, such a menace was not only the stuff of fiction. Canada was sandwiched between two superpowers who might start to take pot-shots at each other with ballistic missiles. The Soviets saw Canada as the first battleground, the Americans considered it a security buffer.

Alert, on Canadian soil, was then, as it is today, manned by Canadian personnel, mostly military. But everyone involved knew the Yanks were running the show. After all, since it was their equipment Canada was using, it was only natural that they give the orders and that the Canadians rigorously obey. And Alert itself had been the

Yanks' brainchild, since they had no location on U.S. territory, even in Alaska, that could provide an intercept station so close to the Soviet Union. Such an abrogation of sovereignty was not something Canada's political leaders would boast about, of course, nor even admit. In fact, everything was done to cover up American involvement — even though U.S. military "advisors" regularly visited the base and stayed for two to three weeks at a time. These advisors and their superiors, right up to the top of the renowned spy-catching National Security Agency, "tasked" the Canadians and collected their data. But Canada was as powerless in relation to American dominance as it was against a Soviet strike. The former, although far from ideal, was infinitely the more desirable of the two.

Mike Frost didn't know it at the time, but he was about to become a crucial pawn in a much bigger game. It would engulf the next twenty years of his life and catapult him into the world of international intrigue and espionage. He couldn't have suspected it, since in peacetime this was not a likely activity for a Canadian government employee, simply because no Canadian government would sanction it. Espionage on that level was out of Canada's league and left to the big boys.

But what if the big boys took Canada onto their team? The Americans would do the training. A Canadian uniform, passport, residence and government job would make the perfect cover for someone who would really be an American spy, paid for by Canada but working for the United States.

This was all foreign to Frost the day he got the letter from Frank Bowman. As a Navy-trained communications intercept operator, Frost knew something about the intimate co-operation between the Pentagon and Canada's military surveillance operations. He had listened in on more Soviet fishing trawlers, commercial ships and — if he got very lucky — the odd nuclear submarine than he cared to remember. But his involvement was essentially that of a desk clerk pushing around paper that to him was totally meaningless.

Bowman's letter was highly intriguing. "Would you be interested in going to Moscow?" it said. "We are setting up something in

Moscow that I am not at liberty to tell you about . . . you would be posted as a military clerk."

Frost was on the next plane out of the cold. That caused quite a stir among his colleagues in Alert, who were envious of the fact that, although posted for a six-month sentence, he had served only four. What connections did he have in high places?

None to speak of, really. But Mike Frost liked what he did and believed it was right. He had the know-how, the talent and the dedication that made him an ideal candidate for something that would test his loyalty to the full.

He was exhilarated at the prospect of something that sounded both exotic and exciting. Moscow had been to him so far a remote puppetmaster pulling strings that he sought to cut with limited means. Now he was being sent backstage to do . . . well, what *was* he to do? No matter. Few intercept operators could dream of such a posting. Whatever the job was, it beat Alert and all his earlier assignments.

As Frost boarded the Hercules, he knew it would be a noisy, uncomfortable and incredibly long flight. He didn't have a clue that the real roller-coaster ride awaited him on the ground, in Ottawa.

In time, this unprecedented operation would turn Canada's Communications Security Establishment (CSE) into an aggressive arm of the American National Security Agency (NSA) anywhere in the world. Frost's baby would become known by a codename so secret it is still capable of sending a chill through Canada's little known and underrated spying community. It would be called "Project Pilgrim".

ONE
WHERE DID MY LIFE GO?

MIKE FROST HAD JUST HIT a 200-yard drive off the tee, straight down the middle of the fairway. He should have felt elated when his golfing companions marvelled at his prowess, as avid golfers always do. Though every avid golfer knows that, secretly, the congratulations really mean that they hate your guts at that very moment. It's a lot like writers who read a powerful piece of prose and praise it, but in their hearts wish they had written it themselves.

Yeah, Mike was happy with his shot. He loved the game, he loved the balmy weather. He loved living in his 1,800-square-foot retirement home in a mobile home-park in Bradenton, Florida, on the Gulf of Mexico, just a little north of Sarasota. "Nice and easy" was the way to describe the pace of life in the resort city of 250,000 souls — most of them "snowbirds", many of them, like Mike, spending six months in Florida in the winter, six months in Canada in the summer to qualify for Ontario Health Insurance Plan benefits. Walks on the beach, swimming in the pool every day, biking all around. His most pressing responsibilities were making sure the mobile home-park community activities went well. His wife Carole was into arts and crafts, on the kitchen committee. He played shuffleboard, organized tournaments. A lot of Canadian friends. Retirement like you dream of it.

He was only 52, clean and sober. His greatest worry of the day was to check on how well his grapefruits were doing in the back-yard. And once in a while he would have a chat with "Alphonse".

That's how he referred to any of the Florida lizards that crawled around just about every lawn and were masters at catching mosquitoes. And, as always, there was golf. Lots of golf.

But as he's walking down the fairway to set up for his iron shot to the green, somehow Mike Frost isn't a happy man. Nobody around him can really tell. After all, for years he has been trained not to show his emotions, not to show who he really is.

At first Florida was so enjoyable that he wondered why he hadn't thought of it sooner. But the memories that he had sworn to himself he would forget forever kept crawling back into his mind. And, along with them, some qualms and concerns about many of the covert actions he had engaged in or had known about.

Mike Frost was a spy. A retired one. But still a spy, who had served his country, Canada, and the U.S. and Great Britain for more than twenty years.

The pace of his life had gone from 200Ks an hour to a dead stop. And, as the quiet days went on, he found himself wondering how "the game" he had sacrificed so much for, and "the players" he had shared so many sorrows and joys with, were doing. He wished he could pick up a phone and find out. International espionage, of course, does not work that way. He realized how much he would like to tell the world, especially his fellow Canadians, what he had done for them. At the same time, he started to wonder whether perhaps he should not do so as a matter of public interest. Because he wasn't so sure what was right or wrong any more.

This was late 1990. A few months before, Mike Frost had resigned from the Communications Security Establishment, the most secret espionage and counter-espionage agency in Canada. So secret, in fact, that few Canadians are even aware of its existence, despite its roster of at least 1,000 employees and payroll of some $40 million — not to mention its well dissimulated budget within the National Defence Department. Even among those supposed "experts" from the outside, who claim to know what CSE is really up to, there are few, if any, who know the real story.

The truth is that Canada has been actively engaging in espionage operations in foreign countries since 1972. And Mike Frost was in on the very first foray, in Moscow. Moreover, he and his colleague Frank Bowman were the first two Canadians to set up what is known within the intelligence community as "embassy collection." Because, as most initiated people in the field know, the days of "James Bond era" spying operations are gone. Espionage is now the stuff of intricate satellite systems and the interception of communications. In other words, you do not need people to pose as friendly "spies" any more, when you can get better information by tapping into the communications of the country from which you seek to gain inside information. Having electronic equipment and the proper location to cover it up is far more efficient.

In Canada's case, these "embassy-collection" operations have been conducted from some of our diplomatic chancelleries around the world for most of the last twenty years. With the help and particularly the muscle of the American NSA and the co-operation of the British Government Communications Headquarters (GCHQ), CSE agents have been sent on missions in foreign lands to do what Canada previously used to do only in wartime: espionage.

Mike Frost was one of the two men who were tasked, way back in 1971, with setting it all up and carrying it out. What they started with very little means turned out to be a lot bigger than any of their superiors — particularly the politicians who authorized it — ever expected. Mike Frost's story is, in fact, the story of how a supposedly "tame" country like Canada inched into and eventually became a fully-fledged participant in international spying operations.

And now in 1994 he assumes Canada is just as active. Why would it not be? Are we now in Beijing? he asks himself. Did the boys get into Baghdad during the Gulf War? How about Teheran? What are Canada and its NATO intelligence allies doing these days in Serbia and Bosnia?

Are the Canadian intercept spies still in New Delhi monitoring Sikh communications as well as they did until the day he left? Is the "Sphinx" operation still on in Moscow? Did CSE ever establish a permanent site in Bucharest — a city he holds dear to his heart if only because he almost left his life there? And is CSE, as he would expect, still monitoring the Soviet embassy in Ottawa from the corner of Charlotte and Laurier Streets?

How big is "Project Pilgrim" now? Not only was it Frost's baby, it was named after his boat. There were about thirty people involved in "embassy collection" at CSE when he left. It's got to be bigger now, because "embassy collection" just kept growing. What kind of budget do they have to work with? That was always a concern. Because when you're involved in espionage, the last thing you want to worry about is money. You simply have to have it when the need arises.

He smiles as he remembers all the stuff that came out on the British royal family, Lady Di, Fergie and Charles. That must have come from foreign agencies' intercept, he thinks. If GCHQ was involved, it would not have done that job itself. It would rather have asked a trusted "ally" to do it, maybe even the Canadians. Too sensitive, even within the intelligence community, for anybody to admit it. His experience tells him that if GCHQ was involved, it would refuse to identify the source and put itself in a position to say "no, it never came from us."

But Frost knows better. He knows how, in "the game", intelligence of this kind is shared between the partners that are Great Britain, the U.S. and Canada. But when a final report arrives on a minister's or a Prime Minister's or a Queen's desk, the source is never identified.

He wonders what his NSA buddies are up to in 1994, and about the latest developments at College Park, the secret American "special-collection" operation that is alternately run by an NSA and a CIA appointee. He chuckles when he thinks that, even within NSA, most people don't even have a clue College Park exists. He does. He was there. Several times. When Frost resigned, the CIA was technically in charge. But Frost knew that it didn't matter who had the top job at College Park: NSA ran the show, with orders coming directly from the White House — when they didn't make them up themselves.

Reverting to Canada, one thing bothers him more than any other. Is CSE still trying to spy on Quebec separatists? In 1994, there would be more reason than ever. Despite his devotion to duty, he never liked the fact that Canadians were running espionage on their own citizens, no matter what their political option might be. "We were spying on ourselves," he tells himself. "Or maybe we asked the Brits or the Americans to do it for us. Is that right?" After years of rarely questioning it, these days Frost is shocked by the enormous potential for abuse CSE has. He is a decent man. But he finds himself telling his wife Carole: "Can you imagine if my neighbour knew what I could do to him?" His neighbours happen to have a so-called portable phone — a "spy's dream," as Frost calls it, because it radiates so much you can pick up the conversation from two blocks away. All you need is a receiver and a spectrum analyser, stuff you can buy at Radio Shack. Indeed, with the electronic gear available, CSE can get basically whatever it wants, from anywhere. It can pipe into a phone line without even having to plant a "bug" in it.

Long-distance telephone conversations are easiest to pick up. Locally, it's more complicated because you have to get into the "land lines". But even then, if the local system gets overloaded, it automatically switches from the "land line" to microwave communications. Basically Frost knows that if CSE wants something badly enough, it can intercept whatever it wants, whenever it wants and never get caught.

From the top floor of the CSE building, on Heron Road in Ottawa, there is a room that faces southwest straight down Baseline Road. There are receivers in there that can intercept any telephone conversation that goes through microwave towers. And a lot of communications traffic goes through Ottawa — from Newfoundland to Vancouver. So many times, just for the heck of it, Frost and his colleagues would turn the equipment on and "listen in", plain as day, on anything their electronic gear could catch. Nobody would question it.

There was no watchdog. They just did whatever they felt like doing. Theoretically they were "testing the gear" to see if it would work once they got it into foreign countries. But, in fact, they were intruding on the privacy of the people they were supposed to protect.

Increasingly Frost finds himself thinking about how scary this power is. How do the Canadian people feel about CSE's capability for doing this kind of thing? Sometimes, it was a little eerie for him to hear certain conversations, knowing that the persons speaking believed it was entirely private. This was different from his days as a Navy intercept operator. Back then, he was trying to get the "enemy", the Russian Bear. But these were Canadians whose privacy he felt he was invading without them having any authority to challenge the action.

It had really started to bother him deeply when CSE was asked by the Security Service of the RCMP to spy on the then Prime Minister's wife Margaret Trudeau. "It's not that I'm that much of an ethical person," he once told his boss Steven Blackburn. "But we are being asked to spy on the Prime Minister's wife, for chrissakes! We are a handful of people here who have the power to abuse the rights of the entire Canadian population." He also wondered where the order came from. Did the RCMP decide to investigate on its own or did they take their orders from a higher political source?

And what about the operation they did for British Prime Minister Margaret Thatcher? A little paranoid that Iron Lady, he thought.

He asks himself: "When there are abuses, who the hell knows? Who cares? Something's not right here."

CSE does not answer to anybody, really, except a committee of bureaucratic mandarins. It does not have to report to the House of Commons Intelligence and Security Committee. In the final analysis, it really benefits, in Canada, only the senior bureaucrats who control it and, ultimately, the Prime Minister, who is directly responsible for CSE. "We don't really answer to anybody at all," Frost once said to Bowman. "And even the people we answer to don't really want to know what we're up to. They just want to cover their ass all the way, so they'll be able to say they didn't know."

Mike Frost sacrificed a lot for CSE. His family, his friends, his health. Did his country really benefit from it? Because, all in all, that is all he wanted to happen. Was it all worth it? He thinks about his CSE colleague who blew his brains out by putting a shotgun in his mouth. He remembers the CSE employee who committed suicide in broad daylight in the parking lot of the Establishment by putting a garbage bag around his head and strapping his head to his car's exhaust pipe. Was he trying to send a message to the world? Nobody at CSE seemed to care, as long as the news didn't get out. Just replace him. His seat is still warm and there's another body in there to do his job.

In a way, Frost is lucky to be alive himself.

In his last two years at CSE, from 1988 to 1990, he was tasked with a range of jobs no normal human being could have possibly accomplished. He was still in on the "embassy-collection" operation, was in charge of upgrading the information-processing lab at CSE — a monumental job — and was also the Canadian representative for the NATO Advisory Committee for Special Intelligence (NACSI). On top of that, he also represented Canada on another little-known international committee known as SIGDASYS, where intelligence is selectively shared with allies who are not members of NATO. (He can't help but be puzzled as to how these committees operate today. When he spoke for Canada at their meetings, the U.S.S.R. was still whole, and German reunification was just around the corner. Are we now sharing intelligence with yesterday's enemy?)

He feels frustrated as he remembers how many hats CSE asked him to wear in his last days with the Establishment. Maybe he took on too much. But Mike Frost was not one to turn his back.

Frost was also, by that time, battling the cunning disease of alcoholism, attending as many AA meetings as he could. He was sober, but he knew in his heart his sobriety was not strong. And, as so often happens when people are saddled with this kind of pressure, he looked for an escape. He had an affair with his secretary, who introduced him to smoking pot.

Three weeks later, he was drinking again. Heavily. Once that started, things got worse by the minute. He was drinking two forty-ouncers a day, and more. His marriage was falling apart, as well as his professional life. Whether he was suffering from burn-out or breakdown, he doesn't know. But he knows he was not the smooth-operating efficient machine he once had been.

One particular weekend, he was on his boat *Pilgrim*, with his wife and another couple. He got so drunk that he went into a black-out and came to on July 31st, 1989. There were empty bottles of vodka, cognac, brandy, rum, wine, beer, whatever was there, all around him.

His wife Carole had left a note on the dashboard of the boat, along with a quarter. It read: "I've left you 25 cents to call for help, when you decide you need help. I love you."

He had no car keys, no boat keys, nothing. He staggered to the pay-phone on the dock and called CSE. He was on holiday, but he figured at that point that the first people he should make aware of his condition were his employers. He got in touch with his new boss, Lloyd Taylor. By that time Frank Bowman had retired.

"I need help," he said.

"You don't have a drinking problem," said Taylor.

"Trust me. I do. I've had two years of sobriety, I've now been drunk for about three weeks. I need help."

"Where are you?"

"I'm on my boat at Indian Lake Marina."

"Stay where you are. I'll come and get you."

Taylor made the two-hour drive from Ottawa to Indian Lake and picked him up. He brought him to the Royal Ottawa Hospital, where they sent him to the Detox centre. He spent seven days in what can only be qualified as hell on earth. Going "cold turkey" when you have been consuming somewhere between 80 and 100 ounces of vodka a day is a terrifying experience. He went through the shakes, the sweats, convulsions, delirium tremens, moments where his heart was pounding so hard he felt it was going to burst out of his chest. At times he was just rolling on the floor screaming in pain. All this in a room with five other guys in a similar condition.

At some point, the Detox orderly suggested perhaps he should be in the hospital. But that was against Frost's training in life. He felt he had to suffer the pain he had inflicted on himself. Finally, after a nightmarish week, he was sent back to the Royal Hospital for another two weeks of "coming down", and eventually ended up at Meadow Creek for a 28-day rehabilitation program.

Frost would realize later that, in those terrible three weeks, he was actually trying to kill himself. In fact, just a couple of days before he made the phone call to CSE, he had let himself roll off the deck of his boat into the water, wanting to drown. Somehow, he had just kept floating back to the surface. During the same period he had also tried suicide by locking himself in his car with a propane tank and turning it on. It was empty.

He had had enough. Of life, of his alcoholism, of CSE. He was in a classic tailspin, trying to pull an airplane out of a dive, but not really wanting to. "I guess God had other ideas," he says now. "Carole did the only thing she could do. She left me a note and a quarter. . . . She didn't know if she'd ever see me again."

These days, in Canada as in most civilized countries, most government agencies and departments, and most corporations, operate on the principle that, if you have an addiction problem and ask for help, they will not only provide it but will accept you back within the work force once you have gone through the program. As long as you don't screw up in a big way again.

Frost knew something was wrong, though, when one of the counsellors at Meadow Creek took him aside one day and said: "I don't know what position you hold within the government, but it must be important, because you're getting some visitors tomorrow." That was strictly against the rules at the rehab centre. No visitors to disrupt the program.

"What visitors?"

"Your director of personnel Sharon West and a man named

Victor Szakowski." Right there and then, Frost knew the jig was up. Szakowski was the CSE bouncer, head of security within the agency, an intimidating figure of a man, ex-RCMP, who acted the part you would cast a Texas Ranger in.

"They're coming here?"

"Yeah. I've been fighting it all the way," said the counsellor. "But somehow I couldn't stop it."

They showed up as scheduled.

"Will you talk to us?" asked Szakowski.

"Do I have any choice?" shot back Frost, who already knew the answer.

"No," said Szakowski.

"Okay," said Frost, "but I want one of the counsellors with me here too. . . . We're not going to talk classified information, are we?"

"No, no. This is more personal stuff . . ."

After the usual "how-are-you-making-out?" formalities, it was Sharon who asked: "What do you think you will be doing if you go back to CSE? Where do you see yourself fitting in?"

Frost didn't pick up on the "if" part right away.

"Well, I'll just go on with what I was doing."

"No. We'll find another spot for you," said Sharon.

"What do you mean?"

"There will be no reduction in salary . . . but we'll find a new spot for you."

"Like what?"

"Something that's easier on you. . . . Working in the storage, or the mailroom . . ."

"I beg your pardon?"

"Don't worry, your salary will remain the same. We'll just find another job for you if you come back."

He finally caught on to the "if".

"What do you mean 'if'?"

"Well, after you leave Meadow Creek, we'd like you to go through a complete psychiatric examination."

"Why?"

"We just want to determine your stability and your suitability for employment."

"Do I have any choice?"

"You can refuse if you want," she said, "but I would advise you not to. CSE will pay the psychiatrist. . . . You'll be on sick leave and then administration leave until this is all cleared up."

"Well," said a downcast Frost, who could read the writing on the wall, "I'll be out of here in a couple of weeks. Do you want me to report to CSE?"

"Oh, no. Just go home. We'll be in touch with you."

This account, as personal and painful as it may be for Mike Frost, has to be given, if only to show how spy agencies deal with those individuals who, despite their extraordinary services, suddenly become "liabilities". He couldn't help but think that just a year before that he had been Canada's official spokesperson and negotiator on NATO's crucial intelligence committee.

The very next day after he left Meadow Creek, he got a phone call from a clerk in CSE's personnel department telling him he had an appointment with a psychiatrist picked by the agency.

For some strange reason, the doctor was located on the Quebec side of the Ottawa River, in Hull. He had been hired by cse to assess Mike Frost's ability to go on with his work — in other words, his sanity. To this day, Frost believes that the psychiatrist was under orders from CSE to provide them with the conclusions they wanted. "Knowing the way CSE operates, that would be the most logical thing to do," he told his wife Carole.

From October 1989 to February 1990 he went to the Pierre Janet psychiatric hospital in Hull to do what he calls "stupid little tests and inkblots". He was hooked up to a machine by wires to his head and fingers, had to count backward in threes, forward in fours and was put under hypnosis. They even showed him pornographic films to determine his sexual drive and orientation. He felt degraded. If his body hadn't been violated, his mind and his soul certainly had.

And when it was all over, Mike Frost asked the most normal question in the world for any patient who has been under such scrutiny: "Can I see a copy of the report?" The doctor said he couldn't, since the work was being done for CSE. If he wanted a copy, he would have to get it from the agency.

Frost phoned Sharon West, whom he knew to be a decent person.

"What's going on?" he asked.

"Well, Mike, we have found you a place to work at CSE if you want it. Or we can offer you a nice little package if you choose early retirement."

"What sort of job do you have for me at CSE?"

"To be honest with you, it would be pretty degrading. . . . The only thing we can offer you right now is to deliver mail within the building."

"You mean you want me to walk around the building with that stupid little cart to deliver mail to all those guys who used to work for me?"

"That's all we have open right now."

There was still some pride left in Mike Frost. He opted for early retirement, with the severance pay he was entitled to under his CSE contract, plus his pension. To this day he has never been allowed to see the report from his psychiatric examination. He felt they had robbed his soul and kept it to themselves.

Over the previous years, when he was a fully-fledged, highly efficient spy, Frost had seen a lot of good people, men and women, "squeezed out" of CSE. But, in his naivete, he had never thought it would happen to him. He had no axe to grind, in that CSE had given him what he considered the best years of his life. But when they took his job away, he felt they had done it with no class at all, suggesting that a man with the equivalent rank of Lieutenant-Colonel become a mailman.

Frost remembered what CSE had done to Mary Cook. She went back to the days when CSE was just a house on Alta Vista Drive.

Cook also had the honour of having worked in close collaboration with Canada's most famous spy in wartime, William Stephenson, otherwise known as "The Man Called Intrepid".

"She was a walking encyclopedia," says Frost. "You could ask Mary anything about what had happened at such and such a time. And it didn't matter how far she had to go back, she'd remember dates, names, everything. People would go to Mary for anything from family to professional problems. . . . She was a good-old-aunt kind of person. She was just loved by everyone at CSE."

She didn't hold a very senior position, but was considered more essential to the workings of the place than most people with flashier titles.

Then one day CSE just told her that her job had become redundant, she was no longer needed. She was still in her fifties and, as Frost says, "believed she was going to work for CSE until she was 90." They offered her some meaningless job that she couldn't accept and, that day, Frost saw her bawling her eyes out in the Establishment cafeteria. "I was hurt, everybody was hurt and we would ask: 'Why Mary?' " She was replaced by a university graduate with a degree in ... archeology.

Now it was his turn.

He could see the pain in Sharon West's face the day after she gave him the bad news, when he went in to see her and say that he would accept a retirement package.

"Fine," she said, "you'll be hearing from Security. They'll want to see you to sign your de-indoctrination forms."

Sure enough, two days later, Victor Szakowski's secretary called him for an appointment.

Mike Frost walked into CSE through the guardhouse, which is the only way into the building. He turned left, went up the walkway and looked up at the sign that read "Sir Leonard Tilley Building". He thought it appropriate that the sparrows who used to nest inside the letters making up the sign had left excrement all over it on his last day on the job.

He went up to his office. He couldn't get in. The access code had already been changed. Victor Szakowski's men had taken care of it. He went down to see Sharon West to explain that he had personal items in there he would like to take back with him.

"They're already all packed up in a box and you can get it on your way out," she said.

"They've cleaned out my desk . . . ," he said simply, more to himself than to the personnel manager.

"Yes . . . you know how it is. I would just like to thank you for all the years of service you put in at CSE. Goodbye and good luck."

He still had to see Victor Szakowski, a man who, Frost felt, disliked him and was now having his moment of ultimate glory as far as Mike was concerned.

Inside the office Szakowski told him: "I have some forms for you to sign. . . . Your de-indoctrination from 'Pilgrim', from 'Gamma', from 'Guppy', from 'Daisy', from 'Artichoke' . . ." And he proceeded to go down the list of just about every operation Frost had ever taken part in over the previous eighteen years. There must have been about thirty signatures required in all.

"De-indoctrination" meant he was not to reveal anything to the outside world about his work for the government agency. Frost's head was spinning as Szakowski went through the motions of specifying how many years each "de-indoctrination" consisted of, because they varied from one operation to the other. Finally, Victor Szakowski said: "Your box of personal stuff is on the loading dock. You can get it over there."

A shattered man, he walked down to the loading dock and tears came to his eyes as he remembered all the equipment he had personally shipped out through there for espionage operations. And there he was, picking up his family pictures and desktop statues.

As he got into his car, he swore to himself he would wipe CSE and everything that went with it out of his memory banks. "Oh well, I guess I'm just going to play golf and swim in Florida."

He went home. Carole was working. He turned the TV on and watched Sally Jessy Raphael, wondering if this was what his life was going to be like from that day on.

Then, four years later, we bumped into each other at an AA meeting. As I was walking out of the meeting, this tall, slender man with a friendly demeanour, a white beard and thinning blond hair came up to me. He knew who I was, what I had done as a journalist and writer for the previous twenty years. And he had been given a sense that somehow I was the kind of "cowboy" to take on seemingly insurmountable odds.

Even though I had worked in Prime Minister Mulroney's office for almost three years, I didn't have a clue what CSE really was. I left him my phone numbers. A few days later, he called. We agreed to have coffee. I almost choked on my first cup when I heard what he had to say.

The story that follows is one every Canadian — and indeed citizens of other countries — should know, and we have Mike Frost's courage to thank for it. It is, yes, about the ultra-secret "Project Pilgrim". But it also exposes what CSE, the American NSA and the British GCHQ can do to their own citizens if they only press a button and aim an antenna or a satellite in the right direction. It is a tale of how we spy on each other, on ourselves and on the perceived villain. It just happens to be all true.

TWO
THE INTELLIGENCE CONSPIRACY

SINCE FEW CANADIANS ARE even remotely aware of CSE's existence, and even fewer know how broad and possibly abusive, certainly intrusive, its mandate is, perhaps a few historical and logistical explanations are in order before we begin Mike Frost's story.

What is now known as the Communications Security Establishment, nicknamed "The Farm" by its employees, is really the final product of a Canadian espionage agency that emerged out of World War II. It has not only changed names often over the last fifty years but has had its different "services" gradually amalgamated in such a way that it has increasingly come to resemble the U.S. National Security Agency, possibly the most powerful spy network in the world now that the KGB's — or rather its successor's — status has been somewhat lowered by the break-up of the Soviet Union.

Up until 1975, CSE was known as the Communications Branch of the National Research Council (CBNRC) — where it was "cleverly" hidden behind supposed scientific research walls. When its existence and real purpose were exposed in a special television report by the CBC's public affairs show *the fifth estate*, an embarrassed government then shifted it to the Defence Department and changed its title to what it now is. This move also had the advantage of protecting CSE from prying eyes, since the government of the day, whichever it might be, could always invoke "national security" to keep it secret.

Not all CSE employees are espionage operators in the James Bond sense of the word. But they are all "indoctrinated" to act as if they are part of a vast espionage network and so is every other government bureaucrat or even private-enterprise person who comes in contact with them and their secrets.

What does CSE do? Well, as explained by Philip Rosen in his booklet "The Communications Security Establishment: Canada's Most Secret Intelligence Agency," it "provides government institutions with advice and guidance on the security of their electronic communications; this part is largely defensive and uncontroversial."

The last phrase is important, because it is what has protected CSE from greater scrutiny for years. What it means is that CSE is charged with making sure crucial government communications are secure and not intercepted by "hostile" countries.

CSE personnel, for instance, install "jamming" equipment outside cabinet meetings on Parliament Hill to make sure the signals radiated by the translation devices within the cabinet room are not picked up by people on the outside. They advise ministers of the Crown to be careful about what they say on their cellular phones — though it's conceivable that sometimes they would not, if they should ever be tasked with "watching" a given minister. By whom? Nobody knows, since CSE answers to no one but the Prime Minister and, as this book will show, has a unique talent for "free-lancing" operations on its own.

Rosen also says of the second part of CSE's mandate that "it deals with foreign intelligence; it allows CSE to intercept and process foreign communications between Canada and other countries. . . . This part of the mandate takes up most of CSE's resources and is more controversial because its intrusive nature has the potential for violation of the rights and freedoms of Canadians."

This is true. What is missing, however, is the subject of this book. CSE has also been given a mandate, without parliamentary approval or scrutiny, to intercept communications in other countries of the world. It has sent agents and sophisticated electronic equipment to Canadian embassies since 1972 to spy on foreign countries such as Romania, the Soviet Union and Venezuela to "collect" information which is then used as intelligence in Canada, and is largely shared with the American NSA and the British GCHQ.

CSE has also gone further than that in doing "the dirty work" for those two friendly agencies on foreign soil and has also spied on countries Canada would call without a doubt "allies".

And, yes, it has spied repeatedly on Canadian citizens.

This all started rather innocuously as part of an agreement in 1947 between Canada, the U.S., Great Britain, Australia and New Zealand, that they would share information at the so-called secret level of intelligence. Canada was tasked mainly with taking care of the Soviet Arctic.

The Canadian role then evolved into military intercept, where the country's naval ships were tasked with tracking communications from Soviet vessels when they came into the area patrolled by Canadian ships. Other military intercepts were to follow shortly after, and in the mid-fifties CSE (an acronym we shall use to cover both CSE and its predecessors) got involved in the role of trying to pin down KGB ("civilian") and GRU (military) Soviet spy communications.

CSE was also a member of the Atlantic and Pacific High Frequency Direction Finding (HFDF) network, which consists of a network of bases that circle the two oceans for purposes of intercepting communications and locating their sources. In the Atlantic, the Canadian sites were in Bermuda, Gander (Newfoundland), Frobisher Bay (Arctic), Moncton (New Brunswick) and Leitrim (Ontario). NSA was the controlling agency for this network, but once or twice a week that responsibility would be shifted to the Canadian base in Moncton. Control meant the base would be responsible for warning all the other sites of what to look for, usually Soviet ships, aircraft or other marine trawlers. On the west coast, Canada had stations in Masset and in Ladner. To these were added the two crucial Arctic sites of Inuvik and, especially, Alert, on Ellesmere Island. In addition to those "local" sites, CSE would often give tasks to Canadian military ships going overseas and man them with its intercept operators.

CSE was, in a few words, the controlling authority for all Canadian intercept operations. The operations just listed, however, are known as "overt" intercept, and considered normal protective measures for any country conscious of its own defence.

CSE did engage in some "covert" intercept attempts, for instance when a Canadian ship docked in Vladivostok, the Soviet Union's main military port on the Pacific. But this was really kid's stuff compared to what the other major espionage agencies were doing and to what CSE would engage in later on.

Officially, the orders to task these ships and stations around the globe came from CSE. But, in fact, as Mike Frost puts it: "The director of NSA treated CSE as just another branch of NSA. We did an awful lot of just carrying out orders from the Americans." He gives the example of the Inuvik intercept site. "Soviet bombers would fly over our territory sometimes as far down as the American mid-west states. . . . We were told by NSA what to do with the intercept. Just track them."

Many Canadians may shake their heads in disbelief and wonder why those planes weren't either forced to land or shot down. But, for people in the intelligence world like Mike Frost, this was a common occurrence: "The Soviets would do it and monitor our own communications to see what we were doing. . . . They were testing our defences. They'd come in with one bomber and a couple of fighter aircraft. We let them do it, first because the alternative was to shoot them down. But the real reason is that the Americans were doing the same with their bombers, testing Soviet defences. . . . We were just going along with the 'rules of the game'."

It was so common, in fact, that NSA could predict when it would take place. The Soviets would do these exercises only on certain days of the week, and in certain kinds of weather. Before they took place the Soviets would tip their hand by changing their grids, altering their codes, increasing their traffic. "We knew well in advance when these flights would come," says Frost. NSA would warn the whole network: "Okay, there will be a Soviet bomber testing our defences on such a day at such a time. Track it and report back." As an example of how NSA actually ran the show, the Canadian Inuvik station would get a copy of the information directly from the American agency, before it even got the "action order" from CSE in Ottawa. This was standard, everyday stuff. But, in a strange way, NSA's muscle was enabling CSE itself to grow into a more and more powerful organization.

In the 1950s CSE (then CBNRC) was moved to a four-storey building on Heron Road in Ottawa that had earlier housed the Department of Agriculture. Before that the true CSE component was operating from a small former private home on Alta Vista Drive — and using the National Research Council's facilities and the Department of Defence for its operations.

The move to Heron Road was the beginning of the real growth of Canada's international agency. The building was meant to accommodate people and desks, certainly not the kind of equipment and technology CSE would eventually bring in there, so there has been lots of evolution over the years.

During Frost's years at CSE, this was roughly the lay-out of the building: The basement was a cafeteria and storage room. The ground floor of the building housed the mailroom, the administrative offices, the CSE travel office, the photography lab, part of internal security, the loading dock and platform, and a huge "training area" with classrooms for aspiring spies.

The second floor was where the chief of CSE and all his directors-general were. There was also a library and the top-secret "Talent-Keyhole room," which was where NSA and CIA satellite data was received and processed. Access to it was extremely limited within CSE itself. The second floor also had a huge engineering section, where CSE experts modified and customized their intercept equipment.

The third floor included the "Pilgrim" office, from where Mike Frost and Frank Bowman mounted Canada's "embassy-collection" operations. Soviet military and fishing analysis was also done on this floor, along with counter-espionage.

The fourth floor was almost entirely taken over by the "crypt group", the code-breaking experts.

In 1994, though, if you had driven past the inoffensive-looking government edifice — ironically located between the headquarters of the CBC and of Canada Post — you would have noticed two unusual things. First, there is an addition to the Agriculture Department building in the back, which looks something like a four-storey bunker. This was known in Frost's days as the "Annie" project, but quickly got the derogative nickname of "Granny" since it seemed as if the proper bureaucratic authorities could never get their act together to build it. It's there now, however. A massive, concrete block with no windows, in an area that CSE employees once used as a playground during break hours. It is what is known in the intelligence world as "Tempest-proof", which means that any electronic equipment inside does not radiate emissions to the outside. The only access to it is through the old building. Frost was not around to see the completion of "Granny", but can logically speculate that it now houses all the code-breaking equipment and the big Cray computer, the engineering section, the "Talent-Keyhole" satellite office, the counter-espionage unit and probably the "Pilgrim" operation too. Anything that could radiate compromising information.

The other oddity an innocent observer may have noticed while driving by CSE was scaffolding — later removed — surrounding the old building. It was in fact physical evidence of why "Granny" was built. When CSE built up very quickly from a house on Alta Vista Drive to a major espionage network it moved all kinds of electronic equipment into a building that was not designed to hold it. For instance, they had to add a concrete floor on the fourth floor to make sure the code-breaking Cray computer wouldn't fall through the ceiling. The dream invention of NSA's research chief Howard Engstrom Cray, when the first model was produced in 1976, it was considered the most advanced device of its kind, capable of processing 320 million words per second. It apparently weighed more than seven tons.

So much electronic equipment was stuffed into "The Farm" and so many people that the edifice literally started to burst at the seams. By the mid-seventies, bricks started falling off the outside wall. The building became so unsafe it probably would have been closed down if city regulations had been observed. Some offices had to be moved to three floors in the government offices at Billings Bridge Plaza.

Inside the building, CSE operates with a special telephone system. Originally, most office managers' offices had two phones, an out-line black phone and a green-coloured internal one. On the "green line" you could speak freely right up to the highest security level, because it didn't go out of CSE. The communication was scrambled within CSE itself. There was also a "fail-safe" mechanism to make sure that if you picked up the black phone while the green was in use, the internal communication would automatically be cut off.

CSE then progressed to a three-phone system, adding a red one to the arsenal, a direct line to NSA — scrambled, of course. These phones are totally encrypted, which means that although you can carry on a perfectly normal conversation between two people on the line, anybody trying to intercept it would find nothing but static — at least theoretically, though in the intelligence world, where technology evolves at a meteoric rate, you're never too sure what "the other side" is capable of.

Another important feature of the CSE building is that, from that location, anything within the radio environment of Ottawa can be intercepted — Soviet satellite communications; microwave towers, which carry tons of information, especially long-distance calls; cellular phones, which are tapped on a daily basis, sometimes just for the heck of it.

CSE also owns at least two white vans, which look roughly like closed-up chip wagons. These they can move around the city — or anywhere else they please — to mount an intercept operation. If they need to, they can mount an intercept with very little equipment (the equipment is getting better and smaller all the time) from the back of a station wagon. Officially, the two vans are used for an "overt" role, to protect Canadian government communications from foreign intercept. But, in fact, they are regularly and quickly modified to mount "covert" operations when the need arises. As we shall see later, these vans can be very efficient when it comes to their covert role. The vans carry two to four operators, depending on the complexity of the operation, and have all kinds of receivers and recorders on board. The vans are air-conditioned and have their own generators.

The CSE building is surrounded by a nine-foot-high fence with barbed wire on top. There is only one access gate, and only the higher-ups in the agency are allowed to park their cars inside the perimeter. The main parking lot for the 1,000 or so employees is outside the gate. Before an employee gains access to his or her office, they have to show their identification three times, to three different commissionnaires. On the final check, the commissionnaire sends out information to internal security that the employee is expected to arrive at a specific office in the following minutes, either by one of the two elevators or by the stairwell. Although Mike Frost has never been inside "Granny", he suspects it functions on the same system, with even more modern and efficient equipment.

This, then, is the environment in which "Project Pilgrim" was born.

"Pilgrim" would never have happened, though, without the pressure put on the Canadian government by the U.S. National Security Agency and the co-operation of Britain's GCHQ.

In the early seventies the two espionage agencies were already sharing their intelligence with Canada, to a certain extent, under the CANUKUS agreement. Under this agreement Canada received a good deal more intelligence from the U.S. and the U.K. than did Australia or New Zealand, but Canada had little of great value to offer in return, and certainly wasn't engaging in the risky spying ventures of its two allies. It is crucial to understand the different relationships CSE had with its partners. NSA was perceived very much as the bully in the picture, while GCHQ had a rather stereotypical "Bobby" image.

NSA, as mentioned before, considered CSE as part of its organization. CSE operators were regularly sent down to its main centre of operations in Fort Meade, Maryland, on a U.S. army base, between Laurel and Baltimore. Nothing tells Canadians where CSE is but, secretive as its operations are, the NSA building is not hidden from view. In fact, if you drive along Interstate 95, you will see a sign that says "NSA".

Mike Frost came to see Fort Meade as his second home — although not necessarily his fondest. It didn't take very long to "feel" the power the place held. The first thing that would impress you in approaching NSA is the parking lot. Frost was told it contained up to 10,000 cars, all used by the agency's employees. The second thing to strike a neophyte would be the two "ray-domes" on top of the roof. They look exactly like giant golf balls, and house antennas that pick up signals from orbiting satellites or anywhere else NSA chooses to aim them.

To get into the parking lot, you have to clear an armed guard — in Frost's day a Marine (although the security of the establishment has now been contracted out to civilian armed guards). You have to say who you are and where you're going, and, of course, show some form of identification, including your social insurance number. Once inside the parking lot, you have to stop at another gate, with a guardhouse, another Marine sentinel and a barbed-wire electric fence. He checks on his master sheet to see if you are expected. You can't just walk in. Your arrival has to be announced days in advance.

Before you even get inside the building you've already cleared two checkpoints. There are four main entrances to the building that Frost swears must be bigger than the Pentagon — which is generally said to be the largest edifice in the world. But visitors, like Frost, are allowed through only this one main door. You are greeted by more armed guards as soon as you get through the door. In the reception area you are met by the person whom you're supposed to meet. If there's nobody there waiting for you, you're stuck, can't get any further. Your host takes you to a clerk who, once again, checks on the list to see who you are. All your clearances and your ID badge are waiting for you and the clerk knows exactly what kind of pass to give you. You are photographed every single time, no matter how often you have visited the place before or how recently. The badge will identify you by name and SIN and will indicate the duration of your stay at NSA. Badges are colour-coded. Yellow is for visitors. The pass is encoded with a magnetic strip of all the offices you have access to. From then on, every time you pass an armed guard — and they are everywhere inside NSA — you are expected to hold your pass underneath your chin, so the soldier can check your photograph. This includes places like the cafeteria, the hairdresser, the bank, because within NSA there is a little city with all the necessary commercial services and amenities. If you happen to be carrying something, like a briefcase, each time you bump into a guard you have to show the contents — unless, exceptionally, you have it specified on your pass that you are exempt from this check.

It's the same procedure when exiting the building. And you can't leave NSA carrying anything, even your lunch, without having it searched.

"You need a map to get around that building," says Frost. "It is so big it seems to go on forever." In fact, while it looks like one building, it's really like a box, and in the middle are flowers, trees, gardens, walkways, park benches. Frost can't get out of his mind the image of the trucks in the basement where all papers generated at NSA are sent for incineration. "They have 18-wheelers in there. It's like a road down in that basement, where trucks just roll up to the incinerator."

As often as Frost went to Fort Meade, however, it was in another NSA highly secret location known as College Park that Frost would share his best intelligence with the Americans.

Overall CSE looked upon NSA as the people to provide the money, the equipment and the muscle. And, as so often, the Americans flaunted what they had.

It was very different with GCHQ. CSE's international spies came to consider the British as the providers of the expertise, the knowledge and the subtleties of what made a successful operation. "NSA would tell us what we were going to do," remembers Frost, "and how we were going to do it. GCHQ would ask us if we could possibly do something, and, if we possibly could, would suggest that this might be a good way to try to do it. We looked at GCHQ as sort of 'family'; NSA was like the 'Godfather'."

Even the difference in physical installations of the two agencies blatantly showed the difference in attitude. Frost always felt more relaxed travelling to GCHQ, which is located just outside the English town of Cheltenham, near the Cotswold Hills, and closer to the Atlantic than to London. The countryside is beautiful, typically British. Frost would always lodge at a bed and breakfast place by the name of the Cotswold Grange: two old houses, one on each side of the road, run by a couple and their son, and guarded by a sheepdog. From there to GCHQ is a nice, mellow drive on country roads.

When you get to what is perhaps the most efficient — as opposed to the most powerful — espionage agency in the world, you think you've stepped back in time by about fifty years. Run-down army buildings. Some are stone, some are wood, most need a paint job. The grass grows wild. No manicured lawns, not even walkways to take you from one of the many scattered buildings to another, just dirt paths. You are met at the door by a clerk who offers you a cup of tea and you are taken down to the male-dominated office with a clock on the wall so old it has Roman numerals. The furniture is worn out, the walls are yellowed.

But, as Mike Frost puts it: "What NSA can do with a hundred people and a $2-million budget, GCHQ can accomplish with ten people and $100,000. . . . Totally dedicated people, who know exactly what to do on a shoestring." They have beaten the Americans at the espionage game time and time again for years. Even NSA recognizes their competence, although it doesn't like to broadcast it.

GCHQ operators weren't as cocky as their American counterparts. Where NSA guys would say things like "We'll get you a plane, we'll buy you this computer." GCHQ agents would simply state: "We'll do the best we can and see what happens."

What made Mike Frost feel even more comfortable in the British surroundings was that they knew Canada. If he said "Ottawa" or "Winnipeg", they knew where it was. NSA people, with a few crucial exceptions, knew CSE existed, but didn't have a clue where Ottawa was or whether it was the capital of Canada or not.

There was no huge parking lot at the Cheltenham site. The Canadian agents would just pull up their cars and park them alongside the building they worked in, on the side of a hill or under a tree. There were security and gates at GCHQ, but nothing close to Fort Meade. A "bobby" would let you through and say: "Good morning, sir." No military. He'd let you in and salute, no matter who you were. Frost never noticed any guns.

This was the context, back in the early seventies, in which Canada tasked Frank Bowman to mount its first-ever international espionage operation in peacetime.

It was intended to be just a smoke-and-mirrors show put on by CSE, but it gradually developed into CSE's crack unit and put Canada on the international spying stage in a way none of its leaders or citizens had ever thought possible.

THREE
FOR THE LOVE OF "STEPHANIE"

HOW LONG HAD IT BEEN SINCE they first started working on this cursed project? Two years, maybe three, thought Frank Bowman. Now he was being told it was a "go". After all the political and bureaucratic wranglings, the numerous trips to NSA and to GCHQ, they had the green light. The Americans had finally got their way with the Canadian authorities, and as far as Frank Bowman was concerned, that was only fair and just. Now, though, he was being asked to head the team that would venture into totally uncharted waters for the Canadian espionage establishment in peacetime.

Bowman, in his late forties at the time, was perhaps the best man for the job—a pipe-smoking, dark-haired, stocky type, about 5'8", impeccably dressed in a suit and tie, reserved, very private, soft-spoken, a man who never seemed to lose his cool, never questioned orders and accepted failure as much as success with the same quiet demeanour, as if it was all part of the law of the universe. He spoke softly, but with authority. People knew they couldn't put a fast one by him, because he had a memory like an elephant. Throughout his years with CSE, he was given some major responsibilities and was generally given a free hand to handpick his own staff when a job needed to be done. So when the pressure came from NSA for Canada to mount an "embassy-collection" operation in Moscow, or risk being cut off from American intelligence data, Bowman was chosen to handle it. "Just go through the motions to satisfy the Americans," he was told by his superiors. "Go to Moscow, see if you can intercept anything. . . . That will make them happy and they'll get off our backs."

That was underestimating Frank Bowman's dedication to duty. As usual, he just said: "Okey-doke." But, in the back of his mind, he had no intention of just putting on a show to satisfy his intelligence allies, be it NSA or GCHQ; instead he saw a golden opportunity for Canada to "get in the game".

Politically, sending Canadian agents onto foreign soil to spy from within the country's embassies was not a popular prospect among the country's leaders in those days. It is uncertain whether it will be popular today. What Frank Bowman was being asked to mount was really a "token effort". The high-level politicians and bureaucrats involved believed that the Americans would eventually realize the Canadians couldn't do the job anyway and forget about it.

But Frank Bowman had been asked to do a job—a bigger, riskier one than he had ever done before professionally—and he would do it, even if it took many long, frustrating years.

He had just the one condition: that he could handpick his people. They gave him the OK.

Sitting in his Ottawa office, Frank Bowman wrote down some trusted names.

At the top of the list was Mike Frost.

"You can't get him, he's in Alert," he was told.

"Like hell I can't," said Bowman. "If I can't, I ain't doing it."

Who was Mike Frost and why was Frank Bowman so insistent on getting him on board?

The man's story is both tragic and at times funny. His early life took unexpected turns that were exciting and tumultuous but also painfully stressful. Frank Bowman knew him as a man who accepted orders, whatever they were, did his duty at all costs and had built an uncommonly patriotic Canadian heart, a man who was ready to go to any lengths to serve his country, sometimes at the expense of wife and family he loved.

He was born in Kingston, Jamaica, in 1938, in the days, as he puts it, when "white was right and black was wrong". He was white. His parents divorced when he was only five years old. He lived with his mother, who held various clerical jobs, but, in Jamaica back then, this still permitted her to have three house servants — a cook, a butler and Mike's nanny — plus two gardeners.

His mother, he would later find out, was a fully-fledged alcoholic who drank every day. He never saw his father. "I was not raised," he says today. "I just got older."

When he turned twelve, his mother came home one day and simply said: "I'm leaving Jamaica. . . . Some day, I'll send for you." He had no idea where he was going to live, he had no idea if he would ever see her again, he was just left there.

He didn't know exactly where she was headed with a British man he knew as John Frost, except that it was somewhere in North America. He doesn't even remember her telling him where he should go or how he should live. His older sister, Marguerite, who was sixteen, found a solution to the homelessness issue by getting married.

After his mother left, Mike recalls getting on his bike and riding to his grandmother's house. His father's mother seemed to be the only person who cared about Mike. Her son certainly didn't. "I knocked on the door and asked her if I could stay there," he says. "She was a real sweetheart." She found room for him in a bedroom he shared with the cook, behind the kitchen.

It was a traumatic time. Mike remembers vividly one day writing the word "Mum" on every line of every page of an exercise book in school.

He spent most of his days away from school, a barefoot boy hanging around with black boys, just roaming the streets of Kingston. At some point, with the help of his grandmother and his sister, he tracked his mother down in New York City, where she was working as a domestic and was about to marry John Frost. The next thing he knew, she had moved to Vancouver, British Columbia.

Through his grandmother, he was told by his father that, if he wanted to join his mother in Vancouver, he would have to board a merchant ship and get a job, perhaps as a cabin boy, to pay for his passage. He was given the option of staying in Jamaica with his grandma but chose to leave.

It was the summer of 1951 and he had just turned thirteen. He got on a freighter called the *Loch Ryan* that sailed through the Panama Canal and up the west coast of the United States and Canada. He left Jamaica with just his bicycle and a few clothes. It took six weeks for the ship to reach Vancouver.

The ship docked, but although his mother knew he was coming, there was no one there to greet Mike. He waited on the *Loch Ryan* for at least two days, maybe three, before she finally showed up. It was October, and even in relatively mild Vancouver, it was a little cool for a boy who owned nothing more than short pants and T-shirts, and usually walked barefoot.

His mother didn't have a car. She took him by bus to where she was living with John Frost. He dropped his suitcase and his mother told him right off the bat: "I'm going to show you the boarding school you are going to tomorrow."

"Tomorrow?" said a stunned Mike, who thought he had finally rediscovered his family life.

"Yes. We've got you registered. Tomorrow, we're going to take you to the bus stop, show you how to get there."

The next day he was enrolled in St. George's boarding school, one of the most highly rated in the country. His mother had taken care of acquiring him the compulsory uniform, grey flannel trousers, blue blazer, white shirt and tie, and — rare for a boy from Kingston — a pair of shoes. They put him in Grade Eight. Why? He doesn't know. He had no real schooling to speak of; he hadn't even graduated from Grade Seven. He felt as if he'd just landed on an unfriendly, forbidden planet. Mike, whose surname was still Earle at that time, spoke English with a Jamaican Black accent. He acted as if he was black, he even wished he was black. He was told he would play cricket and rugby. He had played a little cricket, but he had no idea what rugby was. He also didn't know that, four classes ahead of him, was a boy by the name of Peter Hunt, who would later play an important role in his life.

His stepfather, an insurance salesman, was making a lot of money in those days. In the mid-fifties Mike's family moved to a house in Vancouver's exclusive British Properties district, a huge five-bedroom house valued at $250,000 even back then. "It was a very elitist place," says Mike. "I had my own bedroom, anything I wanted, but it was all a facade for me. I would much rather have been in Jamaica, running barefoot or riding a donkey." He felt out of place the whole time he spent in the British Properties house and St. George's. But he managed to get through to Grade Twelve in five years. He worked hard to rid himself quickly of his Jamaican accent so he wouldn't stand out so much.

At age sixteen, he enrolled at the University of British Columbia. It took him two years at UBC to decide he'd had enough of school. He decided to join the Canadian Navy in 1958. In theory he could have joined as an officer but, first, there was a waiting period for officers and he wanted to join immediately; second, he failed the requisite colour-blindness test that relates to identifying red and green lights at sea, which, at night, tell you if a ship is heading for or away from you.

Joining as an ordinary seaman, he ended up at the Cornwallis Navy School and was asked to pick a trade. There was one that particularly struck him because they wouldn't tell him specifically what it was.

"What's that?" he asked, always curious.

"We can't tell you."

"Why not?"

"Because it's top secret."

That's all they had to say. "I want that!" said Mike.

From Cornwallis, he ended up in the fall of 1958 at the now dismantled Gloucester base (it was to be replaced by nearby Leitrim), where he was taught to be an intercept operator. He graduated in the summer of 1959. Mike was a dashing nineteen-year-old when he was posted to the Gloucester base. Over the four previous months, following a suggestion from a friend at the base, he had become pen-pals with a girl he knew in Ottawa by the name of Carole Lester. She was seventeen. When he finally got to the capital, Mike phoned Carole and asked her out for a date. They went to a restaurant called L'Esterelle on Sparks Street. There was no looking back. He loved her enticing smile and her sense of humour. A year later they were married in Ottawa's St. Augustine's Church. They would eventually have three children together, all boys. And, in many ways, over sometimes rocky and difficult years, Carole would become the pillar of strength Mike would reach for when everything else seemed lost. She would follow him wherever he went. Equally, she accepted being left behind whenever she wasn't needed. She was always there in times of crisis. She still is today.

His initial posting was in Moncton, New Brunswick, where he first dealt with intercepting clandestine Soviet high-frequency communications, from the KGB, GRU, the military and even from fishing trawlers. The Soviet fishermen had a habit of giving a false position over the radio when they were in fact inside Canadian territorial limits.

It didn't take long for Mike Frost to come to see "The Russian Bear" as the most dangerous enemy Canada had on the planet. He hadn't really given much thought to international politics before. As Carole puts it: "He was too busy having fun!"

In 1961, his first posting at sea came in. He had to take a course in Electronic Warfare at Gloucester and then moved once again to the west coast to be posted on the *Skeena*, one of Canada's fleet of destroyers. While on the *Skeena* he was sent out to sea to prepare for nuclear world war when the Cuban Missile Crisis took place. That event too contributed greatly to what became an aversion for anything to do with the U.S.S.R.

One day on the *Skeena* Frost and his fellow seamen thought they had scored a great coup in electronic warfare. That kind of intercept is achieved mainly by tracking the enemy's radar. Frost had learned how to identify different types of radar signals mainly from ships and aircrafts, including, of course, all of the Soviets'. The

Skeena was on manoeuvres in the Pacific somewhere off the coast of Vancouver Island, tracking a Canadian submarine, when suddenly the electronic operators picked up what sounded like the radar of a Soviet submarine. It had all the parameters of such a radar, was on the right frequency, had the right pulse repetition. Now to catch a Russian submarine's radar would look impressive on the performance assessment of any Navy operator or the captain of the ship. "We could all smell promotions, and citations, and medals." They reported it to the captain, who came down to the electronic-warfare room to check out the information. He recommended to the squadron commander that he cut off the exercise and go after the Soviet sub.

After several hours of a chase way out into the ocean, a call came from the bridge saying that they could see through powerful binoculars what appeared to be the conning-tower of a submarine. They headed straight for it, full speed ahead. The sea was very rough. The conning-tower kept disappearing. "We thought: 'The son-of-a-bitch is diving!' " says Frost. "But moments later, it would re-emerge and we thought they'd decided to play games with us. It was really exciting, and the closer we got, the more it looked like a conning-tower."

Then, as the *Skeena* gained on the "sub", things started to look a little wrong. Somehow, it didn't quite look like a conning-tower any more. Then they saw, ahead of the Soviet submarine, a tugboat. "We thought: 'What the fuck is a tugboat doing there?' Then we figured, geez, the sub has broken down and the Soviets are towing it home. This is really great!" As they finally closed in, the collective heart of the *Skeena*'s crew sank to their heels. This was a Canadian tugboat, pulling a barge with a bulldozer sitting on it. The radar they had intercepted was that of the tugboat that had, somehow, all the parameters of a Soviet radar.

"We didn't boast about it too much. We didn't want it known that we had thought a bulldozer was actually a Soviet submarine."

It wasn't the only embarrassing incident Frost witnessed on the *Skeena*. The following one could have had tragic consequences.

They were in the straits of Juan de Fuca, off the American west coast. Again on manoeuvres. But these were firing exercises involving 3.5" shells, the biggest guns the destroyer had. As Frost explains it: "An air-force plane tows a drone behind it, and our job was to fire at the drone. Hopefully, you don't blow the pilot of the real plane away."

On that particular day, in late January 1962, something went terribly wrong: although the gunnery officer calculated where the drones were, he forgot to take into account where the shells would land. Frost remembers hearing the gunnery officer talking to the captain over the ship's radio: "The drone is in place, sir. Request permission to proceed with the exercise."

"Permission granted."

Then the next thing he heard from the man in charge of the shelling was: "Captain, we have a small problem, sir. Request permission to cease the exercise."

"What's the problem?"

"I suggest your presence on the bridge, sir."

What the *Skeena* had actually done was bomb a schoolyard where children were playing outside, in the state of Washington. By some incredible fluke, nobody was injured. The pride of the *Skeena*'s commanding officer was seriously bruised when it blew up in the press that a Canadian destroyer had been shelling an American school.

After the "incident", the *Skeena* got the hell out of there immediately, found a secluded bay and dropped anchor until somebody told them to do something else. "That's the way we were trained," says Frost. "Something like that happens, you do the equivalent of burying your head in the sand. We couldn't go to shore and face the press onslaught."

Tragic as it was, and hilariously stupid as it turned out to be, the shelling of the schoolyard would serve as a great lesson to Frost in years to come: routine as things may seem to be, they can always screw up big time. Another anecdote from his days in the Navy also taught him something about the dangerous world of intelligence gathering and about how strange and secretive his life was to become.

He had been posted, after the *Skeena*, to another destroyer, the *Margaree*, in 1963. The Canadian destroyer had been tailing a Soviet merchant vessel that had been operating on the west coast and was due into Vancouver. They followed it right into Vancouver harbour. When the Russians docked, they did too. The Soviets then pulled one of their propaganda tricks and held an open house on their merchant ship, announced in the press, for the folks of Vancouver to come and see how friendly the communists were.

While in Vancouver, Mike thought it would be a good chance to get in touch with his sister. Marguerite had also moved to Vancouver with her husband by then. She came to pick Mike up from the ship to have dinner at their place.

"This is the second time we've been down at the docks in the last couple of days," said Marguerite as they were travelling to her home.

"Oh," said Mike, "how's that?"

"Well, we went to that open house they had on that Russian ship."

"That's interesting," said Mike laconically.

"Did you know it was in the harbour?"

"No. . . . We just pulled in to get some gas, give the guys some shore leave, you know . . ."

"Yeah, it was great!" continued Marguerite. "We met some great people!"

"Oh? Who's that?"

"We met the captain and the communications officer and, as a matter of fact, we invited them over and they came to the house for dinner. Had a great time!"

"I beg your pardon?" stuttered Mike. He paused for a bit. "Marguerite, can I get this straight? You had the Russian captain and the communications officer over to your home for dinner?"

"Yeah! And we exchanged addresses and we're going to write to each other . . ."

Seaman Frost's heart was pounding: "Sis, would you do me a favour? Could you put a hold on all activity with them at this moment? I really can't explain, but what you did could be very embarrassing for me."

"Sure . . . ," answered his puzzled sister.

"Please don't go back to the ship, don't make telephone calls, just don't do anything until you hear from me."

"Okay . . ."

What had happened was that Marguerite's husband, an old wireless operator himself, had struck up what he thought to be an innocent but fascinating conversation with the Soviet vessel's communications officer and, eventually, the captain. This communications officer was probably doing intercept work, the same thing Frost was up to on the *Margaree*.

The very next morning, he went straight to the commander of the *Margaree*.

"Come on in," said the CO.

Frost saluted, took his cap off and said: "Sir, I have to report to you that two of the officers from the Soviet vessel were at my sister's house, two nights ago."

"Yes, I know," responded the commander. And he showed Frost a piece of paper that ordered him to find out from Frost what was going on. Obviously the Soviets had been tailed to his sister's place by the Canadian Security Service. "I told him that the whole thing had been done out of total innocence. . . . And he said, 'All right, I'll write my report that way. . . . And I suggest that you tell your sister to stop her relations with the two Soviet officers.' "

"Yes, sir!"

It would come up time and time again over the years, but that was the first time Mike Frost had to ask a member of his family to do — or not do — something, without really explaining why, other than that it would hurt his career.

The year 1965 was a benchmark in Mike Frost's rise in Canada's espionage community. He was posted to a Long Range

Technical Search (LRTS) Intercept course in Ladner, B.C., largely because his ability as a top operator was starting to show.

The most important thing that happened during that course, apart from the fact that he finished first in his class, was that he met and chatted to a man by the name of Frank Bowman. Bowman was already working for CSE and had come out to Ladner in order to give a lecture.

From that course Frost was posted to Inuvik, at one of CSE's Arctic intercept sites, in what was known as "an elite position", where he dealt with advanced electronic gear that other operators were not up to handling. He had been promoted to the rank of petty officer within eight years, which in those days was considered a meteoric rise.

Another unusual incident happened in Inuvik that almost put an end to his career once again. While in Inuvik, his son Danny got bitten by a rabid cat. He ended up in Vancouver with his mother, Carole. Mike asked his CO if he could join the members of his family in the hospital, since they had been told his son had only a 50 per cent chance of living.

The Navy CO denied him the request. "Your son is getting the best medical treatment possible, your wife is with him, you're needed here," said the CO.

Heartbroken and feeling totally powerless, Mike phoned his sister in Vancouver. Unbeknownst to him, though, his brother-in-law had political connections — to the point where the case of petty officer Frost and his dying son was raised in the House of Commons, where the Defence Minister was asked to explain such a lack of compassion.

"I had no idea all of this was going on," says Frost. "But a few days later, the CO phones me in a blind rage, threatens to punch me out and asks who I think I am to go over his head and to the Minister of Defence. . . . I didn't have a clue what he was talking about."

"Frost," said the CO, "you're a petty officer and I'm going to make sure you retire from the Navy as a petty officer! Your career is over! I've got your fucking plane ticket. Get out of here. I don't even want to see you!"

He still has a copy of the letter he asked his brother-in-law to send to both the Minister of Defence and his commanding officer explaining that all of this had taken place without his prompting or knowledge. But for the rest of his days in the Northwest Territories posting, where he went back with Carole and a healthy Danny, the co never even looked at him again.

He continued as an intercept operator, becoming better and more knowledgeable in the field. But, after that incident, he realized that, given the way the military is structured, he was a marked man. Fortunately Frank Bowman had come into his life. In Inuvik he was tasked by Bowman for certain duties. Frost went back to the Gloucester Navy school as an LRTS instructor in 1969 and had more regular contact with the man he had met in Ladner four years earlier.

"Anything Frank would ask me to do, I always delivered on."

In due course the CSE man requested he go to Alert to try to identify a new Soviet radio signal codenamed "Trimline" that nobody could even hear. They didn't know when it was on or what frequency the Soviets used. And that is how Frost, and another man who would later become part of his espionage team, went up to Alert.

Not even time seems to move in Alert.

In summer — if this is summer — the white sun just seems to sit up there forever against the white sky, as if painted on the cheap backdrop of a low-budget science-fiction movie. Alert itself is much like the sun. Just there. Not seeming to belong in the vast emptiness of the Canadian Arctic, on top of the world where a human being feels he couldn't get any lower. The loneliness, the cold, the silence, the desolation, the monotony, broken only by the eerie splendour of the Northern lights, in the always dark winter, beckoning in the distance like dancing angels at the gates of heaven.

But Alert itself is more like hell: the hell of mythology where the damned spend day after day repeating tasks that never get done and lead nowhere, for ever and ever. In the end, it is only fitting that Alert be there, a monument to the folly of humankind, a beacon to Armageddon.

You have only one wish when you are posted to Alert: to get out. The military assignment lasts 183 days, and you start counting down the day you get there. On every table, desk, wall, you can read the acronym "I.H.T.F.P." carved or scribbled angrily. It stands for "I hate this fucking place."

Back in the summer of 1971, Mike Frost was taking the punishment in his stride. Complaining was not in his nature to begin with, and thirteen years in the military had made sure it wouldn't be. Alert was a little much, though: a few thousand yards of dirt roads, wooden huts, a curling rink and, of course, a mess with lots to drink. You couldn't get any closer to nowhere, with nowhere to go. At least a ship, confining as it was, could always eventually pull into port; there would be places, things, women to see. In Alert, not even television, not even a telephone, no escape. Except booze. Cheap booze. Fifteen cents a shot or something. And if you happened to be broke — God knows why! — you could always run a tab. The military wanted the boys happy and mellow. Mike Frost found that way out quickly and often. But that was fine, even respected by his superiors. He had to drink to stay sane and forget about reality, somewhere far away, where Carole was raising the three boys. At least he and his colleague had managed, after painstaking work, to track the new Soviet signal.

Sitting on his cot, Frost was carefully opening the week's mail. There was always a mild sense of anticipation, since the postman came to Alert only once every seven days. The excitement was usually unwarranted. The letters from home only did more to remind him of the months he had left to his sentence.

But Frost was nearing the halfway point. Pretty soon he'd be over the hump. He had no idea, on this dreary Alert August day, that this mail run would be different. In fact, it would change his life forever. As he read the letter, his heart started to race, his hands started to shake. This time, it wasn't the booze.

Mike Frost's first instinct was to rush out into the street and shout it to the world. No way. There was no street and the world couldn't be told. Also Frank Bowman had made it clear this was not the kind of letter you circulate. The best he could do was write back. He couldn't phone. There was always the shortwave ham radio, but that was no use either. For one thing, just over the horizon, the Russians were doing the same thing he was and listening in on every communication they could intercept. He would have loved to discuss the matter with his wife, who was back in Ottawa, but such ham-radio communications to and from Alert were broadcast in the mess at Alert for every "inmate" to hear, like calls from astronauts to Planet Earth.

But even writing was frustrating as he had to wait for next week's mail plane to post his answer. It was affirmative of course. He didn't care what was involved. Anything but Alert, to start with. But Moscow . . . that gave him a rush. All he had known about the Soviets until then was the gibberish he had been picking up while intercepting their communications. He had been trained to loathe them as the enemy. Now he was being asked to step right into the lair of the Bear. That was perfect. The more he could do to trip them up in their plans for world domination, the happier he was.

Three long weeks went by before Frank's reply finally arrived. Mike Frost was in heaven. Not only was he getting the job, but Bowman had thrown in the bonus of yanking him out of Alert before the end of his six-month term. Frost could hardly believe his good fortune; he had always thought even Jesus Christ couldn't pull that one off. All Frost knew was that he was going to the government's foreign language school in Ottawa to learn Russian.

Frost's commanding officer was suspicious. Not only was this guy being removed from Ellesmere Island two months ahead of time, but he was going to language school. That didn't jibe at all with Frost's military training. He had specialized in LRTS, the technical side of intercept operations. Only transcribers were asked to learn Russian, not the boys who played with the hardware.

Frost's envious colleagues now called him "short-timer" and never stopped razzing him. But Mike was laughing all the way to Moscow. The last night in the Arctic was predictable. Everyone had to leave Alert with a hangover and Frost was only too glad to indulge. He boarded the Hercules the next morning for the thirteen-hour non-stop flight feeling sick as a dog. But in the Navy that was the equivalent of a badge of courage. The more you drank, the less you showed the effects the next day, the more of a man you were.

He settled himself down in the net-binding "seats" in the plane's cargo bay and tried to forget about the thunderous noise of the engines echoing against the metal fuselage and in his throbbing head. He landed at Trenton's military base, took off his northern gear and quickly hopped on another flight to Ottawa.

Carole was waiting with their three sons. His youngest, six-year-old David, went hysterical when his dad went to pick him up and desperately tried to escape his grasp. Mike was wearing a four-month beard and David didn't have a clue who this strange man was. Little did Mike know that, in the years to come, he would become even more of a stranger to the members of his own family as a result of a much deeper transformation.

That night Mike and Carole fantasized about the exotic new posting. Carole was almost as excited as her husband. In another highly unusual move that raised eyebrows within his unit, Mike's wife had also been granted permission to attend language school. That made her part of the adventure, although she would never be told what was really involved, even in the slightest detail.

Frost reported to his home base in Gloucester, south of Ottawa, the very next morning for a cameo appearance and was in Frank Bowman's office the next day. He had been behind the forbidding doors of the intercept establishment several times before. But Frost's adrenaline was pumping furiously that September day.

Bowman went right to the point. "We have been asked by NSA to go to our embassy in Moscow, set up some receivers and antennas, and intercept Soviet communications in VHF and higher frequencies. . . . They want us to see if we can pick up anything that is unique and different from what the U.S. and the U.K. are getting at their two intercept sites."

"U.S. and U.K. sites where?" Frost asked naively.

"In their Moscow embassies," replied Bowman.

"You mean the Americans and the Brits are doing collection from their embassies?"

"Sure. They've been at it for years. The American operation is codenamed 'Broadside' and the British is 'Tryst'. But there are some holes in their intercept and they wonder if Canada could perhaps go in and have a look. Maybe we can fill in the gaps in their collection."

Bowman went on: "We have agreed to do it, we got approval from the Prime Minister's Office and External Affairs, and you're our man for the job."

Frost was transfixed. This was getting better by the second.

"The code name of the operation is 'Stephanie'. We named it after Peter Hunt's daughter," said Bowman, referring to his superior in CSE's L Group. "You're going to go in undercover as a military clerk, working for our military attaché, and you'll have another military clerk working for you — he'll be our second man."

"How on earth are you going to justify sending two additional clerks for one military attaché?"

"No problem. The colonel in our embassy has been complaining for years he needs more clerical staff. So we're sending him two extra clerks."

"Yeah, but does he know the two clerks won't be doing any clerical work?"

"No he doesn't. He's just elated he's getting more staff!"

The two men laughed out loud like kids planning a practical joke.

"So that's it. You'll be posted for a minimum of two years. What do you think?"

Frost would have paid to go. He had been flabbergasted to learn about the American and British embassy operations, and even more surprised to find out that Canada was even thinking of doing the same thing with the apparent approval of Prime Minister Pierre Elliott Trudeau. But such thoughts were being drowned out by total exuberance at the opportunity and the sense that he was being allowed into a select universal club of spies, where you do things you're not supposed to, carry secrets few people would ever know or even think about, and do it all with the blessing of a government that looks the other way.

He was, as normal procedure requires at CSE, "indoctrinated" for "Stephanie". That meant he could not discuss any part of the work he was doing with anyone who was not "in-the-know", not even other CSE employees. And the onus was on the indoctrinee to know whom he could discuss the project with and to what lengths he could go in his explanations. This was a practice Frost would become very accustomed to over his years at "The Farm". Bowman had one thing to add, however, that reminded Frost of the dire warning in the Alert letter. "Should you ever get caught over there, you're on your own. The government will deny everything." Frost just brushed it off. That was standard procedure. Besides, he simply wouldn't get caught.

Mike and Carole immersed themselves in language school with unrestrained enthusiasm. Although she didn't have a clue that her husband would be only posing as a military clerk, Carole was ecstatic about their new life in the foreign capital. At home they practised their Russian on each other. The kitchen was plastered with Russian words for spoon, fork, knife, milk, potato, window and door. They were getting the three boys ready for the adventure too. Never had they been involved in Mike's work together like this, never had they been so close.

It was too good to last.

Just before Christmas, a little more than two months into the course, Frost's world seemed to collapse when he was called into the office of the language school's commanding officer.

"You wanted to see me, sir?" he said, trying to cover up his growing anxiety.

"Yes . . . I've been asked to inform you that you and your wife are not to complete the language course."

Even the military hadn't prepared Mike for this kind of nasty surprise.

"What do you mean?" he blurted out.

"Your stay here is terminated as of now. Word came from your superiors."

"Who? Why?"

"That's all I know."

Feeling punch-drunk, Mike found his way back to the classroom, walked over to his wife and said sternly: "Come on, we're going home." They were devastated.

Early the next morning, after a sleepless night, he phoned the only person he thought could shed some light on this disaster, Frank Bowman. Yes, he knew what had happened all right. Word had come back from the Canadian ambassador to Moscow, Robert Ford, that there was currently no suitable housing for a family of five in the Soviet capital. The only available housing was a two-bedroom apartment on the thirteenth floor of a walk-up. By Russian standards, that was normal. But the ambassador didn't think it was adequate for a Canadian family.

"I don't give a shit if you put me up in a barn! I want to go to Moscow!" pleaded Frost. "Tell Ford I'll go anyhow."

Bowman complied, but to no avail. The ambassador rightly believed the stress of adjusting to life in the Soviet Union would be bad enough without adding to it by forcing the family to climb thirteen flights of stairs every day and live in cramped quarters in a dingy Russian flat, where the heating and the plumbing were considered luxuries that didn't always work. Add to that the kind of work Frost was sent to perform behind the Iron Curtain and it was a sure recipe for breakdown.

Mike was near tears when the final word came. He had been used not to question orders, but how could they have built up his expectations so high, for so long, without even checking out the housing beforehand?

Frank Bowman felt personally responsible for the fiasco. Once again, as he had when he took Frost out of Alert, he pulled a few strings in an attempt to set things straight. Frost was going to get an honorable discharge from the Navy and come to work for him as a civilian employee of CSE. He would head the "Stephanie" team from Ottawa and co-ordinate all the planning and the unfolding of the operation.

It wasn't Moscow, but, as Frost was to find out, he was still very much involved. In fact, it would turn out to be a very minor setback.

Frost was still bitter when he was sent down to NSA in Fort Meade, for a six-week course. With him were the two Canadian military men who had been picked to go to the Russian capital. The government put them up in the Sheraton Hotel in Silver Springs and rented them a car for the duration of the course. They were the first Canadians ever to attend this specific course provided by the agency for its own agents. NSA had classified most of its contents as "top secret", but not only were the Canadians allies, they worked for them, didn't they?

The need for such schooling had never arisen before since the type of intercept Canada had engaged in against foreign powers was strictly long-range, nothing of this highly aggressive sort. The Canadian government hadn't bothered to train its people for something they never intended to do —like embassy collection.

As with most things NSA does, the course was good and it was thorough. It was purely technical, dealing with the VHF, UHF and SHF frequencies, and teaching the prospective American and Canadian spies what the signals they could expect to hear in these frequency bands looked like, sounded like, what they could do with them, how they could demodulate them, demultiplex them, get a page copy or an audio tape.

In layman's terms, "modulation" is the way information (voice, fax or video) is carried over the airwaves. When several messages are sent on the same frequency they are "multiplexed". The interceptor first

FIGURE A

BLOCK DIAGRAM OF "STEPHANIE" EQUIPMENT

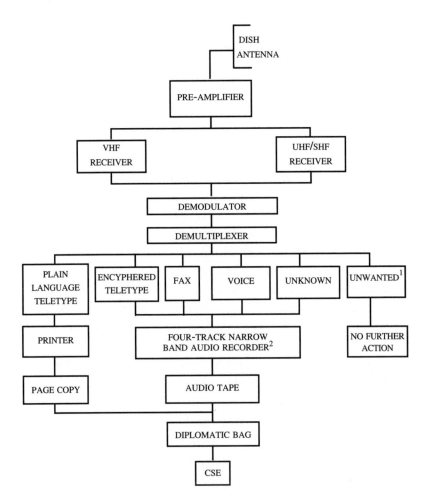

1. Radio, TV, press, etc.

2. Three tracks were used to record intercepted signals.
The fourth track was used to record an internally generated reference signal.

(Diagram by David Frost)

has to demodulate the signal to recover all the messages. Once that's done, he has to demultiplex all the messages to find the one he wants.

The easiest example, simplistic as it may seem, is a telephone conversation. When you speak on your ordinary home telephone, your voice is alone on the line only from your house to the nearest major carrier, whether that is a land line or microwave tower. There it is mixed — multiplexed — with hundreds of other voices. How is it, then, that your interlocutor hears only yours? Because when your voice gets to a switching station, it is demultiplexed based on the number you dialled, and isolated from the rest.

Frost set out to finish first of his class. The cancellation of his Moscow posting only fuelled his determination. And he did finish first. The other two "Canucks" were second and third in the class of forty-odd agents.

In six weeks, they had learned what being an international spy in a modern world dominated by technology really meant and now they wanted to do some mischief. This was going to be fun.

NSA went out of its way to make the birth of "Stephanie" as easy and painless as possible. When their Canadian counterparts complained that they didn't have much money for this kind of delicate operation with little political will behind it, the Americans took care of it. They provided all the necessary equipment, all developed by and at NSA, on loan, never expecting to get it back. The only requirement was that the Canadians make sure the NSA serial numbers were erased so that the agency couldn't be linked to the operation in any way. This was very expensive equipment, most of it one-of-a-kind developed specifically at NSA's request. The research and development costs were understandably astronomical for products you couldn't market outside the friendly spy community.

Frost and Bowman sat down in the Heron Road office they had been assigned to plan and execute their special project. Two men, two desks and the world to conquer. Bowman soon figured out a way to get them a little more working space by going up to the roof of CSE headquarters, where the furnace room is located. (You can also enter it through a white fire-exit door that, from the right location, you can see from the street.) Bowman asked and got permission to build a cinder-block wall within the furnace room that would house the electronic gear for "Stephanie" and give his operators a chance to "test" it. That room, although Bowman or Frost had no such intention at the time, would later on be used for some questionable CSE operations.

Their first problem was to figure out a way to make the equipment "Tempest-proof", which meant it wouldn't emit radiations that could be picked up by Soviet listening devices. The NSA equipment, good as it was, did not meet that requirement since the Americans operated differently. Wherever they had an embassy listening post, they would make the entire room "Tempest-proof", so the equipment itself didn't have to be. The Canadians couldn't undertake such extensive renovations in their Moscow embassy without blowing their cover, with both the embassy staff and the Soviets.

Frost and Bowman quickly came to the conclusion that there was no way they could isolate each and every black box of gizmos they had to use. As they sat there in their office, staring at each other, the walls, the ceiling, their eyes finally came to rest on what had been the answer all along. There, between their desks, stood a majestic government-issue safe. The safe could be a mini-room of sorts. They could modify it to house the equipment and "Tempest-proof" the safe itself.

"At the end of the day, we would simply close the door, spin the dial and that would be the end of the equipment. The room would look just like another office."

The CSE engineers went to work modifying the strong box, putting in brackets to fit in all the equipment and providing access for antennas. They customized two safes. One was the "Moscow Surprise", the other a prototype to be kept in Canada in case something had to be rearranged once the equipment was behind the Iron Curtain. Every piece of electronic equipment was also duplicated.

FIGURE B

"STEPHANIE" EQUIPMENT AS MOUNTED IN OFFICE SAFE

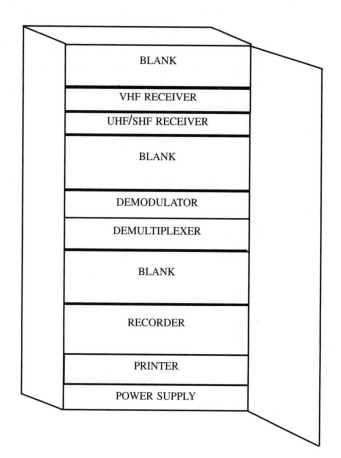

(Diagram by David Frost)

For all its complexity, that was the easy part of the exercise. Now they had to figure out the horrendous task of getting a safe to Moscow, while keeping a low profile. They couldn't exactly use their usual means of communication: slip the damn thing in a red diplomatic bag and have a courier pick it up.

First they had to find a reason for sending it from Canada to Moscow that would satisfy the Soviets' curiosity, given that safes could easily be purchased, if not in the U.S.S.R., then nearby in Europe. Also, never mind the Russians: Frost and his team were having enough trouble explaining their actions to Canadian bureaucrats from External Affairs.

Finally, Frost and Bowman dreamed up the rationale for the safe: the military attaché in Moscow had documents that had to be stored in a safe that met military standards. There were no such safes in the Soviet Union or indeed elsewhere in the free world, so it had to be sent from Ottawa. They bought it. As for the military attaché in Russia, he was basking in all this sudden attention. Two new clerks and a safe to boot. And he thought the Trojan Horse was a fairytale. . . .

The really tricky part was yet to come, however. How were they going to get it over there? They couldn't fly it to Russia: too much paper work, too many people involved, too heavy a load on an airplane not to raise suspicion. The safest way, they thought, was by sea. And so the most important piece of spying equipment ever used by Canada for a foreign operation up to that point left Ottawa by truck and was put on a ship in Montreal for a good old-fashioned transatlantic voyage.

Before sending it on its way, Frost had made sure to cover the entire inside walls of the safe with lead panels — similar in appearance to aluminium foil. They were necessary because, although the electronic gear was to be sent separately, the engineers had drilled holes inside the safe that corresponded exactly to the mounting brackets for the gear. It wouldn't take long for the Soviets to figure out what the holes and the safe were for if they decided to X-ray it when it got on their territory.

Two or three months went by, as the safe crossed the Atlantic to the port of Murmansk, where it was unloaded in full view of the Soviet war fleet, was put on a train and finally arrived — to sighs of immense relief in Ottawa — at the Canadian embassy in Moscow. However, when the special delivery arrived at the embassy it had to go to the top floor. The only way to get it there was by elevator. Frost had never thought to look into the matter before expediting the safe, but the aging elevator in Moscow — where such a device was a big luxury anyway — could not carry the load without the risk of the cables breaking and the elevator crashing down the shaft. And there was no way to bring the safe up the stairs. There it sat, for everyone to see, in the foyer of the embassy for weeks before the embassy's telecommunications technician finally took a chance and put it on the elevator, by itself. The safe made it to the top floor and into the room where it was supposed to go.

But that wasn't the end of this silly saga. When the decision was made to remodel the inside of the safe, one operation had had to be left out. A hole needed to be drilled at the bottom of the strong box through which the antennas could be plugged into the equipment. To ship a safe with a hole in the bottom made no sense at all, so they left instructions with the embassy technician — one of the three members of the diplomatic personnel briefed on the operation — to perforate the floor of the safe. Now a coded message came back to Ottawa from Moscow: there was no drill strong enough in the embassy to pierce the metal.

Frost and Bowman were getting used to this obstacle course. Undaunted, they went to a heavy-equipment hardware store and bought a drill the size of a jackhammer. They stuck it in a diplomatic bag — in fact two red diplomatic bags sewn together — and sent it to Russia.

Finally, word came back that the "Tempest-proof" safe was ready to receive the intercept equipment. The two Canadian agents left for the Soviet Union in their military clerk uniforms. Once there, one of their first tasks was to brief the military attaché as to the real reason for their presence and that of the new safe with the hole in the bottom. The clerkless colonel then had to sign forms swearing him to secrecy, which were sent back to Ottawa.

One piece at a time, the electronic gear arrived in Moscow, all by diplomatic bag. The major snag came when it was time to send the antenna. Frost and Bowman had consulted NSA as to what kind of device could cover all the frequency bands they were expected to intercept. They came up with a five-foot-high dish. That didn't fit in a diplomatic bag and certainly wouldn't go undetected. They had no desire to go the shipping route again, since the safe expedition had taken more than enough precious time. Frost came up with the idea of cutting the dish up into pie-shape slices and sending them over a period of a few weeks. This was not that easy, since the pie-shapes had to be hinged together to preserve the integrity of the antenna. But they risked it anyway, cut the dish into twelve pieces, mailed them by diplomatic courier four pieces at a time and had them in Moscow within three weeks.

Finally, a coded message came from the team leader in Moscow. The first few paragraphs confirmed that all the equipment, including the antenna, had arrived without any problems, and everything was in working order. Then came the clincher: "Incidentally, how the fuck do you get a five-foot antenna into a four-foot attic?"

To be functional, the dish had to be set up as close to the roof as possible, while also being hidden from sight. It had been decided that the ideal place to put it was the embassy's attic. Except nobody had bothered to check the height of the cramped space.

Imagination had got them this far, however. They weren't going to quit so close to the goal. The insulation used in the embassy building was nothing but good old earth, a common practice in Russia. So the Canadian spy went to work digging a one-foot hole between the beams and somehow managed to nestle the NSA antenna in the attic. But there was still a problem: you couldn't rotate the device once it was installed. Frost and Bowman had picked a type of antenna that had to be rotated by hand, since the sound of a motor could have been heard by Soviet listening devices planted in the embassy. So another message arrived from Moscow with a puzzling question: "What azimuth do you want the antenna on?"

Frost and Bowman looked at each other. They didn't have a clue. They wrote back: "Pick one."

The spy did. The antenna was hooked up to the receivers and D-Day finally came. Months of hard work and setbacks were about to come to fruition. The team leader in Moscow sat down in front of the receiver with his earphones on and, with a tingle running down his spine, turned on "Stephanie".

What he heard made his heart sink. It was something like: "Shhhhhhhhhhh . . ." Nothing else. Not even a taxi driver. Once the moment of extreme disappointment had passed, Frost and his colleagues tried to figure out what the problem was. They didn't have to look too far. The very-high-frequency waves they were attempting to catch were highly directional. The closer to the frequency of light the waves get, the more directional they are. Everything has to be just right for them to be intercepted. The antenna has to be on the correct azimuth, the receivers have to be tuned just right and the polarity also has to be exact. To get the idea, move the rabbit ears on a television set just an inch and see what happens to the reception. Then multiply that a hundred times for VHF waves of the kind Frost was trying to intercept. All in all, the dish was simply facing the wrong way. The agents in Moscow had dug the hole in the most convenient way they could.

Frost and Bowman weren't going to give up now. They sent back ruthless orders for their men to perform a job that turned out to be about as enjoyable as a few months in the salt mines. While one of them was sitting at the receiver, the other agent was up in the attic with a shovel and a handsaw. His job was to turn the antenna by hand, five degrees at a time, and then spin the dish on its axle five degrees at a time. For each of the 72 positions (360 degrees) of azimuth, there were also 72 other positions of polarity. In total, over 5,000 positions to catalogue. All the while, as they cut through supporting rafters and made piles of dirt, the agents were hoping the ceiling wouldn't collapse. The agent sitting at the receiver would go through all the frequencies and log each position. When he was through, he would bang on the ceiling and the dish would be moved another five degrees.

The working conditions in the attic were horrific. There was neither heat nor air conditioning; the earth insulation was like moondust that would fill the nostrils and the lungs as soon as it was moved; you couldn't stand up straight; you had no one to talk to; it was like being stuck in a chimney for days on end. The two agents couldn't even speak to each other. The Soviets had the embassy bugged and, although they didn't know where the listening devices were, the agents had to assume they were under audio surveillance. They communicated by sign language. It was bad enough that they had to risk using the handsaw.

They also had to brush the dirt off their military clerk uniforms at the end of every day, since the embassy staff, all except now four being unaware of their activities, would have naturally wondered what they had been digging up in a top-floor office. No matter how hard they tried, they couldn't quite erase the harried look on their faces when it came time to quit.

Once the tedious and filthy job was finally over, Frost studied their report and chose the azimuth that appeared to be the most productive. The team leader in the embassy was surprised to find out that the degree he picked made the dish face straight into a brick wall: apparently waves from the world-renowned Ostenkino tower were being bounced off that wall back into the Canadian embassy.

That would have to do. "Stephanie" was born. She may have come out sideways but she was there and the Canadians could proudly report to their overseers in NSA that the mission was accomplished. They were on the air and they hadn't been caught — not for lack of trying, however.

In fact, "Stephanie" was up and running in time for one of the most memorable confrontations between Canada and the

U.S.S.R., in September 1972. When Canada's bruised and battered hockey stars travelled to the Soviet Union for the final and decisive four games of the first-ever, gripping hockey series between the two countries, "Stephanie" was listening in. For the budding electronic spies, this goal was as important as Paul Henderson's magical moment 34 seconds before the end of the last match-up, that gave Canada the come-from-behind, pyrrhic victory — although "Stephanie" didn't help find Vladislav Tretiak's weakness in nets. Ironically, the Canadian hockey players had been complaining openly about the Russians spying on their every move in their hotels and elsewhere. While the Canadian media was waxing indignant about these underhanded ways, here were Canadian spies trying to do the same thing under diplomatic immunity. Meanwhile the "Stephanie" operation indirectly came in mighty handy for Frost and Bowman back in Ottawa: they used the duplicates of the equipment loaned by the Americans to listen to the radio transmission of the final game in their CSE "furnace room" — where such a thing was normally forbidden under the agency's strict rules.

Over in Moscow the equipment actually had to be turned off for part of the series because a high-ranking Canadian government official was visiting. From the start, following American and British practice, CSE's policy was that embassy listening posts would be shut off when the country's politicians happened to be passing through. Frost disagreed with the policy, since he figured that, especially in the case of the Prime Minister, the operation could contribute to the Canadian visitor's protection. But the politicians wanted to be in a position to deny the existence of a listening post should the Soviets ever ask about it.

"Stephanie" had no problem hearing things, mostly voice communications, but also frequently TASS press agency transmissions and detailed weather forecasts — lots of those.

At this early stage in Canadian electronic espionage history on foreign soil, very little analysis of the collected material was done on site. The Canadian agents had instructions to alert the ambassador should they intercept any earth-shattering information, but almost all the fruit of their labour was put on audio tape or print-outs and sent back to Canada in diplomatic pouches. Frost had arranged for the diplomatic bags to be identified by an agreed-upon number. When the courier arrived at External Affairs, the product of espionage was left under seal and shipped immediately to CSE for analysis. The material was sent south of the border to NSA as soon as physically possible.

The secure diplomatic route was also used for other insidious deeds, a few months into the operation, by a new Canadian agent who had just arrived to replace one of the original two and saw, literally, a golden opportunity to get rich. Avoiding both countries' customs and controls, the Canadian spy started buying solid gold samovars and sending them in the pouches, along with the audio tapes and other espionage material.

Both Frost and Bowman looked the other way. Frost, a good military man, figured it was up to his superior to take action if he deemed it necessary. If anything, he envied the man's inventiveness and luck although he was fully conscious Canadian law, never mind Soviet, was being broken.

It was as fool-proof a method of smuggling as you could imagine. Nobody but the people involved in a top-secret operation knew of it, since they were the only ones to handle and see the contents of the bags at either end. Realistically, who could Frost or Bowman tell? The police? The government? Too many questions would be asked. Chances were that if word ever leaked out, that would be the end of "Stephanie." Canada's eager spies were used to keeping things quiet. Besides, they were also convinced they were already breaking every law in the book with the operation itself.

The samovars kept coming every week. At least one of the two or three bags headed for CSE had gold in it. Frost and Bowman diligently stored it in the two bottom drawers of a locked filing cabinet. This charade lasted for three or four months until the drawers were both nearly full and the shipments stopped abruptly. Frost didn't ask for an explanation, but there was a sense of relief. For one thing, such an initiative was making an already dicey enterprise even more dangerous in terms of possible reprisals. It was also making the Canadian agent involved an ideal target for blackmail, which is usually the preferred way to recruit double agents.

When the "Stephanie" operator finally returned to Canada, he made several trips to CSE with an empty case that would leave the building at the end of the day full of gold samovars. The operator couldn't have got away with it at NSA, from which you can't exit with a brown paper bag. But at CSE no one was ever checked as they left the agency for what they were carrying.

A perfect crime. No record whatsoever to this day.

"Stephanie" ran relatively problem-free for its first year of operation until trouble came from an unexpected source. Frost received a message from Moscow that the intercept equipment, in a room that was off-limits to most embassy personnel, had been viewed by a chauffeur who was also in the Canadian military. The man wasn't supposed to be on the top floor of the building and had "accidentally" stumbled onto the operation. A red alert was sounded at CSE and, this time, the RCMP was called in to check on the chauffeur in question. To their horror, Frost and Bowman were told the man was suspected of being a KGB agent. Very shortly after the incident, the chauffeur was mysteriously transferred to another embassy . . . in Beijing.

Frost scratched his head in puzzlement at the logic behind such a move — putting a suspected KGB agent in our Chinese diplomatic corps. Who was he really? Was he really KGB? Could he perhaps have been working for the RCMP counter-espionage unit? Or were the Mounties setting him up for a bigger fall? He never knew. He found out years later that the man had returned to Canada and lived a life as a successful businessman.

If the KGB was ever told of what was going on in the Canadian embassy, they never did anything about it. "Stephanie" lasted about three years. But, for all their hard work and persistence, the Canadians reached the sad conclusion that they couldn't provide any "unique" information that wasn't already being obtained by "Broadside" at the American site, or "Tryst" at the British. The other more seasoned operations were churning out better and more timely material that made Canada's effort redundant. For Frost and Bowman, though, "Stephanie" had been a success. They had made stupid mistakes along the way, but, as their American mentors would say, they were learning. They couldn't fill the "holes" in the American and British intelligence-gathering that had justified "Stephanie" in the first place, but that wasn't their prime concern. The objective had been reached: they had smuggled equipment into Moscow undetected, got it running in extremely difficult circumstances and intercepted signals. Four of their agents had functioned for three years without being exposed.

NSA told them to shut "Stephanie" down. The agents were called back and every piece of equipment used in the operation was returned to Canada in the same way it had gone out . . . except the safe, which most likely still sits there, with its hole in the bottom.

This was the end of Canada's first foray into embassy collection. It would not be the last. "Stephanie" had been set up, according to Bowman, with the approval of External Affairs and the Prime Minister's Office. Was the Prime Minister told? It is hard to believe he was not. Yet in a debate in the House of Commons on January 10th, 1974, Prime Minister Trudeau stated:

> We have never, to my knowledge, certainly not under my government, engaged in any espionage abroad in the sense that we have not been looking for information in an undercover way in any other country.

FOUR
CATCHING SPIES

IN OTTAWA, MOST OF CSE'S WORK from the seventies through to the end of the Cold War was targeted on the Soviets, who used the Canadian capital as a preferred target to get to Western intelligence. In the seventies CSE was interested in the Chinese to some degree, but they had to leave that counter-espionage to the Americans, because they had no expertise whatsoever in the language and no resources to get at the methods of operation of China's spies.

It is important to recount how Canada, especially CSE, dealt with the Soviet threat in the seventies and eighties for two reasons: first, it served as the main training ground for CSE employees who were later asked to conduct international espionage abroad, against the Soviets and against other countries; second, it was used by CSE to go totally outside its mandate of being strictly a "protective" body and become an active part of the spy-catching network that is supposed to be reserved to CSIS and the RCMP. In other words, the perceived Soviet threat transformed CSE from what is supposed to be strictly a "defensive" and data-analysis establishment into an aggressive intercept operation.

Not long after "Stephanie", Mike Frost went to work in section N1A of CSE, a group of about fifteen CSE employees tasked with the "analysis" of Soviet intelligence. CSE did a lot of that. Some of it came from the two American spy satellites, the NSA's Keyhole and the CIA's Talent. Since one of the problems with those super-spy satellites is that they spit out so much data, the Americans made a deal to share the data with Canada if CSE agreed to help them process the massive amount of material they got.

Frost was one of the first CSE employees "indoctrinated" for the "Talent-Keyhole" room that was, back in the seventies, considered one of the most restricted areas at CSE. In those days even the existence of such orbiting devices was still the subject of speculation and even fiction.

Frost's main professional preoccupation in the mid-seventies became figuring out what the Soviets were up to with their own spy satellites. In 1975, both the American and British spy agencies were aware that Moscow had a network of orbiting communications satellites whose main purpose was to send messages to its spies around the world. But they were puzzled as to where those spies were, and how the system worked. Frost was one of those who contributed to the eventual solution of the puzzle, for once you know how the satellite operates, you can intercept its signals; once you can do that, with long, painstaking work, you can eventually pinpoint the destination and the receiver of the message sent from the Soviet Union. In other words, you have caught a spy.

And all you needed to do it was electronic equipment. It was the beginning of the end of the "James Bond era" of spycatching and also led to a meteoric rise in power for agencies such as CSE, NSA and GCHQ.

Mike Frost was picked to help solve the mystery of the two Soviet satellite systems that would be codenamed by the Americans "Amherst" (the "civilian" KGB system) and "Yanina-Uranium" (the military GRU tool). It took the CANUKUS partners about a year to figure it all out.

Frost was chosen because of his knowledge in the field of technical or non-Morse intercept and for his "Stephanie" experience. He was given a promotion and became one of the two sub-section heads of N1A, where he was also put in charge of intercepting more conventional high-frequency (HF) KGB/GRU communications between the Soviet Union and its agents in North America.

"Amherst" was the first one they broke. It is a belt of eight satellites that orbit the Earth at a 64° angle to the Equator and was used by the KGB to communicate with its agents around the globe.

"The Soviet spy satellites were just coming into play in those days," says Frost. "They were used to supplement the normal HF communications network. The Russians didn't yet have enough faith in their satellite system to cut off the HF link. . . . We knew very little about it and we just had to find out how it worked."

"Amherst" operated like this: with its eight "beachballs" at some time in any given day over any geographical part of the planet, a particular agent would eventually be within reach of one of these satellites. They fly in a low orbit, at roughly equal distance from each other. Their lifespan is about six months to a year and they are constantly being replaced, as all spy satellites are, mostly for lack of fuel.

The way it works — and, to the best of Frost's knowledge, the way it still works — is that Moscow "loads up" the satellite with "traffic" as it passes over Russia. Once the information is received by the orbiting device, it is also programmed to "dump" it at a given time over a specific area of the earth. Once it is over the area in question, down goes the information. When the KGB agent, Soviet or otherwise, receives the transmission at the other end, he lets Moscow know with an HF "burst transmission" that is very hard to track or intercept because it lasts for only a short time.

To explain: when using HF you don't need satellite link. It's basic wireless radio communications. A "burst" technique means that the sender compresses his HF message so that his transmission lasts perhaps only milliseconds — a couple of seconds at most — much like listening to a tape recorder on "fast forward". He sends it at a pre-determined time to make sure it won't be missed at the other end where they can leisurely decompress and decipher it.

"It became a very routine thing for the agent," explains Frost. "He knows that on a certain day, at a certain time, he sends a burst transmission."

Trying to figure out where it comes from is the tough part for counter-espionage people, because the duration of the "burst" is so short. The only way to be sure of the source of emission of the signal is to target what is believed to be the base of operations, get close enough to intercept a signal directly, and be there and listening when it happens.

Figuring out a satellite downlink can be just as tricky. The problem is that the "footprint" it leaves is so big, the agent receiving it could be — if we are talking about Canada — anywhere from Quebec City to Winnipeg. The signal is very much like a flashlight beam. It starts in a very small circle but keeps growing until it fades (except that satellite radio signals are strong enough to reach the earth, whereas a flashlight beam just fades into the night). So, if you can intercept only one transmission, all you can say is that there is a Soviet agent operating somewhere between the Gaspé Peninsula and Hudson Bay.

All messages sent by the Soviet spy agencies are sent in what is called "one-time-pad code" (for aficionados and amateur cryptologists an example of one-time pad code is provided on p. 81). In Frost's day, neither CSE nor their allies were ever able to break the Russian code. Which meant that capturing a satellite or HF transmission meant very little in itself, since they had no idea what it meant. But the reason for persisting was that, eventually, despite the huge "footprint" left by the satellite downlink, there was a way to find out where it was destined to go and possibly isolate the receiver.

"The key to it," says Frost, "is to intercept enough downlinks to be able to overlap them. Sooner or later, orbiting satellites being what they are, you will find that there is a very small area where all those transmissions overlap." In other words, the "footprint" is never exactly the same. But there is at least one part of it that always touches in the same place. It's like drawing circles all over a page, but making sure every circle includes the same dot at the centre. Sometimes, the interceptor can get lucky, and the two first "footprints" are so far apart they practically tell you where the "dot" is.

FIGURE C
HOW A ONE-TIME PAD WORKS

Random five-figure groups held by both sender and recipient:

97410	36982	12501	22473	71802	14580	
80143	91029	87871	48954	87101	23587	etc.

To encode the following: HAVE A NICE DAY: replace letters with figures as follows:

A = 11	F = 16	K = 21	P = 26	U = 31	Z = 36
B = 12	G = 17	L = 22	Q = 27	V = 32	Space = 37
C = 13	H = 18	M = 23	R = 28	W = 33	Period = 38
D = 14	I = 19	N = 24	S = 29	X = 34	Comma = 39
E = 15	J = 20	O = 25	T = 30	Y = 35	Question = 40

h	a	v	e	sp	a	sp	n	i	c	e	sp	d	a	y
18	11	32	15	37	11	37	24	19	13	15	37	14	11	35

Using one-time pad, subtract figure substitutions using false subtractions (no carrying):

97410	36982	12501	22473	71802	14580
18113	21537	11372	41913	15371	41135
89307	15455	01239	81560	66531	73455

Transmit these five figure groups to recipient[1].
To decode, recipient subtracts these five figure groups from one-time pad using false subtraction.

97410	36982	12501	22473	71802	14580
89307	15455	01239	81560	66531	73455
18113	21537	11372	41913	15371	41135

Substitute letters for figures:

18	11	32	15	37	11	37	24	19	13	15	37	14	11	35
h	a	v	e	sp	a	sp	n	i	c	e	sp	d	a	y

1. Sender usually indicates to recipient in the clear the page/row/column used.

Usually, however, you need dozens or hundreds, maybe a thousand transmissions to figure out who on earth they are aimed at.

CSE hired an engineer in N1A to draw up a computer program that would do the analysis for them. "Amherst" was relatively easy to figure out because it is a network of satellites that transmits an "identifier" all the time, which means it is always sending a signal to confirm it is operating. However, when it "downloads" information to an agent, the "identifying signal" stops. At that point the intercept operators know a communication is imminent. The problem, in the early days, was that neither CSE nor its allied spy agencies had a clue when the satellites would "downlink". So they had to keep a 24-hour watch on them, once they figured out the eight-ball belt. All the "overt" intercept sites of CSE, NSA and GCHQ were tasked with "Amherst" intercept. So were the "covert" ones. What they were trying to find out was the frequency being used, the time of day the message was sent, and who was receiving it.

The "Amherst" satellites were programmed to rewind and replay the tape of the Moscow "upload" should the Soviet agent on foreign land have missed it, for any reason, when it passed overhead. All the agent's "HF burst" said was that he had received the message from headquarters. Most of the time the "burst" lasted less than a second. But it was enough for the KGB to tell the "Amherst" satellite to rewind the tape and erase it.

If the Soviet agent on foreign assignment had a lengthy message to send back to Moscow, he would use one of the satellites to do so. All he had to do was wait to hear on his home receiver the "identifier" signal of one of the eight "Amherst" orbiters and send the message up by VHF — which, contrary to HF, goes straight out into space. The satellite would store it, then each time one of the eight satellites passed over the Soviet capital, the KGB operators would "interrogate" it, asking basically: "Do you have any traffic on board?" If the answer was "yes", Moscow pressed a button and the information was "dumped".

It was a lot trickier to figure out the GRU's "Yanina-Uranium" system. Called in the business a "store-dump" system, the way it works is a lot more "silent" than the "Amherst". It too is "uploaded" in Moscow. But once the information is received by the orbiter, the satellite doesn't then emit any kind of signal, contrary to the Amherst identifier that lets you know at all times where the device is. There is another major difference in what is considered a "passive" system. It contains only three or four satellites, as opposed to "Amherst's" eight, and has a highly elliptical orbit around the earth at a 45° angle to the Equator. So it comes close enough to the planet to "store" or "dump" traffic only once in a while. It zips around the globe at a very high speed and then flies way off into outer space, relatively out of reach.

The "loading" of the satellite sent by Moscow was code-named "Yanina" and the "downloading" to the agent was also code-named "Yanina". Messages sent up to the orbiter by the agent were known as the "Uranium" side of the operation. The "downloading" from the satellite to Moscow was also codenamed "Uranium". It became so confusing that CSE had to refer to the transmissions as "Yanina-up", "Yanina-down", and "Uranium-up," "Uranium-down". The "upload" in Moscow was done on a command from GRU headquarters, but (unlike the preprogammed Amherst) no command was given at all from the Soviet Union for the "download" to the agent. Instead the Russian spy abroad received an HF transmission from Moscow to let him know there was something for him on the satellite. The agent then waited for it to pass overhead and sent a VHF signal that told the orbiter to "dump" whatever it had stored for him.

CSE and the other agencies trying to solve the "Yanina-Uranium" problem figured out that the enemy agent must have been given a timetable of sorts — something like a bus schedule — telling him when a satellite would pass overhead. Because, like them, without an identifier he couldn't hear it coming and he had to know exactly the short period when it was within earshot.

In the early days, the CANUKUS people had quite a hard time solving the "Yanina-Uranium" mystery, because they had no idea where the satellites were, what frequency the agent would be using or how many orbiters were being used. All they could speculate was that the Soviet agents had to be communicating with the satellite by VHF "burst transmissions", but these lasted for only a few seconds, and to intercept them you had to be close enough to do so.

The first step in solving the puzzle was to figure out the orbit and the parameters between the satellites. Once the counter-espionage people had managed to do that by constant tracking, they would at least know when one of the devices was within their reach or an agent's reach.

"We were eventually able to isolate some 'Uranium' transmissions and narrow them down first to cities and then to buildings," says Frost. Now they were close to catching a spy. And they did.

CSE worked very closely with what was then known as the RCMP's Security Service, now the Canadian Security Intelligence Service (CSIS). The Security Service was tasked with monitoring the movements of suspected KGB and GRU agents, because those movements were crucial to their transmissions being intercepted.

Every CSE employee involved in the counter-espionage operation was given a little card — the size of a business card — with red diplomatic car-plates on them. Any licence numbered between 800 and 999 and followed by the letters CDA to Z, XTR to Z, or CCA to Z (the third letter being any one from A to Z) were cars belonging to Eastern Bloc countries. On the back of the little card was a phone number to call, collect, 24 hours a day, should one of those vehicles be spotted in an "unusual" location or movement. The card gave these instructions, in English and French: "Identify yourself — Report plate number — Give location and time of sighting — If possible: make, model, colour, no. of occupants, unusual activity, etc." Employees were to carry it with them at all times, and were on strict orders to use it.

One day Mike Frost almost had a car accident as he was driving down Highway 16 with his family. All of a sudden he spotted two cars parked on the side of the road. The first one, he could see, had a red plate on it and, lo and behold, it was an Eastern Bloc plate.

Interestingly enough, the other car had Ontario plates. Two men were standing there, in the middle of nowhere, having what seemed like a lengthy conversation.

Frost stunned the members of his family when he suddenly said nervously: "I've got to get to a phone! I've got to get to a phone!" He did, and gave a detailed description and the plate numbers of both cars.

He doesn't know the result of his intervention but, assuming the diplomat was not a double agent talking to a Canadian counter-espionage man (which is highly unlikely), both men probably went high on the Security Service's hit-parade list of suspected spies.

That was not Frost's normal role in capturing Soviet spies, however. In 1975 and 1976 section N1A was heavily involved in isolating communications to foreign agents. Frost recalls three interesting cases where CSE's expertise was required by the Security Service.

The first was that of a Soviet scientist by the name of Khvostantsev, who was in Canada working at the National Research Council on an exchange program. He had apparently approached a Canadian scientist at NRC to buy some documents. The Canadian went right to the RCMP and reported him. CSE got involved to see if any radio signals could be intercepted from the man's residence. They discovered rather quickly that he was using the "Amherst" satellite system, which meant without a doubt he was KGB. Not only did they isolate the "burst transmissions", but the man was always home when they occurred. Once they had proven, thanks to the intercept, that the man was indeed an agent, the RCMP mounted a successful sting operation. He was expelled from the country in 1977.

Another Soviet agent, a Lt.-Colonel Smirnov, was also the subject of a CSE-RCMP operation. He tried to buy secrets from Bell Northern. The Soviets often targeted communications and computer firms to copy their research. Once again the Canadian employee alerted the RCMP, who then went to CSE who then found that the Soviet spy was communicating with the "Yanina-Uranium" system, which meant he was GRU. He too was stung and thrown out of the country in 1977.

What is interesting about these cases, and the ones to follow, are that they were broken from a location that really shouldn't have existed. It was the furnace room, on the roof of CSE's main building on Heron Road, that Bowman and Frost had transformed into an intercept site when they mounted "Stephanie". Technically it had been put there to check the electronic gear for "Stephanie". It was where Bowman and Frost had listened to the radio transmission of the last game of the 1972 Russia–Canada hockey series. If you drive by CSE, you can see, on the main roof, what looks like a smaller building, with a white door. Right above that white door are a number of small antennas and a number of cables coming down the side of the building into a junction box against the brick wall. These are the antennas that were used to intercept Soviet satellites, cellular phones and microwave towers.

"This was clearly outside our mandate," says Frost. "We were not supposed to do live intercept. We were supposed to analyse it, but get it through other means. We set up the room so we could do intercept without involving any of our other stations — like Alert, Moncton or Inuvik, for instance. It made it possible to do 'covert' stuff without too many people knowing about it."

Foreign agents, by the way, can't operate with permanent antennas: that would give them away. They use small dishes that are stashed away until they are needed to communicate with a satellite. With the proper equipment, this can be done from an apartment balcony or even, in the case of VHF transmissions, right through the roof of a house. An HF antenna has to be much bigger. It's actually a wire and it has to go outside — on a clothesline, for instance — and be cut to the right frequency. The agent has to get the wire outside and pull it back in. But that is relatively easy to disguise for "burst transmissions".

A good way to understand the difference is that your FM radio is on VHF, which explains why you can hear it nice and clearly inside, because the signals easily penetrate wood or concrete, whereas AM functions on MF to HF, which explains the distortions on certain stations inside a home.

Strangely enough, although it can reach outer space, a VHF signal does not travel "earthly" distances well, because if aimed upward it heads straight for outer space unless it is directed, as regular FM signals are, to serve a given market.

The third case of spycatching from the seventies is the one Frost remembers the best, because it involved a Canadian citizen. The RCMP had told CSE that there was a suspected spy operating from his home, a highrise apartment building on Prince of Wales Drive, in suburban Ottawa. CSE already knew there were "burst transmissions" coming out of and to the area from the intercept in its "furnace room". This time, though, CSE used one of its white vans to get closer to the suspected agent. They determined over time that the chances were high this Canadian was a KGB agent. It took them two or three years to amass enough evidence to be sure since it takes a long time to isolate HF transmissions: when you start looking for them, you basically know nothing more than the fact the Moscow transmission is being directed toward the Western Hemisphere — and there are hundreds of transmissions sent to agents around the world every single day.

"It's a very tedious, frustrating, time-consuming job," says Frost.

Once they had identified the Canadian working for the KGB, as far as Frost knows, nothing was done about it. The man was not arrested, although it is not improbable that the Security Service used its knowledge to turn him into a double agent. The philosophy behind this apparent passiveness, the decision to refrain from prosecuting a Soviet agent, is rather simple. "You spend years trying to catch this guy," explains Frost. "When you finally find him, if you prosecute him, the Soviets will simply replace him and you're back to square one again. However, if you are following him and you intercept his communications, although you can't break the code, you can find out what kind of information he's after, what he's supplying, and assess the damage he may be doing. You may even decide to feed him disinformation. If you know what he's up to and how good he is at it, you can make an assessment of how serious his spying operation really is. . . . Mind you, I don't know who makes the decision as to whether we prosecute or not. . . . The other obvious angle is that you have some-body who could easily be persuaded to become a double agent."

One fascinating and worrisome point Frost raises about his former employer is that he is "one hundred per cent sure CSE has been infil-trated by a Russian mole, perhaps more than one by now. If there is no mole at CSE, it would mean that CSE is the only intelligence agency in the free world that has not been penetrated by the former Soviet Union. And that doesn't make sense. NSA, GCHQ, DSD in Australia — they have all been penetrated."

How did the KGB make a "mole"? Normally he or she was "groomed" from the high-school or university level — usually high-school. An individual was picked because he or she was exceptional-ly bright and maybe had some left-leaning tendencies. There were offers, perhaps of job possibilities in a foreign country, without iden-tifying the country, or perhaps even of a job in Canada with a high-profile prestigious firm. This work was done by Soviet agents, some-times Canadian citizens on the KGB payroll.

It takes years to "mould a mole". Slowly you become friends with the person, the family, the spouse. You suggest specific courses to take in university, claiming to have influence in a foreign country which would hire a person trained in such a way. Then you reach the next step where you start putting down money, paying for their edu-cation, or a special course. You take them on trips abroad and assume the expenses. It's all a way of making the potential mole feel as if he or she owes something to the agent. This goes on for a number of years. "After a while," says Frost, "the person not only trusts the agent, but starts feeling indebted to him."

When the "mole" finally graduates, the agent says something like: "We need your services for just a little while. Try to get a job at Bell Northern, CSE, CSIS. . . ." The agent still doesn't tell the person a spy is in the making here — or rather, near completion. He just sug-gests that it could be made easy for them to get a position with a given company or government department. If the agent has done his work well, the "mole" will have many if not all of the qualifications required for one of those jobs and will make it to the top of the candidates' list. Finally, the unsuspecting spy may end up working at CSE.

The process thereafter is very slow and subtle. Questions are asked by the agent about apparently innocuous things that are going on inside or about how a certain individual is doing. Little bits of information start to slip out. When the KGB agent finally thinks the "mole" is trapped, he goes for the jugular. He says: "If you can find this out for me or get me this in hard copy, I'm going to give you this amount of money. . . ." This is payback time. If the "mole" refuses, then the agent drops the bomb, says he is with the KGB and starts listing the things he has been told. They may have seemed insignificant to the "mole" but, added together, they put him in a situation that makes it look as if he or she revealed a lot of secrets. The question of the money paid for the university courses, the foreign trips is brought up. The agent threatens him or her with exposure. By this time, the "mole" is usually so deeply involved that he or she has no way to turn back.

CSE has been in existence long enough now — at least since the last war — that Frost is certain the Soviets planted a mole there. It's interesting to speculate about the effect of the fall of Communism in the Soviet Union on such a "mole". In all events such a person would by now have risen through the ranks and be right there near the top.

Frost claims that, in the two to three years he spent in counter-espionage, up to twenty suspected spies of non-Soviet origin — mostly Canadian citizens — were being tracked by the RCMP and CSE. Yet if any were ever charged and prosecuted, the media knew nothing about it — which seems a near impossibility.

There were, however, thirteen Soviet diplomats expelled in one swoop by the Trudeau government in 1978. The following January the short-lived Joe Clark government threw another three diplomats from the Soviet embassy out of the country. This time the Kremlin reacted by expelling Canada's military attaché in Moscow, Col. Harold Gold, "for intelligence reasons". Then the Secretary of

State for External Affairs, Flora MacDonald, said there were no Canadians spying in Moscow. Perhaps not at that time. But "Stephanie" had shut down only five years earlier.

Much of the information that justified the extradition of the Soviets was gathered by CSE in conjunction with the Security Service. Mike Frost has a good idea how those diplomats were caught.

When Frost joined the N1A section, he was quickly "indoctrinated" for an operation codenamed "Capricorn". It involved not only the RCMP — or now CSIS — and a very questionable method of intercept but also an outside corporate giant who co-operated in what was really a spying operation on a foreign nation.

"Capricorn" was the tap the RCMP had on all CN-CP communications between the Soviet embassy in Ottawa and Moscow, most of them in those days by telex. (Fax machines were coming into use but had not yet entered the mainstream of the communications industry in 1975.) These communications were being carried by what is known as "a common carrier", a service embassies around the world use to get their messages over to the Mother Country.

Every day, an RCMP courier would show up at the CN-CP communications offices to pick up boxes of hard copy containing all the Soviet embassy's communications with Moscow using a common carrier. CN-CP just handed it over. Whenever the Russians asked to send a message, CN-CP simply made two copies of it, one to send and one for the Canadian counter-espionage people. "We got tons of it," says Frost.

Was this ethical? Well, let's just say that Canadians always raised a fuss when they suspected Communist countries of doing that sort of thing to them. For the RCMP, it was just tit for tat. CN-CP's decision, however, to go along with such a massive operation of providing all raw traffic, without the police having to use any legal justification, is staggering. But at the time the Russians were "the bad guys" for everybody.

Did the RCMP or CSIS ever obtain information from this same source, in the same manner, that had to do with Canadian citizens and nothing to do with espionage? Frost has no answer to that. The potential for such abuse, though, was clearly there.

The material received from the CN-CP "tap" was so voluminous that a whole section of CSE was dedicated to analysing it. Some of it was encoded, some wasn't. The key, however, to breaking a code is to get enough traffic that you can eventually figure out a pattern. We don't know if CSE's cryptologists ever succeeded. If they did, they wouldn't have told anybody.

"Capricorn" was Frost's gateway to another operation that was a little more down the technical side of his alley. Again, he had to be "indoctrinated" for what was known then — and probably still is — as "Kilderkin".

"This was very hush-hush," says Frost of "Kilderkin". It was an intercept site that the RCMP and CSE set up together on Charlotte Street in Ottawa, right across the road from the Soviet embassy, on the corner of Laurier Street. It was located in a typical Sandy Hill house, in the rather exclusive downtown Ottawa neighbourhood that now houses a lot of embassies and ambassadors' residences. "Kilderkin" was designed to target the entire Soviet embassy complex, which is surrounded by an eight-foot-high gate, for any emanation or radiation of electronic equipment that might seep out.

"If that embassy was radiating anything, we wanted it," says Frost, "and we needed to be very close to do that."

Frost figures the "Kilderkin" site is still in operation today. One of the tell-tale signs is that the curtains on the windows are constantly drawn. Since there was so much electronic gear in there, and the Soviets were within eye view, it was only normal procedure to make sure the Soviets couldn't see what was inside.

Despite the proximity and the amount of effort and equipment put into intercepting Soviet signals, the "Kilderkin" house was deemed at some point not to be good enough to do the complete job. The operation there continued, but CSE and the RCMP decided to get even closer to the Soviet chancellery. They did this by putting antennas into the garage of what is now known as "Paterson House", at 500 Wilbrod Street, the Queen-Anne-style home of Canadian Senator Norman Paterson from 1941 until his death in 1983. The garage literally hugs the wall of the Soviet building.

When Mike Frost put on his spy cape one more time and went on a reconnaissance mission at "Paterson House" in June 1994 for the sake of this book, he discovered that it has become not only a "Heritage Home" and tourist attraction but also the home of the Maharishi Heaven on Earth Development Corporation, a transcendental meditation organization. The pamphlet provided to visitors does not mention that the garage was once a CSE intercept site. As far as Frost's keen eye could detect, the site doesn't appear to be there any more. In fact, even in the seventies the antennas were there for only a few months since it was very risky to be that close, and the site didn't produce much more than they already had anyway.

Why were the Canadian counter-espionage people putting so much effort into this? Because if you can pick up radiation from electronic equipment, it is also possible that you can pick up voice or other kinds of transmissions. You don't just hear a "buzz" when you capture emanations of this kind.

CSE was also able to establish that the Soviets, for their part, were listening to us. CSE picked up electronic radiations from intercept equipment the Soviets were using against Canada. They had what amounted to an intercept site inside their embassy. This was mainly given away by regular power surges when the Soviets turned on their listening devices. CSE also picked up radiation from oscillators, a component of intercept equipment, and found that some of the power surges were occurring outside normal business hours. They didn't see any antennas or huts on the roof.

At one point the "Kilderkin" people became very excited, because their equipment had picked up a video transmission, on a UHF frequency, coming from inside the Soviet compound. "We thought we had something really hot," says Frost. It took them several months to figure out what it was, mainly because such signals are not easy to demodulate and reproduce. They all felt a bit ridiculous when they finally realized that the video camera that they had "intercepted" was actually a security camera looking down Charlotte Street — the sort that just about every embassy in every major world capital is equipped with.

To the best of Frost's knowledge, while he was in counterespionage, "Kilderkin" didn't pay its way. They never really came up with any staggering diplomatic intelligence from this elaborate, close-up surveillance. Compared to the success of the "Amherst" and "Yanina-Uranium" intercepts, "Kilderkin" was not very effective. It wasn't conceived to catch spies either, since the Canadians knew the Soviets did not communicate with their agents through embassy channels.

One final interesting point about the Charlotte-Laurier-Wilbrod sites is that the intercept operators were members of the military from the Leitrim base. CSE piloted the project, but they wanted to be in a position to deny direct involvement if ever asked about it.

Going out of its mandate in even more outrageous fashion was not something CSE hesitated to do when orders came from "higher up". One day, in 1975, totally out of the blue, Mike Frost was called into the office of his section head, Steven Blackburn.

"Mike," said Blackburn, "I wonder if we could do intercept work for the Security Service on an individual living in the Ottawa area. . . ."

Frost sensed right away that something was slightly out of whack. His superior didn't seem too eager to divulge any details of the RCMP's request too quickly.

"Why don't you get Leitrim to do it?" asked Frost.

"Oh no. . . . This is one we have to do right here out of CSE."

"Well, let's get Leitrim *operators* to do it."

"Oh no. . . . This has got to stay within CSE."

"Why?"

"Because the target is the Prime Minister's wife."

Frost just about fell off his chair: "I beg your pardon?"

Blackburn took a deep breath and went on almost reluctantly: "The Security Service was wondering if there was anything CSE could do to assist them in determining whether Margaret Trudeau is buying and using pot. . . ."

"Steve, what on earth can we do?"

"I don't know. Can we listen to phones, can we listen to anything?"

"Steve, I wouldn't even know where to start!"

"Well, can you try it?"

"Sure, we can try it. But we're talking the Prime Minister's wife here, for chrissakes! I don't even know what I'm looking for!"

"Well, the RCMP just asked if there was anything we could do. Can you check?"

"Technically, yeah. I can go to our room on the roof and have a look."

"Well, do it."

"Okay."

Mike Frost was near shell-shocked when he walked out of the office. He was used to obeying orders and all that, but this had to be out of line. CSE was already breaking its mandate by intercepting signals from its Heron Road headquarters; it was intercepting conversations between ordinary Canadians while "testing its gear". Now they wanted him to go after Margaret Trudeau because she might have been smoking pot! It just didn't make any sense to him, whichever way he looked at it. She was in no way suspected of espionage. Why was the RCMP so adamant about this? Were they trying to get at Pierre Trudeau for some reason, or just protect him? Or were they working under orders from their political masters?

Those were the days that preceded the famous McDonald Commission into wrongdoings by the RCMP — barn-burnings, break-ins, etc. The RCMP were a little more free-wheeling than they would be today — this was before their Security Service, as a result of the

Commission's findings, became a civilian department known by the acronym CSIS.

For the first and perhaps only time in his spying career, Frost put in only a token effort. He still did it, though. Orders were orders.

"I went up to the 'furnace room', I hooked up some VHF receivers, some spectrum analysers, some recorders and I started to go methodically through all the car-phone conversations that I heard," says Frost. In other words, he was listening in on a lot of other unsuspecting Canadians too, something he loathed.

"I came in at night, I came in on weekends. I didn't come in early in the morning because I didn't think Maggie Trudeau was a person who would get up and do that kind of business in a car at that time of the day. I wasn't really looking. I didn't think it was right, I didn't like it, I did it more to please my boss, I guess, than anything else, because I'm not the kind of guy to say 'no'.

"I did this for a month or two . . . I would watch the press to learn when she was in residence at Sussex Drive or at Harrington Lake, their summer residence. The Security Service would give us information on when she would be travelling — and therefore possibly using her car phone. I remember telling Steve that they should give us her movements when she was not with the Prime Minister, because that would most probably be when she would be doing it. So we focussed on when she was travelling alone in the area. If it was in the evening or on a weekend, I would come in and go through the frequencies I knew were being used by car phones, though frankly I found it a little ridiculous that if she were using or buying pot, she'd do it from a car phone anyway.

"There was no question in my mind that the intercept was clearly illegal. But it was so easy to do. If she *had* eventually used a car phone for a drug purchase we would eventually have got it. But what would we do with it?"

When Frost first started on the Margaret Trudeau operation, he reported to his section head almost on a daily basis. Then it was every second or third day and eventually the reports of "no progress" came every two weeks or so.

"I frankly think Blackburn didn't care and didn't want to do it any more than I did. We simply did it because of the Security Service request, good relations and all that. Also we didn't really know from how high up the orders came. I'm relieved and glad I didn't find anything."

In fact, Margaret herself would admit to pot-smoking at 24 Sussex Drive in her "tell-all" book *Beyond Reason*, published in 1979. But the story does raise the question of how far Canada's security establishment is willing to go to invade the lives of the citizens of the country it is supposed to protect. If they are daring enough to go after the Prime Minister's wife, where do the rest of us rank on the list of possible targets?

Were other Canadians, not suspected of being KGB spies, subject to CSE scrutiny? No doubt some Quebecers, probably many high-ranking ones, were. Because there is a mysterious "French Problem" section at CSE that is dedicated to "analysing" intelligence to do with Quebec separation. Did they just analyse, or were the employees in the section tasked, like Frost who was technically an analyst, to perform some exceptional intercept? The odds are that they were. It would follow logically from the rest of CSE's way of operating. Later chapters will show just how determined CSE was to tap into Quebec-France communications in other parts of the world.

"My feeling and the feeling of my peers at CSE was that it was almost a given that CSE was doing Quebec intercept," says Frost. He has no direct knowledge of any "covert" operation carried out from CSE headquarters on that question. "I can't tell you that nobody did it," he says. "We're talking here about the Trudeau era and that man would have gone to any lengths to win the battle over separation. On the other hand, I can't say I ever saw anybody actually doing Quebec intercept from CSE or any raw copy coming from there."

Frost strongly suspects that the people from the "French Problem" section went to the Americans, to NSA, asking them to do some intercept against France-Quebec communications with their Talent-Keyhole satellites.

"I don't know for sure. . . . But if somebody were to tell me so authoritatively today, I would simply say that I totally expected it. I mean, if they asked me to spy on the Prime Minister's wife . . ."

Mike Frost's real calling, however, was still around the corner. Significant as spycatching and eavesdropping in Ottawa was, it would pale in comparison with what CSE had in store for him. After "Stephanie" CSE had put "embassy collection" into dry dock. Now, however, "Pilgrim" was about to be built and launched.

FIVE
"MOVE THE BIRDS"

"HURRY UP AND GET YOUR ASS in gear, because we want you into Beijing!"

If it had been any other person speaking to them, if the conversation had taken place anywhere else, the three Canadians would have laughed hysterically. Sure. Just a measly little espionage trick among the Chinese. Chicken feed.

But being inside the NSA compound in Fort Meade was rarely a joking matter. And men like Patrick O'Brien, in charge of all covert embassy and "special" collection operations for NSA around the world, didn't kid about such matters. It was his main, if not his only, purpose in life: seek the "enemy" out, find a way, any way, to intercept his most secret communications, as many as and as often as possible, and use them to further the American cause, for the "good side".

O'Brien was physically, almost charismatically, impressive. Then in his mid-forties, he was 6'4", a heavy-set balding man with a deep James Earl Jones type of voice. When he walked into a room, even in a crowd, you could feel his presence. When he said something would be done, you just had the feeling there was no way it could be otherwise.

Mike Frost, Frank Bowman and the newly appointed chief of CSE himself, Peter Hunt, had made the trip to the American spy centre many times before. But this mission in 1977 was extraordinary. Another foray into "embassy collection" was being seriously considered for Canada.

O'Brien wasn't going to deflate their enthusiasm or let them off the hook. If anything, he wanted to shock them into attention. Not only did he have specific ideas as to how and where they were to go about performing their little tricks; the NSA man had every intention of making their job as easy as it could possibly be. This time, there would be no turning back. "Stephanie" had been fun. Well, the fun was over. NSA meant business. They wanted Canada to jump with both feet into the most advanced spying network on the planet. They were also willing to go to any lengths to make sure the Canadians lived up to their intentions.

For at least a decade now a familiar threat had circulated at the top levels of CSE. It derived from the fact that the Americans thought Canada wasn't doing its fair share of spying on foreign soil, in fact, wasn't doing anything at all in that domain, while nevertheless continuing to benefit from most of the material NSA and GCHQ produced at high risk.

"Stephanie" had been born out of such a complaint when the Yanks had threatened to cut off the intelligence they gave Canada freely — or in return for small, less meaningful services. To those in-the-know, NSA's persistent gripe sounded much like the father who keeps telling his son he'll take away the keys to the Cadillac if the son doesn't put in a tank of gas once in a while. The son shrugs and doesn't really believe in such a reprisal. But by 1977, four years after the shutdown of Canada's first covert operation in Moscow, the Americans were not taking this lightly any more. Embassy collection had mushroomed as the most productive and cost-effective method of getting to information less friendly nations didn't want to fall into the hands of the Americans and their closest allies.

By 1977, the director of NSA, Bobby Inman, was not only showing signs of impatience at the Canucks' take-it-easy attitude. Word came back to Peter Hunt that his American equivalent was willing and very capable of putting a lot of pressure on powerful people in Canada to get his way. Hunt had been head of CSE's L group when "Stephanie" had taken place. To him, Inman's pressure tactics were not only understandable, they were long overdue. He certainly wasn't going to get in Inman's way. If anything, he would provide his own intelligence on who could get the Canadian government moving on this, and how.

Hunt called on Frank Bowman. "Pressure from NSA has been mounting on embassy collection," he said. "They are serious about cutting us off if we don't get in the game."

Bowman showed little sign of surprise, but perhaps a little excitement.

"Why don't you set yourself up with somebody else and do a feasibility study of the matter . . . report back to me."

"All right. But I want Frost."

Mike Frost was not in Alert this time, but he wasn't thrilled with the job he was doing at CSE. After "Stephanie", with all its screw-ups and moments of elation, an office job — even one catching spies — brought very little meaning to his life any more.

No cryptic letter was needed this time. When Bowman called him in casually, Frost thought he saw a hint of a smirk on his face as he said: "Just had a talk with Peter Hunt. They want us to get back into embassy collection."

Frost had always secretly hoped this day would come, but there had been moments when he had wondered if his best spying days were already behind him.

He hesitated as long as a kid being handed a Mickey Mantle rookie card.

"Let's go for it! Tell me want you what me to do. . . . Does this mean we get our own little office with two desks to conquer the world from, just like before?"

"You got it," chuckled Bowman. "But forget about the safe this time."

Then the two men stared at each other and Frost said: "What the hell are we going to call this one?" Operations like these always have to have a name. A name gives meaning, a superior purpose almost. And it is simply the spy thing to do — possibly a holdover from the war days when resistance fighters got their orders from poems read over the airwaves.

"Why don't we call it 'Julie'?" said Bowman.

"Julie?"

"Yeah. . . . That's the name of Peter's other daughter."

"Stephanie" had taken the first steps. "Julie" would learn to run.

"Julie" would also find out very early that thinking of running and doing it are two very different things. Especially in a country like Canada that prefers people who just sit still and don't rock the boat, certainly not this new prototype.

As they sat at their desks in their special little "Julie" office, Frost and Bowman came to wonder how the rebirth of their dream caper had come about. Sure Inman had pushed his weight around. But how had they got to the point where NSA was inviting them further into their inner sanctum of spying methods and equipment than Canada had ever imagined possible?

"Julie" was already under way, although spinning its wheels to a great extent, when Frost, Bowman and Peter Hunt made the crucial trip down to Fort Meade to discuss their "feasibility" study with the people who had been pushing for it in the first place. For Frost, this was one of the most momentous events in his career to date. He travelled in the back of the car, while the chief of CSE Peter Hunt and the leader of "Julie", Frank Bowman, sat in front. Frost carried the suitcases, but that was just fine with him. He had known of Peter Hunt from prestigious St. George's School. But Hunt, who was ahead of him by four years in school, was distant and aristocratic, very pseudo-British in demeanour and language, someone who did not associate easily with underlings.

The three of them had dinner at the Howard Johnson motel, in Laurel, Maryland, the night before the crucial meeting at NSA. The establishment was serving free wine with the dinner. Frost ordered soda water because he was trying to stay on the wagon. Bowman never drank, and had coffee. Hunt, however, said he would like his glass of free wine.

"What kind of wine would you like: red, white or rosé?" asked the waitress.

"I'd like a glass of rosé," said Hunt.

The waitress looked at him with a straight face and asked: "Sir, would you like a red rosé or a white rosé?"

Rose-faced and with his sternest British accent Hunt quipped: "I would like a rosé rosé!"

All entertainment aside, the next day's meeting would eventually change Canada's role in international espionage. Months of backroom negotiations and contact-building had gone into preparing for it. So much so that when the Canadians walked into the office of Patrick O'Brien, the Americans had yet another bomb to drop on them.

"Give us the co-ordinates of the embassies you want to target," started O'Brien, "and we will task our two 'birds' to take pictures and see whatever else we can find."

The "birds" in question were the spy satellites NSA and the CIA had at their disposal. For them to offer their use to the Canadians was so extraordinary that it underlined the full importance of their desire to have Canada get into this game. The Americans use their spy satellites extensively. But they don't move them around at anybody's beck and call. First of all, they have their own preoccupations. Second, it costs enormous amounts of money to do that. However, here was O'Brien offering to "move the birds" to help the Canadians without even being asked.

This was an era when the world knew of the existence of these orbiting observers and had heard fantastic stories about their capabilities — like being able to take pictures so precise you could read the licence plate on a car. But it was still a highly guarded secret as to how much the devices were being utilized, and they seemed much more the stuff of Tom Clancy novels than of reality.

O'Brien's astounding offer and general forcefulness had not developed overnight, however. Behind this high-level meeting between his top people and the Canadians lay the work of another Canadian by the name of Stew Woolner (who became chief of CSE in the late eighties). Woolner was known as CSE's CANSLO. That was an acronym for Canadian Senior Liaison Officer at NSA. He was of course working at the U.S. agency, although far from being an actual part of their operations. Since Woolner's job definition was to maintain a good working relationship between CSE and NSA, he was an easy target for the eager Bobby Inman.

Woolner had started doing some investigative work on his own within NSA, mainly trying to find out who were the best people Canada could deal with to adhere to Inman's incessant request. It wasn't as easy as it sounds. The CANSLO was not viewed as on the same level as other employees of the agency when it came to top-secret matters. He had to be extremely careful about how and who he approached, since the paranoia about "moles" was always present within NSA walls — much more so than at CSE. There's no one like a spy to spot another spy. In fact, Woolner was rather like Casper the Friendly Ghost to the Americans. They knew he was snooping, but wouldn't do any harm.

He had managed, however, to get in contact with Patrick O'Brien and discovered that O'Brien not only knew about embassy collection but was the head honcho of the huge operation. That was a stroke of luck since O'Brien had spent three years himself on an exchange program at CSE — as the Americans' friendly spook — and knew its methods and people well. O'Brien also had CIA agents under his command and was well known throughout the Signals Intelligence (SIGINT) world.

Woolner finally told O'Brien about Canada's interest in reviving "Stephanie". An elated O'Brien said: "Whenever you guys are ready to talk turkey, send your people down and we'll talk to them."

And so came Hunt, Bowman and Frost to hear a message that couldn't be blunter: "Whatever help you need we will give you.

We'll lend you equipment, we'll even give you people if you want!"
That last remark by O'Brien was taken as tongue-in-cheek by the
Canadians. But it may well have been meant.

O'Brien now made it clear that NSA's preferred choice for
Canada's first major intercept site was Beijing. "We want you in
there," he said with a tone that begged no reply.

All the way back to Canada, the three "Julie" operators were as
pumped up as kids on their way to Disneyworld. The Americans had
convinced them this could be done and, more important, that they
could prove to their own authorities it could be done. Maybe, for a
moment, they forgot they were still working for a Canadian agency.
They would soon find out.

Frost and Bowman made one more trip abroad in the course of edu-
cating "Julie", this time across the Atlantic to British Intelligence's
GCHQ. The visit had none of the dramatics involved in the American
encounter, but they did learn quite a bit from the Brits. Their greatest
lesson was that, co-operative as their Yankee friends had been, the
Yanks had also obviously kept quite a few of their secrets from the
Canadians. These mainly had to do with the kind of covers they used
for their agents and the methods they had invented to get their equipment in and out of hostile countries.

Low-key as it was, the GCHQ information on these and other
matters would prove invaluable. It also convinced the Canadians that
you really didn't need the kind of massive investment in technological, financial and human resources that the Americans used to achieve
their goals.

Sitting in their two-man office, Frost and Bowman were like two mad
scientists who had just discovered how to change lead into gold.
Paranoid about anybody who asked after their little project, they were
ecstatic when the two of them were alone. Their conversations with
American and British agents made their report to Peter Hunt a rela-

tively easy essay. Within three weeks of their two trips abroad they highly recommended that Canada go full steam ahead into embassy collection or be left behind in a rapidly expanding field.

This recommendation would have been hotly debated, of course, had the question been put to the Canadian public or, at the very least, to some of Canada's left-leaning liberals or ardent nationalists. But Bowman and Frost were spooks. And they were good at their jobs. They knew that with the formidable advances in communications since the days of "Stephanie", especially with the growing use of microwave, the only way to do truly effective intercept was to be in close — and that meant embassy collection. From a military, economic and political point of view, if the Canadian government wanted that "edge", it just had to take the plunge.

One of their first conclusions was that more people within the government, starting with CSE, would have to be let in on the "Julie" feasibility study. First on the list of new players would have to be CSE's chief of security, Victor Szakowski, the former RCMP rough-and-tumble guy. That didn't exactly thrill Frost, since Szakowski, he knew, was the stereotypical security chief. But it had to be done, since security matters like cover stories for agents and special clearances would be crucial to the operation. Frost and Bowman called him in for a briefing.

"We have been given clearance to establish covert collection intercept posts within our embassies abroad," said Bowman. "We need your help for cover stories, clearances, the usual stuff."

Szakowski was near shock and his first comment came in a tone only cops use: "There's no fuckin' way Canadians are going to do this!"

"May I ask why not?" asked Bowman.

"There's no way Canadians can go on foreign soil and engage in any kind of espionage gathering, it's that simple. . . . People who work here at CSE are hired to analyse material other people gather, not to become goddam spies or James Bond or whatever it is you fuckin' guys have dreamed up!"

"You don't think we can do this?" asked Frost.

"I think you're out of your league. You don't have the mandate to do it, you will never get the approval to do it, you don't have the technical equipment to do it, you don't have the expertise to do it!"

"Anything else?" asked Bowman.

"Yeah, it's too risky. You're gonna get caught."

Bowman looked amazingly unshaken and finally said: "Whether you like it or not, it's going to fly. So, from your end of it, make it work."

After their consultations with NSA and GCHQ, Bowman and Frost had become convinced there was no other way to proceed than to first do "surveys" of the targeted embassies. That decision, inescapable as it seemed to them, posed a problem they couldn't circumvent. They would have to get External Affairs people involved, since they would be doing their dirty tricks on External's turf. It was not a move they relished, being used to keeping secrets of this kind even from colleagues in CSE itself. They would find out in the months to come that their reluctance to involve External was not paranoia or a figment of their imagination.

Chief of CSE Peter Hunt held a special meeting with Secretary of State for External Affairs Don Jamieson to discuss the matter. Given the immense political implications of embassy collection on the scale now being imagined, Hunt couldn't risk going any lower on the totem pole. Jamieson was co-operative. He provided Hunt with the names of two people at External who he believed could be trusted to do the job and keep it secret. One, Guy Rankin, by some incredible coincidence, just happened to be the technician who had taken part — as an External Affairs employee, not a CSE agent — in the "Stephanie" operation. The other, Greg Smythe, was also from External's telecommunications department. And he would prove to be a particular pain in the neck to Mike Frost.

The new working group of four got together for an initial meeting. Bowman and Frost were already working undercover and breaking the rules, since to get into External Affairs and function there freely they had to be given special security ID badges.

Bowman and Frost briefed the group on what they intended to do.

"That's just super!" beamed Rankin, who remembered the excitement of the "Stephanie" caper. "Let's go for this! This is shit hot! We'll man it with our own people, train our telecommunications people and run the whole thing for you."

"You want to do it yourselves?" asked Bowman incredulously.

"No, no. CSE will run the operation, of course. But our people from External will do it, since it's in our embassies."

Bowman and Frost just looked at each other sideways and raised their eyebrows. Trained and experienced spies were being told by diplomats that the diplomats were going to do their espionage for them. No doubt there was a lot of empire-building mentality in the External Affairs people's reactions, but Frost and Bowman didn't like it one bit. After the meeting they swore to each other that External operatives could have all the make-believe plans they wanted; the CSE guys would simply blow them out of the way if they had to. Embassy collection was going to be *their* game.

Setting up "Julie" turned out to be rather like a game of "Snakes and Ladders", however. One moment they were a few spaces from winning, the next they were back to square one.

One of Frost's greatest frustrations was trying to get the co-ordinates of the targeted embassies for the Americans to take their satellite pictures. These were, of course, Canadian embassies. But for some strange reason External Affairs couldn't come up with the geographical co-ordinates of their own buildings. The task — which suddenly seemed like a herculean feat — was left to Greg Smythe.

"Why do you want these co-ordinates?" asked Smythe of Frost.

"We need them, and that's all you need to know."

Smythe, not being a member of the spying community, was not cleared to know about the way NSA used its outer-space technology. And Frost had no intention of letting him in on even a tidbit.

Day after day they waited at CSE. Smythe still couldn't come up with the co-ordinates. At one point, Frost just blew up and told his friend Bowman: "This guy has to be the driest, drippiest, dinkiest twit you have ever run up against. And those are the nice things I can say about him."

Bowman laughed at his comrade-in-arms' frustration. But he also reminded him that the NSA guys had their own problems with the State Department back in Washington, D.C. It had to be expected with bureaucrats. Spies were not bureaucrats. They were adventurers.

It took months, but Smythe finally did come up with the co-ordinates. NSA tasked their satellites as they had promised, Canada got the pictures, and Greg Smythe never got to see them — which was sweet revenge for Frost. The photos didn't show much more than could already have been surveyed on site, but the Americans had proven one crucial point: they would keep their word. That also meant they expected Canada to keep its end of the bargain.

As was bound to happen, things got worse before they got better. Frost and Bowman were stuck now with involving an alarming number of people in their committee, most of them from External Affairs, not from the normal circle of CSE loyalists who understood this sort of thing. And, as such committees usually go in any government of any country, the more meetings you have, the greater the number of people involved, the more difficult decisions become to make.

In Canada, External Affairs happens to be one of the worst departments to deal with when you are considered an outsider, a "non-diplomat". Because the last thing they want is for anybody to come in on their own little secrets, which include mostly the perks they get from being posted on foreign assignments.

Frost and Bowman had now made it clear that there was no way CSE would let anybody but their own people handle the embassy-collection operation. And so inevitably came the zinger from a smartass at one of the gatherings where all the CSE guys wanted to do was hammer out the details of how best they could accomplish the mission.

"We have to get a ruling from Justice on this," said an External bureaucrat.

Frost and Bowman looked at each other in puzzlement.

"Well, it's not as if we haven't done it before," said Bowman. "You all know about 'Stephanie'."

"Yes . . . but that was different. The Americans want us in big this time. We know who Inman's been talking to. We need a ruling from Justice."

First Frost and Bowman had had to pretend to tolerate the External snobs they had come to refer to as "the pin-stripers". Now they would have to contend with the lawyers.

It had all seemed so simple after their brainstorming sessions at NSA and GCHQ. They had come back to Canada firmly believing they could have their first listening post set up within a year. Now things seemed to have become extremely, and uselessly, complicated.

Frost contacted his buddies at NSA to share his commiserations. Expecting angry reactions on their part, instead he got understanding: "Just stick with it. We go through the same kind of shit with the State Department all the time. We always end up getting our way," said Patrick O'Brien.

As they feared, the ruling from Justice came back saying: "There may be a hint of illegality to it."

"It" was of course the embassy-collection operation Canada had already undertaken with "Stephanie" under the same Prime Minister, Pierre Trudeau.

Well, that was all it needed for the External Affairs types involved in an operation they couldn't control to say everything should be put on hold.

And, as if that wasn't enough, now another wrench was thrown in the machinery. This happened to be the spring of 1979, an election year. Joe Clark, then leader of the Progressive Conservative Party, defeated Pierre Trudeau's eleven-year government. So new political masters, like Flora MacDonald, the new Secretary of State for External Affairs, had to be briefed on CSE's plans and convinced

of their needfulness. It was the sort of landmine a minority government like Clark's didn't want anything to do with. And they were in
power for nine months, until Trudeau's miraculous comeback in
February 1980.

During the Tories' short term in office, and even in the
months that followed, with a new Liberal minister in charge of
External, nobody seemed to want to deal with the "hint of illegality"
question. Frost and Bowman, in the meantime, kept going through the
motions of preparing in minute detail what they still hoped would see
the light of day, although perhaps not in their lifetime.

But discouragement was setting in. Two years had gone by
since NSA had pumped them up to do what they considered to be the
most honourable job in the spying profession. And they were next to
nowhere.

One day Frost said to Bowman: "One more time we're spinning our wheels . . . one more time Canada's going to fall behind
because of those candy-ass fuckin' pinstripers." This time, Bowman
didn't laugh. Frost ranted on: "Those guys are so pussy-whipped, none
of them will make any decisions without checking with their boss!"

Frost and Bowman became so frustrated they even thought
about not using embassies for their covert operations abroad. They
would work from a hotel room, an apartment, anything the External
guys didn't have control over. But they both felt sure that, somewhere
else up the politico-bureaucratic ladder, such plans would be blocked
too.

Finally, they turned to their most trusted allies, the people at
NSA. Frost went to see O'Brien.

"Patrick," he pleaded, "is there anything you can do to light a
fire under External Affairs' ass?"

"I don't know what I can do," O'Brien said, "but I can talk to
the State Department."

Bowman later also went down to see O'Brien to register the
same complaint, if only to explain to the Americans that the delay
certainly wasn't CSE's fault.

Amazingly, about a month after Frost's and Bowman's visits to NSA, a strange thing happened at a meeting of the "embassy covert collection group" at External Affairs. The head of the External team announced he had an important message from Under-Secretary of State for External Affairs Allan Gotlieb (later to become ambassador to Washington during the Mulroney regime). Gotlieb had given authorization to go full steam ahead with the project regardless of the "hint of illegality". He had done it in a signed document. That meant the Prime Minister, Pierre Trudeau, had also given approval, although he would be informed only orally to protect him from political attacks. In other words, should things ever go terribly wrong, the Prime Minister could always claim he didn't know.

Gotlieb's directive did have one reservation, however. CSE was limited to surveying "eight sites", or embassies. Gotlieb added that after eight locations had been surveyed, he wanted to "re-evaluate". To the CSE people that meant he was opening the door but leaving himself a chance to shut it at the first sign of trouble. They also could guess, however, how gut-wrenching the decision to go ahead despite the "hint of illegality" must have been for Gotlieb and the Prime Minister. Neither of them were fools. And they knew how revolutionary CSE's plans were. Overnight Canada, normally perceived as a docile, almost naive, country, was going to engage in aggressive overseas espionage, with undercover agents and all the gadgets that come with the job.

Frost said to Bowman, with a touch of admiration for Gotlieb's guts: "It must have been an agonizing decision. . . . He must have thought it through that lives could be at risk somewhere down the line."

Still, for Frost and Bowman, the relief was immense. At last they could go ahead.

NSA and GCHQ were ready to hear the good news. In fact, they had their "wish lists" of target sites set up long before the Canadians finally got their act together — probably because, in the end, they

Above: *Mike Frost, in May 1994, standing on the steps of what used to be the Gloucester Canadian Forces Base where he was first trained as an intercept operator in 1958–59.*

Right: *"Ray domes", containing intercept antennas, at CFS Leitrim. Similar "giant white golf balls" stand on the roof of the American National Security Agency, in Fort Meade, Maryland.*

Above: CFS *Leitrim, south of Ottawa, one of Canada's "overt" intercept stations.*
(All photos in this section courtesy Danny Frost)

Above: *Mike Frost's 25-foot Chris Craft boat, "Pilgrim", whose name became the codename for Canada's top-secret "embassy-collection" project.*

Centre: *Frost's CSE identity card.*

Below: *This "emergency" card was given to every CSE employee involved in counter-espionage in Ottawa to help them identify red diplomatic plates on automobiles registered to Eastern Bloc embassies.*

Above: *CSE headquarters on Heron Road, Ottawa.*

Centre: *Project "Granny", a now completed addition to the old CSE building, looks like a gigantic bunker. In front is the CSE employees' main parking lot.*

Below: *CSE headquarters, showing a white hut on the roof. It is the twin of the hut used in New Delhi to hide the Canadian embassy's intercept antennas that were directed at Sikh terrorists.*

Left: *This satellite dish carries all communications between* CSE *and* NSA, *from computer-to-computer data transmissions to phone conversations to fax. All communications are automatically scrambled. The antenna sits in the parking lot, across Heron Road from the* CSE *building.*

Above: *An apartment block on Presland Street in Ottawa. The apartment located in the top-left corner of the building is the one that was used for what the "Pilgrim" team nicknamed "the Vanier dry run", in the summer of 1979. This is where methods and equipment were tested before agents were sent abroad on more risky missions.*
Below: *One of* CSE's *two white vans used for both overt and covert operations. Although it looks like a closed-up chip wagon, it is full of electronic equipment and carries two to four operators.*

Right: *One of the microwave towers in the Ottawa area that carry a multitude of communications on a daily basis. CSE antennas can intercept them at will.*

Left: *A typical government safe, such as was used in the "Stephanie" operation in Moscow to hide electronic gear.*

The bearer is   Le titulaire est

A MEMBER OF THE
DEPARTMENT OF NATIONAL
DEFENCE.

MEMBRE DU MINISTÈRE
DE LA DÉFENSE NATIONALE.

(Signature of bearer - Signature du titulaire)

3

Above and below: *Frost's diplomatic passport, now void, with sample pages showing his diplomatic visas for Ivory Coast and Romania.*

VISAS   15

Visa Diplomatique

RÉPUBLIQUE DE CÔTE D'IVOIRE
AMBASSADE DE CÔTE D'IVOIRE
OTTAWA

Nom _____ FROST
Prénoms _EDWARD - MICHAEL S._
No Visa _011/82_
Nature du Visa _court séjour_
Valable pour _un Voyage (1)_
Utilisable jusqu'au _10-05-82_
Pour un séjour de _dix jours_
A compter de la date d'entrée en C.I.

AVIS IMPORTANT

Il est interdit au titulaire
du présent visa de s'installer
en République de Côte d'Ivoire
ou d'y exercer une activité autre
que celle qu'il a déclaré y venir exercer

Ottawa, le _11-02-82_
L'Ambassadeur

LOUIS GUIRANDOU - N'DIAYE

VISAS   21

DIPLOMATICĂ

AMBASADA REPUBLICII SOCIALISTE ROMÂNIA
OTTAWA
VIZA Nr. _9439_
Călătorii _UDO_
Valabilă pentru INTRARE în Republica
Socialistă România în termen de **2** luni
de la data emiterii, cu drept de şedere
5 (cinci) zile de la data
trecerii frontierei.
Însoţit de
Puncte de frontieră _TOATE_

OTTAWA, la _7 sept 1982_

This passport contains 32 pages.   Ce passeport contient 32 pages.

This passport contains 32 pages.   Ce passeport contient 32 pages.

Above and below: *The "Kilderkin" site, set up by* CSE *and the* RCMP *on the corner of Laurier East and Charlotte Streets in Ottawa, right across from the Soviet embassy, here seen on the right in the top photo. The close-up picture of the house that contained intercept equipment shows how the drapes are kept constantly closed, even in 1994.*

Above and left: *The roof of the American embassy at 100 Wellington Street in Ottawa, located directly across from Parliament Hill. Suspicious-looking "air vents" can be seen at the left and right front corners of the top photo. Two smaller "heat pumps" can be seen at left front. Frost believes the "air vents" are fake and protect intercept antennas for an American "embassy-collection" site in the rooms below. The drapes on the barred windows below are closed. A close-up of one of the "air vents" shows how it is strangely closed in by a metal plate on one of its four sides and has another strange-looking metal plate sticking out from one side. Frost believes these plates are both protecting some kind of device. The third photo shows another curious box, this one grey, on a slightly lower roof of the same building. It seems to serve no purpose in relation the functioning of the building.*

knew Canada wouldn't have a choice but to co-operate. But when Frost and Bowman read the lists submitted by NSA and British Intelligence, they wondered out loud if these guys were living on the same planet as they were. They weren't really surprised that Beijing was still on the top of NSA's list. But the Brits, who had been very co-operative on the "educative" side of the operation but much less so in terms of committing their resources, had a real doozie as a first choice for covert intercept: Baghdad (this was a decade or more before the Gulf War).

One thing that has always baffled Frost, however, is how the Americans simply barred the Canadians from going into Israel. "Don't go there," said O'Brien. "We've got it covered." NSA never blacklisted any other capital in the world — even though they themselves had blanketed most of them. "They had to have a special deal going with the Mossad [the Israeli Secret Service]," says Frost. "Because they were adamant about excluding us."

The Canadians also presented their own list of "possibilities". At the top were Oslo and Vienna. As Mike Frost put it back then: "We want to go to an area where we can get our feet wet, we can screw up severely and it won't matter very much. . . . I don't think Baghdad is the place to do that. Nor is Beijing."

The decision on CSE's first embassy-collection operation rested directly in the hands of Frost and Bowman. "No fuckin' way," was the answer both NSA and GCHQ got on their top-of-the-line requests.

Bowman had already made a dry-run in Ottawa, prudently reckoning that they should fake the operation on friendly soil first, close to their offices along the Rideau River. This was in the summer of 1979. This was also when Mike Frost, feeling he had contributed plenty of patience and pain tolerance to the whole endeavour, asked his buddy Bowman: "Do you mind if I get to name this project?"

"Go ahead. . . . What do you want to call it?"

"How about Project Pilgrim? That's the name of my boat. And a pilgrim is a wanderer and a traveller."

"Sounds perfect to me," said Bowman.

Project Pilgrim began in one of the most innocuous places you could imagine. Just outside the French enclave of Vanier, in Ottawa.

They tried — oh, how they tried — to simulate a dry-run from the safe confines of CSE's building on Heron Road. Frost finally told Bowman: "Look, there's no way we can get our operators into the spirit of what it's really going to be like. It just doesn't wash, it's too phoney. Here we are moving equipment from one floor of CSE to the other, trying to pretend we're mounting an intercept operation and, shit, man, it doesn't make any sense! How can you expect these men to go out there in a foreign country, in an embassy where they will have to live undercover, when we're pretending we can train them in the building where they come to work every day?"

There was no argument from Bowman. "So what do you think we should do?"

"Maybe we should rent an apartment, somewhere in Ottawa, to see what we really can do?"

So they did what every normal spy would do: they searched through the want ads. Then Bowman and Frost just went out, like any normal couple, to look at apartments.

They had decided they needed at least a two-bedroom place. One bedroom would be used to store equipment and act as a kind of an office, another would be the "com-centre" where material would be encoded and sent back to External Affairs, and the living-room was to be the intercept operation. They would try their best to simulate an actual embassy site. Their cover story with the landlords was that they were coming to town for a couple of months and needed a furnished place. Employees of the (bogus) business they worked for would use the apartment when they "travelled" to Ottawa.

The whole object of the exercise was not to see if they could intercept signals. They could have done that from CSE itself, as they did all the time. Frost and Bowman wanted to know if they could get away with doing it in a strange location, in broad daylight and still remain undetected. The chosen location would have to be in a relatively safe, quiet neighbourhood and be in sight of microwave towers such as the ones near St-Laurent Boulevard in Ottawa with their tremendous communications traffic, so that they could at least pick up something to really test their equipment. But they didn't want to be located in a highrise where too many people might be aware of their comings and goings. They also needed an elevator. Not any kind of elevator — one that was fairly well protected from view so people on the street wouldn't see all the stuff being brought up and down. Finally, the "operations room" would have to be about 150 feet from the street, because they were also going to test the equipment to see if it was "Tempest-proof."

The landlord who eventually rented them the apartment on Presland Street was a short woman who always seemed to wear an apron and who lived on the ground floor of the four-storey building. The CSE guys wanted a corner apartment on the top floor, for a decent shot at the microwave tower. When they finally found this ideal location, they rented it for two months. The plan was that they would work in it for two weeks, but they would come and go for the two months. CSE agents would show up at the apartment at the same times of day as people working normal hours and doing normal jobs.

On their way home from work at the real CSE building, Bowman and Frost would walk into the apartment, bang things around, flush the toilet, pretend to take showers, leave dirty dishes lying around. The only thing they never did was sleep at the place. "How the hell am I going to tell my wife I'm not coming home tonight if I do that?" said Frost to Bowman. Wives, of course, knew nothing about what their husbands' profession really was. Sometimes, though, they would spend an entire day in the apartment, watch television, have a few drinks, cook meals. They would walk in and out with dufflebags, anything to suggest they were the most ordinary boring tenants in the place.

Their one major technical problem in those early days was that their equipment was not "Tempest-proof". Again, they went south of the border to NSA to find the solution. They borrowed an

"RFI" tent, which looked like a dining tent but was actually made of copper mesh. It had a copper floor, copper walls, copper top and double doors, so that you came in one, closed it, then opened the next. The tent had a big patch panel on the side of it for the power source and the antenna connections. The whole tent was "Tempest-proof" and no signals were supposed to emanate from it.

Hard as it may be to believe, the CSE people actually put up a 12' x 12' tent inside an apartment living-room. (NSA had told them they did it all the time.) The living-room was L-shaped, so that all any stranger opening the door would see was a couch and a TV. As for the windows, they never opened the drapes, but did check them to see if they would prevent signals from coming in. The only pieces of "authentic" paraphernalia they didn't use were the official External Affairs red diplomatic bags. In Ottawa that would have given them away.

They finally got all the intercept equipment into the apartment over about a day or two, in dufflebags. It took Frost four or five car trips from CSE. Then Frost and Bowman had a meeting with the two operators who were going to behave as if they had recently arrived in a foreign country and just gone to the embassy to set up. The operators had to keep a strict log book of the problems they encountered as well as their successes. They also had to see how well the equipment had survived one of CSE's sacred procedures, the transport test. This involved having every piece of packaged electronic gear dropped from a height of six feet to see if it could survive. The logic was that they couldn't count on baggage handlers anywhere in the world to treat their stuff delicately and they couldn't exactly print "FRAGILE" on it.

The Ottawa intercept operation lasted two weeks. Special locks were put on the doors of the apartment — with the landlord's approval — and they installed motion-detectors that were turned on at night to check if anybody had been snooping around. Another crucial part of the operation was to have the CSE's COMSEC people come around the apartment in their specially equipped van to check if any radiations were coming out of the intercept site and see if anything abnormal seemed to be going on in the building. There were no radiations, but the COMSEC operators did report that, when the intercept equipment was turned on in the morning, the power surge was quite noticeable. This meant that any counter-espionage agency monitoring the AC 60-hertz line in a foreign country would know right away something weird was going on. That was rectified in future operations by having the operators turn on the equipment gradually. Eventually, they decided to keep the equipment on all the time, and accept the fire hazard.

They learned a lot. For instance, some equipment survived the six-foot drop, some didn't. So it was decided that everything to be sent on a mission would have to be duplicated. Once at a real site, they wouldn't have the luxury of going to Radio Shack to replace the broken parts. What had started out as a few hundred pounds of equipment had just jumped up over a ton.

From an intercept point of view, the "Vanier" operation (which in fact took place in the neighbouring area of Overbrook) worked beautifully. CSE had material coming out of their ears — telephone calls, fax communications, even escort services' paging systems.

Then something dramatic happened to Mike Frost. For the second time in his spying career that now spanned more than twenty years, he felt guilty. It was one thing to be fooling the "enemy". It was quite an eerie feeling, though, to be listening in on so many conversations between fellow Canadians. Being rabidly patriotic, he felt it was wrong. He saw the incredible potential for abuse in the power they held, and he didn't like it.

It also dawned on Frost and Bowman that they just might stumble onto something like a terrorist plot, or a planned assassination, or even a bank robbery. That became a real moral issue for them. They never made the decision on whether to tell or not. They just crossed their fingers hoping it would never happen. Their instincts would have been to blow the whistle on the potential criminals, but the code of conduct of CSE would have dictated that they pretend they had never heard a word.

They realized how much they were infringing on the civil rights of the people they meant to protect from outside aggression, and came to the painful realization that this invasion of privacy could be practised on them just as easily as they were practising it on others. And all this without anybody ever knowing it.

Mostly, though, Frost and Bowman didn't give a damn about the content of what they were intercepting. They just wanted to know if technically they could be successful. They were. So much so, in fact, that they found they could actually intercept digital signals and play them back. One of the most important findings of the "Vanier" run was that they were pretty good at guessing at what time of the day most of the crucial communications would take place. From 9:30 a.m. to 11:30 a.m., for instance, they had the two operators working full tilt, because that's when they would be most likely to catch important stuff. But the best conclusion of all was that, yes, they could do it. Get in, get out, intercept and not get caught.

They were now ready to risk it on foreign soil.

"Vanier went well," said Bowman at their next meeting. "Now we have to try it in another country. . . . But it's got to be a relatively safe place, where it won't matter too much if we get caught."

Frost had a brainstorm.

"Why not Jamaica?"

After all, as Canadian as he had become, that was his home country. He knew the capital, Kingston, like the back of his hand, and, besides, the weather was nice. There was a bit of a political problem since Michael Manley, a Prime Minister with socialist tendencies, was in power. But they weren't too worried about that since Manley was a good friend of Canada and its Prime Minister, Pierre Trudeau.

There was also the added possibility that, from Jamaica, they could intercept some interesting communications from Fidel Castro's Cuba, which would please NSA no end.

Frost, of course, volunteered for the job. He never got it. Not because he wasn't the best man, but because in 1980 Jamaica still had mandatory military service and he had never gone through that process before emigrating to Canada. In other words, if they found out who he was in Kingston, they just might decide to keep him there for a long while, perhaps even in a Jamaican jail.

Frank Bowman ended up going to Kingston to discuss the operation. He told the High Commissioner he would try to disrupt normal operations as little as possible, that this was not a real intercept operation, just another dry-run leading to more important things. There was no argument. The High Commissioner just said: "Don't tell me what's going on."

The Jamaica operation was codenamed "Egret". To this day Frost still doesn't know why. The same two operators who had done the Vanier run were sent down for "Egret", with orders to intercept government, military, business and any other kind of communications they could possibly snatch out of the air.

First things first, though. Frost had to find a "low profile" way to get the equipment to Jamaica, through External Affairs, in the red diplomatic bags. The External guys, who by now had become slightly more co-operative, said: "Just ship us the equipment in bulk and we will get it there piece by piece." Fine, thought Frost. But CSE doesn't normally ship things to External Affairs. So what's the best way to do it without being noticed, without having to deal with the handlers at the receiving dock and sign forms that will only cause unnecessary headaches? Well, Frost thought, there's no better way than in my car — which happened to be a Renault station wagon. At External's receiving dock, one of his allies in the "Egret" group would pick the equipment up, ask and answer no questions, and everything would be smooth.

Mike Frost was just about to get the car ride of his life. First, he had to get special permission from CSE security chief Victor Szakowski even to bring his station wagon inside the fenced compound of CSE, where only the directors and a few other top mandarins were allowed to park. That was in itself a breach of the "low profile" rule, but Frost couldn't exactly carry the equipment out to the parking lot, in full view of the CBC building next door. Finally Frost and one of the "Egret" operators, Tom Murray, loaded up his car with classified equipment in red diplomatic bags and set off for External Affairs.

They didn't get very far. On Ottawa's Riverside Drive, just past the Recreation Association Centre for public service employees, the laws of physics foiled their perfect plan. The equipment in the car weighed so much that Frost got a flat tire. This was on one of the heaviest traffic-carrying streets in the city. Now any normal person with a flat would go into the trunk, get the jack, get the spare tire and put it on as fast as possible. But in Frost's case, he first had to get all that top-secret equipment out of the station wagon and lay it all out on the street before he could even gain access to the spare tire. He and Murray worked frantically to get the stuff out and reach the spare tire and jack before too many people driving by noticed how strange their cargo was. Before trying to fix the wheel, they hurriedly put all the equipment back into the station wagon. Another brilliant move. The car was now so heavy that the jack broke right in half.

"Jesus!" screamed Frost. "What do we do now?"

They didn't have to wait too long for an answer. A police cruiser just happened to show up. The cop got out and walked slowly over to the funny-looking pair whose car was loaded up with what definitely looked like suspect merchandise.

"What the hell are you doing?" asked the police officer sternly.

"We got a flat tire," said Frost sheepishly.

"Well, fix it!" said the cop.

"I can't, my jack broke."

It was only a matter of time before the cop looked in the back of the car and asked in a tone only police can use: "What's all that?"

"I can't tell you," said Frost.

Before the police officer pulled his gun and asked him to spread, Frost opted to flash his CSE badge. "I'm a diplomatic courier," he explained, "and this is classified material I have to bring to External Affairs."

The police officer bought it. Then he went to the back of his cruiser, got his own jack and helped them put the spare on.

For the rest of the five-mile trip, Murray had to sit in the passenger seat with a dirty flat tire in his lap since there was no way they were going to take all the electronic gear out of the station wagon again.

"Now this is what I call 'low profile'," commented Frost. "Keystone Kops, that's us." The two spies couldn't help but laugh hysterically.

Their trials and tribulations weren't over, though. Guy Rankin, who was cleared for "Egret", was no longer at the External Affairs receiving dock when they got there. He had given up on them ever showing up. Frost steadfastly refused to go through the usual procedure of declaring what he was delivering. That didn't make the loading dock foreman too happy.

"What the fuck is going on here?" he asked. "Here you are in a civilian car, loaded up with diplomatic classified bags and you won't even tell me what you're doing here! I don't even know you guys!"

Frost just told him to track down Rankin and everything would be all right. "It's just telecommunications stuff. We do this all the time," he said to the foreman.

"Sure you do. And I'm Allan Gotlieb!"

Rankin finally showed up with a dolly. Frost and Murray loaded everything onto it and hoped they would never see it again. On his way back to CSE, Frost couldn't help but wonder, if things could go so terribly wrong in Canada, in their own city, what disaster awaited them in Jamaica.

The two CSE operators who were going to man "Egret" were sent down with a very loose cover. They posed as communications specialists from National Defence who were bringing down a load of equipment to see if communications between External Affairs in Ottawa and Kingston, Jamaica, could be improved. It worked. Partly because the Jamaicans would never have suspected the Canadians of mounting an espionage operation, partly because there was no reason for them to believe the story wasn't true. "Egret" was in fact a great success. The Canadian operators picked up all kinds of communications: police, military, government, even high-level diplomatic conversations. Nothing, though, of "intelligence" value. But they did send all their transcripts down to NSA to make sure there wasn't anything they might have missed.

The men came back to Canada safely after a two-week mission, and so did the equipment. For obvious reasons, Frost changed the *modus operandi* for shipping the electronic gear from External Affairs to CSE. Instead of trying to haul the entire load back in one shot, they simply sent a few pieces of equipment at a time, adding one or two diplomatic bags to the normal courier run between the two departments.

Bowman and Frost were now confident they were ready for bigger and better things.

The time had come to look at the "wish lists" for feasible targets. Much as the Americans and the British wanted Canada to plunge into what they considered to be high-priority locations, there was no way Bowman and Frost were going to expose their people to such a risk on a first real mission.

After several discussions, the working group of CSE and External people decided to pre-survey three sites: Mexico City, Caracas, and Havana. All three had the advantage of offering potentially valuable intelligence. Havana, however, was far from safe, even though Cuba did not consider Canada an espionage threat. In fact, CSE had thrown it in more for NSA's benefit than any other reason, the Americans having no diplomatic relations with Cuba, because the chances of the "Pilgrim" people choosing it as their first embassy-collection operation were practically non-existent.

Frost and Bowman split up the pre-survey work between them. Frost went to Mexico, Bowman to Venezuela with a brief stopover in Cuba on the way back.

Frost's trip to Mexico turned out to be almost as laughable as his "flat tire" ride to External Affairs. When he got off the plane in Mexico City, Frost thought this was going to be a piece of cake. He was met at the airport by the embassy's communications-centre operator and driven to his hotel where he spent a pleasant evening sipping a few rum and cokes in the bar and listening to a mariachi band.

The next morning, he met with the ambassador. It was the first time Frost had had to play the role of the bureaucrat and explain he was really a spy who could possibly mess up that ambassador's leisurely life. It was not an easy thing for him. The conversation had to take place on the street, since CSE people had been trained to be wary of listening devices anywhere. If you've ever walked the streets of Mexico City, you have an idea of how dreadful it was: cars by the thousands always honking their horns, pollution levels superior to those of just about any other capital on earth, torrid heat and humidity. To make matters worse, the ambassador kept walking at an incredibly fast pace. Frost was trying to explain things while being constantly out of breath.

Finally they got to the embassy. Frost took one look at the building and said: "Is this the only chancellery we have?"

"This is the pride and joy of Canadian embassies anywhere," said the ambassador. "This is our gem!"

"Yes," said Frost gloomily, "but this is all glass!"

"Yes," said the diplomat, "isn't it beautiful?"

"It's gorgeous, but how on earth do you think we can conduct espionage in a glass house? . . . I'm afraid, Mr. Ambassador, we have been wasting each other's time."

Frost got the impression the ambassador was rather pleased about that; he hadn't seemed that keen on the whole idea anyway. Frost couldn't get over the fact, though, that this kind of information could have been made available to him before Mexico City was even considered as a possible collection site. Those guys at External had a unique way of getting to him. What he learned from the experience was that a lot more homework could be done at home.

Meanwhile, Bowman had gone to Havana. He came back with confirmation that the place was a hell-hole. The embassy building had a slightly higher status than a straw hut, leaking pipes, not enough space, boxes piled up to the ceiling, no security and, thank God, no good reason to go there just to please NSA.

The first embassy-collection venture would take place in Caracas. It was codenamed "Artichoke". It was 1981, four years after "Julie".

SIX

PILGRIM'S PROGRESS

"YOU KNOW, FRANK, WE CAN'T just buy a return ticket, hop on a plane with all the electronic gear, and waltz into the embassy."

"I know," said Bowman. "And this also isn't 'Stephanie.' "

"Right," said Frost. "And the last thing we want is to get caught. . . . It's easy for NSA guys to get away with that. They're so big they just move on. . . . But, at this early stage of the game, you know what will happen to us if we're busted on foreign land."

"Yeah. The politicians will pull the plug," said Bowman.

"And fast! They'll say we never existed and they'll make sure that we don't. . . . And Canada will have to pay the price because we'll never get the intelligence-sharing with the Americans and the Brits that we had before or that we could get now."

"And we'll end up at desk jobs . . ."

Casual as the conversation may seem, it went to the very heart of what "Pilgrim" meant to the CSE men in charge. There simply could be no mistakes at this stage of the game. Canadian embassy collection was still at an infant stage. It would take only one embarrassing diplomatic incident for the country's leaders to kill the project, while hanging Frost, Bowman and Hunt out to dry. They had been told this way back in the days of "Stephanie", and they had no doubt it was still the policy: Canada simply had no spying operation abroad. The Prime Minister would deny any knowledge. Any compromising documents would be shielded from Access to Information for reasons of national security — or would simply be shredded.

"Stephanie" had been a one-shot deal: one mission, one location, one mandate. "Pilgrim" was a concerted effort to get into embassy collection on a permanent basis and in several locations around the world where the Canadians were needed by their CANUKUS allies. CSE could not afford to fail. So preparing for "Pilgrim" was a massive operation in itself. Frost and Bowman had to come up with a strategy that would be as close to perfection as humanly possible.

As we have seen, the "Pilgrim" team had already decided to conduct "pre-surveys" before actually setting up the intercept site according to the guidelines given by Allan Gotlieb. Frost was picked as the survey manager and took on the responsibility for most of the pre-surveys. A pre-survey was a fact-finding mission mainly to check out the locale of the embassy — the height, the location, the ventilation of the intercept room, the best place to locate the essential antennas, the degree of isolation from the rest of the diplomatic staff, etc. Frost also had to look at the surroundings. Was the embassy vulnerable from a counter-espionage point of view? Were there microwave towers easily within intercept reach? In short, was it safe and was it worth the effort?

But before they could even think of getting on an airplane to a foreign destination, there were numerous important problems to resolve. To the uninitiated, these may look like mere details. To a spy, they could be a matter of life and death, and at very least make the difference between success and utter failure. Among the thorny problems to be solved were:

1. The cover: What would the spies pose as? What would be their status within the embassy? What would explain their mysterious walks with the ambassador?
2. The equipment: What kind of equipment would be used for pre-surveying and then for the intercept operation?
3. The location: Could the collection be done from a site outside the embassy?

4. The duration: How long would a pre-survey take? How long could a survey last?
5. Transportation: How would the agents get to the survey site? Who within government would make the travel arrangements? Who would pay for the travel, and how?
6. Security: How would they keep the lid on "Pilgrim"? (This last became one of their most mind-boggling problems. The "Pilgrim" agents were living double, triple, even quadruple lives.)

Each and every one of these questions had to be resolved. Frost could not count the hours or number of brainstorming sessions that went into putting them under the microscope. And that's without including several trips to NSA and GCHQ to discuss exactly the same issues.

It's worth looking at these six items in more detail.

First, what would the cover be?

The problem was that the CSE agents had to hide their true roles not only from the immigration and counter-espionage people of the targeted country but also from nearly the entire staff of the Canadian embassy itself. It became clear that the agents would have to have two distinct covers. For immigration, it would be best to say they were members of National Defence visiting the embassy with a mandate to upgrade the telecommunications between Canada and the chancellery and discuss communications with the External Affairs technicians on site. So, for visa purposes, they would admit to being employees of National Defence. It was plausible and they could talk their way around it easily.

Dealing with embassy staff was much dicier. External Affairs is an extremely tight-knit organization. Inside gossip is currency. Everybody knows who's who, what their government ranking is, which boss is having an affair with his secretary, and so on. Members of External do not suffer "outsiders" well, especially if they're from another government department. They are even more protective of their turf in foreign embassies, where they enjoy revolving in a world of their own, a private club where the unwritten rules are clear. It's one of the reasons that they often freak out when the Prime Minister of the country decides to pay them a visit and are immensely relieved when he leaves. Non-External people don't often go to snoop around an embassy, and these intruders are spotted the moment they walk through the door, prompting inevitable questions and discussions among the regular staffers as to what that stranger is doing in "their" chancellery.

No matter how much they racked their brains, Frost, Bowman and the External Affairs people cleared for "Pilgrim" simply couldn't come up with a cover that would fit everywhere and satisfy the staff's curiosity. Diplomats and their staff are moved around the world and talk to each other on a regular basis from one capital city to another. So if Frost were to pose as a communications expert in one location and in the next pass himself off as an immigration officer, it would be entirely plausible that somebody at some point would say something like: "Hey, this Frost guy was here for communications, and you're telling me he's now doing immigration?" CSE agents would be wearing their spy badge on their forehead everywhere they went.

After hours of debate, they simply gave up on the cover. It was impossible to find one that wouldn't eventually blow them away.

Frost and Bowman decided to go a totally different route. The ambassador — instead of taking a clumsy, phoney walk on the street with the "Pilgrim" man, as in Mexico — would ideally be brought back to Canada and be briefed in Ottawa about the upcoming operation. He would then be asked to circulate a memo to his staff before any CSE agent arrived. The note would say that there would be a visitor from National Defence coming to the embassy for whatever wishy-washy "related business" the ambassador could think up. The staff would be asked to co-operate fully with the military representative, with the implication that they shouldn't ask any questions. The "Pilgrim" people knew that such a memo in itself would raise eyebrows, but figured it the least of all evils. It cut down on the compulsory lies. This became standard procedure and, in Frost's case, seemed to work as far as staff asking him what his business was on their premises.

Along with cover came the question of the diplomatic passport. Despite strong objections from External Affairs, Frost was adamant that he would not go on any mission without a red diplomatic passport. External balked. This was against the rules. He had no right to a diplomatic passport because he was not a diplomat. They believed he should be content with a green, so-called "special" passport—as opposed to the regular blue one issued to ordinary Canadian citizens. He had to fight tooth and nail to win this issue and finally exclaimed in frustration at one of the joint CSE-External meetings: "If I don't get a goddam diplomatic passport, I'm not going!"

The External guys reluctantly gave in.

But Frost wasn't finished causing them headaches on the subject. After his first major pre-survey tour in West Africa (to be discussed later in this chapter) it dawned on him that his passport was stamped with visas from five different countries he had visited within the previous year. It was more than likely that, at some point, immigration officers in a foreign country, probably a hostile one, would wonder why this "technician" was travelling all over the globe so much. Frost would later recommend that CSE "Pilgrim" agents be given a new diplomatic passport for each country they visited on pre-surveys or surveys. You can imagine the kerfuffle. Not only did this non-diplomat heathen want a red one, but he wanted a brand-new one every time. Absolutely unthinkable.

"That's against the regulations," said an External member of the "Pilgrim" team.

"Well, change the fucking regulations!" shot back Frost. "Our passports will give them the whole story of where we've been. That's crazy! Might as well tell them where our antennas are!"

Somehow by now "Pilgrim" had become so credible that, although it took several months and a few extra surveys on his part, he won that battle also. And when he shared his recommendation with NSA people, the Americans thought it was a brilliant idea and wondered why they hadn't figured it out themselves. Thanks to Frost's forethought, it has now become standard procedure also with the U.S. agency.

The passport snag would not be the only time- and energy-consuming confrontation between External Affairs and CSE. High on the list of the diplomats was the question of "status". One has to understand the mentality of Canada's diplomatic corps to grasp the implications of this internal squabbling that, to the outside world, would appear totally ridiculous. When you hold a certain title in an embassy (or, as a matter of fact, anywhere in the bureaucracy) you are entitled to certain perks that your underlings cannot have. In Ottawa, for instance, it can be the size of your office or the quality of your carpet, or the number of paintings you are given to put on your wall. These regulations are all spelled out in bureaucratic lingo in government books as thick as the Gutenberg bible that only experienced mandarins can decipher. They are even more carefully defined when it comes to diplomatic missions and the rules are strictly adhered to by those who profit from them. They cover everything from expense accounts to the availability of a chauffeur and even the size and price of the car a diplomat with a given rank is allowed to have at his disposition. Although this is all public knowledge, technically speaking, the perks are essentially a well-guarded secret within External Affairs. There just might be a public outcry if the extent of what our representatives abroad get at taxpayers' expense were really known.

For these reasons, External people are extremely status-conscious. So when somebody like Mike Frost visited an embassy, even though he was posing as a technician, according to the External bureaucrats involved in "Pilgrim" he had to be treated according to his rank — which was the equivalent of a Lt.-Colonel. That meant, for instance, that he would have a chauffeur and a car waiting on him every hour of the day. The CSE guys had to use a lot of persuasion to explain that they did not want such perks, because they would automatically blow their cover — which was always of a lower rank. This would, however, remain an on-going problem. And it would be compounded when "Pilgrim" started to mount permanent operations and CSE operators under cover had to move to the targeted country with their families. What kind of housing were they allowed to have, for instance? For pre-survey and survey purposes, however, Mike Frost and other "Pilgrim" agents lived their full cover, no matter what their rank entitled them to. There was no other way to go without arousing more suspicion.

Second, what equipment was to be used on a reconnaissance mission? NSA agents were, as usual, pretty bold about it. They brought receivers and antennas in heavy briefcases.

"That's just too risky for us," said Frost to Bowman. "Especially in a pre-survey, when we don't even know if we're going to mount an operation there. Why risk getting caught?"

"I agree. In most countries, NSA doesn't care about getting caught. But this could jeopardize our whole project."

Once you turn on a receiver, it starts radiating, and the "Pilgrim" agents had to admit they were still too green at this game to walk through foreign customs with electronic gear. They would satisfy themselves with a strictly physical examination of the location, jotting down notes and perhaps taking a few pictures. A camera was not a very compromising piece of equipment. As far as Frost was concerned, from a purely selfish point of view, that was a great decision: he would much rather travel with a briefcase full of paper than one loaded with electronic gear.

Third, where would they set up the intercept? Once again NSA was fairly free-wheeling when it came to choosing its sites for embassy collections. NSA agents would sometimes rent an apartment in a foreign city to do it. At other times, they would work directly from a hotel. For a long time — perhaps still to this day — their permanent intercept site in Mexico City was the whole top floor of the Sheraton Hotel. Frost has no idea how they got away with that, and can only surmise that although the Mexicans must have known, they either didn't care or didn't dare do anything about it.

Once again the risk factor was just too high for the Canadians to try an operation from anywhere but within the chancellery itself. There at least they were, according to international law, on Canadian territory — even though the activity was illegal in the country concerned. So a decision was taken that, if it couldn't be done from within the embassy building, they wouldn't even attempt it.

Compared to the other issues, the question of duration was relatively easy. The Canadians knew they couldn't imitate the Americans, who would make a pre-survey last for several months. They could never get that past the Canadian authorities and, besides, the longer the pre-survey and the survey that followed, the longer it would take for them to establish a permanent site somewhere. So the pre-surveys would last a couple of weeks at the most and the surveys would not exceed two months.

The most mind-boggling problems the "Pilgrim" people had to face were those of the security of the operation and of travel arrangements for the agents. The two were intimately linked.

The situation the "Pilgrim" people put themselves in was as close to absurdity as you can get. At the root of the problem was the absolute necessity for keeping "Pilgrim" activities secret within CSE itself. In other words, apart from Peter Hunt, Frank Bowman, Mike Frost and Victor Szakowski, in the initial stage of an operation nobody within the agency itself could be aware of what they were up to. These men had already been trained to hide their real jobs from their wives and families. But this was different. Now they couldn't even tell their fellow agents from other departments that they were going to a foreign capital. If Frost had let slip that he was going to Mexico City, for instance, or later to Bucharest, questions and speculation would have been rampant since everybody within CSE knew he was a SIGINT operator. CSE was also worried about moles inside its own organization working for "the other side" finding out that something very fishy and unusual was suddenly taking their agents around the world.

Outside the walls of CSE, however, Frost's destinations were known to External Affairs people. In the early days, at least half a dozen External bureaucrats were cleared for "Pilgrim". Frost and his colleagues were put in a situation where they couldn't share their concerns with their friends at CSE, but had to put their trust entirely in bureaucrats who lived in a universe of their own and would have liked to control the whole operation themselves. Travel arrangements, for instance, had to be done through External, rather than through the people who would normally handle that at CSE. Since the cover came from External along with the diplomatic passport, and the intercept would be done on their premises, it was the only way to go.

NSA operated differently. They simply posted their embassy-collection people out of the main Fort Meade installations to College Park, which dealt exclusively with covert intercept operations. The American agency was big enough that it could afford to move its people around like that without raising too many eyebrows. CSE was just too small and confined for the "Pilgrim" people to operate that way. This created a lot of stress for Frost. Personal friends from work would sometimes come to the house for dinner. He had insisted that his family be told of his real destination in case of an emergency, and his bosses had agreed. But then one night, when a fellow CSE employee was coming over, he had to tell Carole:

"Oh, by the way, don't mention I'm going to the Ivory Coast."
"Why not?"
"Just don't say anything about it. I can't explain."
"Where shall I say you're going?"
"Just say I'm going down to NSA."

The kids would be asked to lie in the same way. A world of lies for Queen and Country. Lie to your fellow workers, keep the truth from your wife, lie to foreign countries, lie to embassy staff. Most of all, remember who you're lying to because the story might have to change from one person to the other.

Innocent mistakes would inevitably happen. One day one of Frost's sons was wearing a T-shirt his father had clearly bought in Bucharest, with the Romanian capital's name plastered all over the front. They were on Mike's boat, *Pilgrim*, and he had a CSE friend on board — but the man wasn't cleared for the embassy-collection operation.

The actual espionage operation abroad added the complication of playing one part for the host country and another for the embassy staff. It was enough to drive any "Pilgrim" spy into a psychiatric ward to be diagnosed with multiple personality. On the day Frost finally left CSE in 1990, the problem of agents living so many covers still hadn't been resolved. And Frost believes it is still one of the weakest links in the whole operation.

In those early days of "Pilgrim", though, they learned to live with it, just as they had to accept working with External Affairs. There were moments when Frost just exploded: "Why do we have to work with these fucking jerks? Sorry, but that's the only way I can describe them, Frank."

"Do we have a choice?"

"Maybe we don't need them. . . ." But Frost knew that was next to impossible. He just wished that somehow they could have circumvented External Affairs, who by now had more of their employees involved in "Pilgrim" than did CSE. One incident in particular stuck in Frost's mind. At some point during a regular brainstorming session about the cover, status and passport of an agent due to be sent abroad, the head of the External team brought out his pocket calculator and started to balance his cheque book. Frost and Bowman just looked at each other in total disbelief. The meeting ended abruptly shortly after.

"Can you believe that?" hissed a red-faced Frost as they stormed out of the CSE boardroom. "What a rude sonofabitch! Here we are discussing a goddam espionage operation where lives could be at stake and he's balancing his fucking cheque book!" He wanted to kill.

In fact this was par for the course as far as External bureaucrats — with a few exceptions — were concerned. They had wanted control from the start and they weren't going to make it too easy for the CSE guys, no matter what Allan Gotlieb said. In time, though, Frost and Bowman would learn to laugh it off. And, for years to come, whenever they didn't feel like doing something, one of them would say: "Let's go balance our cheque book."

Even this brief outline does not do justice to the countless hours invested in making sure nothing would go wrong. It was a little like climbing Mount Everest. Who would want to know the details once you returned from the summit? Yet those "details" are what got you there alive and back in the first place.

With some issues still unresolved, but many lessons already learned, CSE was ready to attempt its first real survey, in Caracas. "Artichoke" was on.

CSE had no problem convincing the Canadian powerbrokers that Caracas was a valid location for embassy collection in 1981. For one thing, Pierre Trudeau's Minister of Energy, Mines and Resources Marc Lalonde was just introducing his controversial National Energy Policy. From an intelligence point of view, any communications relating to the OPEC cartel that had been responsible for the world oil crisis in the preceding years were a primary target. Venezuela being a major petroleum-producing and exporting country, it was part of the cartel along with Arab countries. That logic worked equally for the Americans, who had suffered the brunt of the energy crisis.

But CSE was also looking to find anything that had to do with drug trafficking and terrorism. As usual, NSA had provided a list of "key words". Among them was one standard name that always appeared on all key-word lists worldwide: Carlos, the infamous terrorist called "The Jackal", who was finally apprehended and handed over to the French in August 1994. With Carlos came a list of other "key words" that might give a clue as to how and from where his terrorist network was operating. Nobody really knew where "The Jackal" was hiding, but perhaps CSE could just fluke into intercepting something extraordinary on that front.

So, both from a potential intelligence point of view and in terms of benefit to Canada, Caracas made sense. It was also, according to Bowman's pre-survey, an ideal site from a technical point of view. Venezuela was also not considered a hostile country — as opposed to, say, an Eastern Bloc or a Middle East one — and for their first main survey, Frost and Bowman wanted to play it as safely as possible.

Still, their hopes were high as they prepared to ship the equipment down and later send their two top operators, Alan Foley and Tom Murray.

NSA was more than co-operative. The Americans told them the best times of day to do intercept in Caracas and what type of transmissions to look for, and gave them all the technical information they would need — in intelligence jargon, TEXTA info, Technical Extracts from Traffic Analysis. Thus before they even got to the site, the "Pilgrim" people had not only specific targets and a list of "key words" to look for but also every possible frequency that was worth intercepting. They also knew what to do with the signals once they caught them, whether to record them in their entirety or demultiplex them.

By this time, NSA had also let the "Pilgrim" people in on their top-secret College Park installation where the Americans would set up strategies and invent and build more advanced technology for the sole purpose of doing intercept operations at home and abroad. College Park was also equipped with what NSA calls "the live room". This is a special room with antennas running around the ceiling, where American engineers actually re-create and radiate at very low power the electronic environment of any world city where an operation is planned. In this case, Frost and the two operators from CSE who went down to College Park for four days were actually able to "hear" Caracas.

It was a simulation, of course. But the operators could swing through the band from VHF to UHF to SHF and start to believe they were already in Caracas. The only slight difference was that the simulation was based on the American embassy — or perhaps a satellite intercept. The intercept would probably be different from the Canadian embassy in terms of getting unique information, for geographical reasons. But the signals were the same, and the operators would at least be familiar with the sort of things they would hear once they got there — which saved an immense amount of time and effort. These NSA electronic briefings would become standard procedure in future missions.

The "Pilgrim" team was so intent on succeeding in their first real survey that they went a bit overboard on the equipment they sent: they had four of just about every piece of electronic gear they needed, from receivers to demodulators. The total shipment, sent in diplomatic bags to External Affairs over a period of several weeks, weighed over 5,000 pounds. In the "Artichoke" caper, all the electronic gear was sent to Venezuela in one shipment. The procedure for later operations would be safer, with the equipment sent to the foreign embassy in separate diplomatic bags, one or two pieces at a time.

The intercept gizmos used in Caracas were also far superior to those they had utilized before, and miles ahead of the "Stephanie" safe. After all, almost ten years of meteoric improvements in electronics had gone by, and NSA was at the forefront of them. There were no more five-foot dishes. They had been replaced by desk-top antennas of much higher performance whose smaller size made the task of dissimulating them immensely easier.

Frost and Bowman were to realize after "Artichoke" that some of the equipment was overkill. Once it had been trucked from CSE to External's loading dock and received and handled by "Pilgrim"-cleared personnel, a courier from External (but paid for by CSE) then had the thankless task of accompanying the equipment from the loading dock all the way to the embassy, in this case Caracas. The courier was expected to remain in sight of the equipment at all times,

FIGURE D
TYPICAL "PILGRIM" EQUIPMENT[1] CONFIGURATION

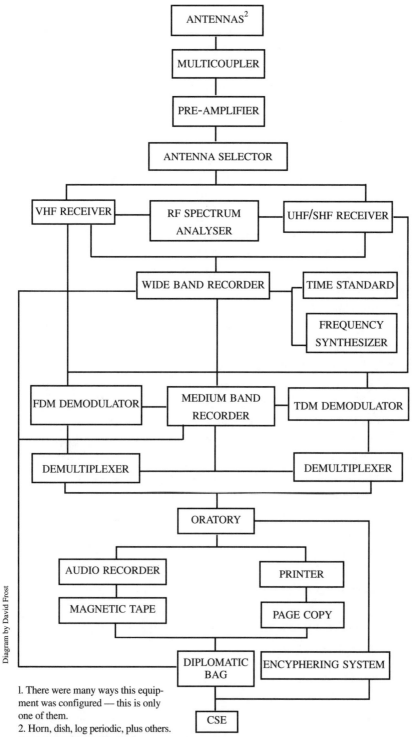

Diagram by David Frost

1. There were many ways this equipment was configured — this is only one of them.
2. Horn, dish, log periodic, plus others. A rotor was also usually used.

except while it was in the belly of the aircraft. His instructions were to make sure the crucial diplomatic bags were loaded onto the aircraft last and be the last passenger to board the flight. He would then be the first one off to see the bags unloaded from the plane. All this on a commercial flight.

This was, at times, a demanding job for the courier, especially when baggage had to transferred from one aircraft to another several times. The only consolation was that he got to fly first-class. The courier arrangements were a bit of a weak link in security since couriers would change and could talk among themselves. They had only cursory knowledge of what it was they were protecting.

The ambassador and an embassy technician had been briefed and cleared by the time the equipment started arriving. If at any time a member of the embassy staff was deemed untrustworthy, either CSE would kill the operation before even starting or the employee was sent on holidays for its duration.

Once the equipment had all been stored in the embassy's communications centre in Caracas, still in the red diplomatic bags, there was a deliberate lull, then the two "Pilgrim" operators left Ottawa two or three weeks later. Within three days of Alan Foley's and Tom Murray's arrival the listening post had been set up inside the necessary copper-mesh tent.

The coded message came back to CSE: "Artichoke is up and running." Frost and Bowman crossed their fingers. It helped that they were dealing with an ambassador who was enthusiastic about the whole project and wanted to make sure everything would go smoothly.

The survey itself lasted about three weeks. At this stage, the intercept lasted only eight hours a day, five days a week, during working hours when the agents could safely live their cover. That would change in subsequent operations. On the technical side, Caracas was a tremendous success. The intercept material was so voluminous that a special courier had to be sent to bring it all back. Normally it would have gone with the External Affairs messenger who swung through various South American cities including Caracas.

When Frost and Bowman realized how big the shipment was, they asked Peter Hunt to detach an analyst to deal solely with the "Artichoke" material. He gave them CSE's top man in the field on a full-time basis. The "Pilgrim" office was now cramped with three desks. The analyst arrived as the sun rose and left long after it set in order to get through tons of data. To make sure he hadn't missed anything, everything was then shipped down to NSA, who put two analysts on the job. CSE had first made sure they kept to themselves anything that was for Canadian consumption only.

It took six to nine months to analyse the Caracas collection product. Then CSE had to confront a devastating reality: they had come up empty. Nothing of any intelligence value from microwave trunk lines, wide band, narrow band, car phones, radios, government and military communications, lots of OPEC traffic. Zero, despite a gigantic effort. They couldn't even produce a single end-product report for their government, the Americans or the British.

Frost and Bowman were crushed. They couldn't believe it. All that time, that money, that effort for something that turned out to be utterly useless. NSA's conclusions were the same, and Patrick O'Brien was just as surprised as they were. He too felt they should have picked up at least a tidbit of valuable intelligence.

What worried the "Pilgrim" people most was that higher-ups like Gotlieb needed ammunition to keep the project going. But they had none to provide. And they couldn't fabricate it. That they could get their men there and back without a hitch and had proven they were wizards at catching airwaves hardly counted. It was a dismal intelligence failure.

They did learn some important lessons from Caracas, however. First, they had sent far too many pieces of equipment. Second, operating eight hours a day was not necessarily the best method, even though they had concentrated on Venezuelan peak business and communications hours. They had not been intercepting during what would be, for instance, peak European working hours. NSA had already told them they would eventually have to operate 24 hours a day, seven days a week. CSE's answer had been that they simply couldn't do it. Now it became obvious they would probably have no choice.

Disappointment was part of the game. They still had the green light to survey seven more sites and they had no intention of slowing down. From Caracas on, though, their priorities started to change. They had gone to Venezuela primarily because it was both safe and easy as a first hit.

"Maybe we have to look at something with a slightly higher risk involved," said Bowman.

"I agree. Eventually, we'll have to go behind the Iron Curtain."

"Somewhere down the line we'll just have to come up with some good intelligence before the eight surveys are over."

"We'll get it," said Frost.

It was more wishful thinking than confidence speaking. But surely, he thought, if they just took a few more risks, sooner or later something would break.

A rather bizarre incident did happen shortly after Caracas, before "Pilgrim" really got back on track. It came totally out of the blue, as the "Pilgrim" team was trying to decide on their next target: NSA wanted them to go to Algiers as soon as possible. Frost was never too sure why, but strongly suspected it had more to do with Algeria's neighbour, Libya, and the fact that the recently sworn-in U.S. President Ronald Reagan planned to wage open war against Mu'ammar al Gaddafi. In the spring of 1981 the Middle East and especially the terrorist problem was high on the hawkish President's list.

Frost was picked for the pre-survey job. His passport was sent to the Algerian embassy in Ottawa, the visa was stamped. In record time he was all set to go. His plane reservations were made, his cover was official, the ambassador was expecting him.

His bags were all packed and he was having a last meal with the family when, just as suddenly as the urgent request had come, somebody pulled the plug on the operation.

Bowman simply told him: "You're not going to Algiers. The operation has been cancelled."

"Do you know why?"

"I haven't got a clue why, who or how. Peter Hunt just said to scrap it. Who knows? Maybe you're *persona non grata* there." The Algiers operation was so short-lived, it never even got a code name. Once in a while, Mike Frost goes over the diplomatic passport he still has in his possession, looks at that Algerian visa and wishes he knew why.

Still, the "Pilgrim" operators decided that West Africa could be a good target. That's where Frost was now headed — to the Ivory Coast, Senegal and Morocco. Bowman, meanwhile, went to Central and South America to pre-survey San José, in Costa Rica, and Brasilia.

NSA was not too thrilled about West Africa.

"What on earth are you wasting your time there for?" asked Patrick O'Brien. "Go to Beijing! Go to an Iron Curtain country! Why fuck around with West Africa?"

Despite NSA's puzzlement, if not outright annoyance, CSE had its own reasons to go to West Africa. On top of their list of targets were French communications. Back in 1982, although the Quebec referendum had been lost by separatist leader René Lévesque, Canada was still reeling from Pierre Trudeau's patriation of the constitution without Quebec's approval. The federal government was deeply concerned about private discussions and negotiations going on between Quebec and Paris. The Quebec government also had a consulate in Paris that had better diplomatic relations with the French government than the Canadian embassy there, as former ambassador and Trudeau minister Gérard Pelletier would sadly explain in his farewell report in 1981. CSE believed it to be its duty to find out if anything unusual was going on between the leaders of France and the separatist government in Quebec.

There was also an economic value to the intercept. The French didn't like the fact that many Canadian companies were intruding on what they considered to be their sacred market, former French African colonies. In many areas, Canadian and French industries were in direct competition. Discussions about forming a French Commonwealth — now known as *"La Francophonie"* — had been stalled for years by both France and Quebec, who each had their reasons to see it fail. (It would take the Brian Mulroney government, some four years later, and a Liberal government in Quebec with Robert Bourassa as premier, to get it off the ground.)

The "Pilgrim" people also knew that a whole section of the African west coast was lined with microwave towers. There had to be all kinds of communications going through there.

Frost and Bowman tossed a coin to decide who was going where. Frost got Africa. He wasn't sure if he'd won or lost. He was on a three- to four-week mission that would take him to Abidjan, Dakar and Rabat with orders not to report home until the end of the trip, except in emergency.

It was minus 27° Celsius when Frost boarded his shuttle flight to New York's JFK airport from Ottawa's Uplands airport. It was one of the rare flights where passengers have to walk out over the tarmac to the ramp of the aircraft. As he approached the plane, Frost glanced at the company name painted on the fuselage. A broad smile illuminated his face despite the Arctic-like weather. It was "Pilgrim Airlines". He transferred to Pan Am at JFK and was on his way to Dakar, then Sierra Leone and finally Abidjan. As the Boeing 747 was coming in for the landing at Sierra Leone, he could see rows of native women planting and cultivating crops between the runways. They didn't even raise their heads to glance at the airplane. When you know the size of mosquitoes over there, 747s don't impress you very much.

When Frost finally got to Abidjan, the temperature was 28° Celsius and, as he puts it, "the humidity must have made it about 190 degrees." He was still wearing his woollen socks, his jeans and a denim jacket covered in Canadian flag pins — because he didn't want to be mistaken for an American. He felt like a polar bear in the jungle.

He was met at the airport by the embassy technician, who had already been cleared for the "Pilgrim" operation. Joyfully the man asked him: "Do you want to come and meet the ambassador?"

"Are you crazy?" shot back Frost. "I've been on this plane for 23 hours, I'm going to my hotel."

At this point he was melting in the heat, and wasn't even too sure any more what he was doing in this strange country.

The technician mercifully dropped him off at the Novotel, about two and a half blocks from the embassy. After a short snooze, Frost was relaxing beside the pool and taking in the warm sun while gathering his thoughts about the task ahead. A woman — or rather a girl because she couldn't have been more than thirteen — came up to him and asked in French: "*Manger?*" With the little French he knew, he figured out that she wanted something to eat and ordered her a sandwich. The girl looked at him wide-eyed and walked away. He was to find out later that when francophone African hookers say "*manger?*" they have another kind of meal in mind.

He had lunch with the ambassador the following day and the embassy technician he had already met was detached to help him throughout the pre-survey. It didn't take him long to spot the microwave towers and the fact that the PTT (Post, Telephone and Telegraph) building was just a few blocks away. "Pilgrim" would have a clear shot at them. Frost assumed correctly that these towers were the main North-South link between Africa and Europe, might carry anything at all and were probably of great intelligence value. He took pictures of the towers and of which way the antennas were facing. He could tell from the type of antennas being used what frequency they were designed for.

He wasn't perfectly happy with the embassy, though. It was a "shared building" as opposed to an "island site". There were other offices and people in the building besides the Canadian contingent, which would make the transportation of equipment and the comings and goings of the CSE operators a little more dicey. However, the Canadian embassy occupied the top floor of the building and they had access to the roof where there was already an encased antenna dome belonging to the chancellery. The dome had a lock on it and was a perfect, ready-made place to put intercept antennas. The only person who had a key was the technician. Even if the "Pilgrim" antennas were spotted by an intruder, the cover story of improving satellite communications with Canada would wash.

It was a relatively safe country. Canada, through foreign aid and CIDA (the Canadian International Development Agency) had good relations with the Ivory Coast. There was some student unrest at the time, but nothing that indicated an imminent major blow-up. This had been the smoothest ride yet for Frost, who already had in mind to recommend the site.

Buoyed with confidence, he boarded the plane to Dakar, a little further north on the edge of the Sahara desert. He was in high spirits as he waited for his baggage at Dakar airport. As he was standing there expecting his flight bag, he saw a loose shirt going around on the carousel. "Nice shirt," he thought. "Wonder how it got there." Then he saw a pair of pants. "Hey, I've got pants like that," he said to himself. Then it hit him when a pair of underwear went by. His face dropped through the floor and his heart started pounding furiously. These were *his* clothes! When his flight bag finally emerged, it had a big rip in the side.

In a state of panic, Frost went to retrieve his loose clothing and verify what had happened to his baggage. It quickly became evident that someone, somewhere, had put a knife to the bag and stolen the expensive government-owned camera. His only relief was that he had taken what could have been compromising film out of it.

But that sort of thing will spook a spook, big time. His bag was the only one that had been tampered with. The very next day he reported to the ambassador, who in turn, through his channels, reported back to Ottawa. Word came back from External and CSE that he should not worry about it too much. It was most probably just a case of theft — something not uncommon in African countries. He was given authorization to go out and purchase another camera on the local market at taxpayers' expense. Which he did — a 35mm equipped with the necessary zoom. The embassy even had his flight bag fixed through an excellent local tailor.

With that annoyance out of the way, Frost still had to take his now-traditional "walk on the street" with the ambassador — and this one hadn't been brought back to Ottawa for a briefing. He hated discussing matters of such sensitivity while pretending to take a leisurely stroll. But by now he was getting used to it, although he was still stepping off curbs and walking into lamp posts.

In Dakar, it was a nightmare. The capital of Senegal is an open-air sewer. There is excrement of all kinds on the street, beggars who won't leave you alone, street vendors who grab at your sleeves and sometimes attack you in droves, walking away with your watch, your rings and your wallet, there are dogs, there are goats. In short it was just about the last place you'd want to have a highly classified conversation with an ambassador who, in the end, doesn't really want to hear what you're saying; he's going along with this simply because he has been told to do so.

"So, what is it you are here to do?" asked the ambassador.

"Well, I'm with CSE and we want to mount an intercept operation. I want to check the countryside for microwave towers and possible targets and, with your permission, find a place to set up our electronic equipment within the embassy. We need a room that will be isolated from the rest of the staff and access to the roof, for antennas, you know."

"Be careful when you talk in the embassy," said the ambassador matter-of-factly.

"Oh, I never talk about that stuff within the embassy. You never know if you're being bugged."

"Right. And the KGB has an office on the floor right above us," added the diplomat.

"I beg your pardon," said Frost, who stopped walking as suddenly as if he'd hit a brick wall.

"Oh yeah! I don't know if they're KGB for sure. But they're Russians and their office is right above ours."

Stunned, Frost walked back to the embassy and went up to the floor where the Soviets were supposed to be. And there it was, plain as the Canadian pins on his jean jacket, a huge hammer and sickle on the door.

So much for Dakar as a "Pilgrim" site. Frost was angry. How could the External Affairs people on their Ottawa team have overlooked this "minor" detail? He had wasted both his time and government money. He couldn't help but remember the Mexico fiasco. Somebody at External Affairs must have known about the Soviet bureau. But they simply weren't trained to react like CSE agents. There was no way CSE could mount an operation with Soviets in the same building. KGB or not, their diplomats are all trained to know what to look for: abnormal movement, strange new faces, work being done out of normal office hours, anything out of the ordinary. The Soviets were masters at this game too: chances were they already had an operation set up in that very building themselves. The cover and the 5,000 pounds of equipment would never get past the Russians. CSE wanted to avoid at all costs the Soviet Union finding out that Canada was in on embassy collection. Because once the Soviets knew, they would be tracking people like Frost all over the globe.

Frost couldn't get over how this oversight had put the whole "Pilgrim" operation at risk. His name was probably on the Soviets' own "key-word" list, since over ham-radio communications back at Alert he would have revealed his true identity and they were sure to have picked up on it. Since he was travelling under his own name, he figured that, if they were watching, the Russians could put two and two together. The oversight gave him a three-day vacation by the sea at the Meridien hotel, while he waited for his scheduled flight to Morocco. But the KGB incident made the holiday a little more stressful than it would normally have been.

Morocco was the final stop on his West African tour. But he first had to go through one more harrowing experience by the name of "Air Afrique". Airlines in Africa don't exactly operate by North American or European standards. Frost had to make the two-hour trip from Dakar to Casablanca on an old DC-8, sitting next to a passenger whose hand-luggage consisted of a crate of live chickens. The meal resembled peanut-butter sandwiches with cold coffee. But what really got to him was the pilot. He didn't look older than twelve.

When Frost saw the embassy in Rabat, he couldn't have dreamed of a more ideal location. It was, first of all, an "island site". It was also in a residential district, which made the "intelligence walk" with the ambassador much easier than those he was accustomed to. There was an empty room on the top floor, with enough power to feed the electronic gear and set up antennas. He took a stroll and then a drive around the countryside. He couldn't see too many microwave towers, but was convinced that there had to be something within the radio horizon. He wasn't as confident as he had been in Abidjan, but he was sure enough to conclude that "Pilgrim" could work here.

While in Rabat, he finally took advantage of the communications link he had secured before leaving Canada and decided to phone Carole. He hadn't had any contact with her in over two weeks, and longed to know how things were at home.

As soon as she said "Hello", he knew something was wrong.

"What's up?"

"Had a few problems."

"What's wrong?"

"Well, Danny [their son] is in the hospital."

"Is it serious?"

"No."

"Well, you sound pretty tired yourself."

"Oh no. Maybe just a little bit upset."

Frost didn't feel good after hanging up the phone. After some 25 years of marriage, he just knew something wasn't right. When he returned to Canada a few days later, he would find out that not only was his son in the hospital but Carole herself was stricken with pneumonia. She hadn't said a word about it or even attempted to contact him, so as not to interfere with his work. And this despite the fact that, since she was kept in the dark about his activities, in her heart she thought he was just travelling around the world having a marvellous time.

There were times, many times, when the sacrifices may have been much greater for her and the family than they were for Mike. And this is true of many CSE, NSA or GCHQ agents who have to lead such crazy, secretive lives. The price is high for everybody. And when he found out about her illness, there were moments when Frost wondered about his calling as a spy. But he was so wrapped up in it at that point, and believed in "the just cause" so much, that he had to go on regardless of the cost and the guilt.

Frost decided to head back home on the Monday. The ambassador tried to convince him to stay for an extra couple of days and accompany him to the legendary town of Marrakesh. Frost would have given his right arm to go, but he knew his cover as a technician did not warrant a trip to Marrakesh with the ambassador — even though his officer's status, had it been known, would have served.

He flew back via Paris and landed in Mirabel in the early afternoon, feeling punch-drunk from jetlag. He phoned Frank Bowman as soon as he cleared Canadian customs. "Hi. I'm back."

"Great! They're waiting for you in the boardroom. Peter Hunt, External Affairs and Privy Council people . . ."

"Jesus Christ, Frank, do they want to talk to me today?"

"They want you to give them a briefing today."

"Jesus, man! My ass is dragging now! I've been in travel status for about 26 hours! What's the problem?"

"We have to discuss our second operation. We have to get recommendations in. We have to get on with it, the pressure is on. . . . Have you got any prospects?"

"Yeah, two out of three."

"Great. Prepare yourself, we'll pick you up at the airport and you're going to do a briefing."

He took the "First Air" shuttle flight from Mirabel to Uplands airport, was picked up by a CSE agent and showed up in the boardroom still dressed in his jeans. All he had were a few scripted notes he had jotted down hurriedly on the way. For a man who loathed writing reports, and in the condition he was, this was a herculean feat. There he faced a group of senior policy makers and his chief, Peter Hunt. Mostly off the top of his head, he went through the scenarios in all three West African countries he had visited. He concluded by saying operations could be mounted in Abidjan and Rabat, but forget about Dakar.

The next morning, when he walked into his office, a letter from Peter Hunt was sitting on his desk: "Mike, thank you for an excellent briefing. Very well done, very professional, very good for the CSE image." The acronym BZ was scribbled on the letter. It stands for "Bravo Zulu" and is the ultimate form of congratulations in the intelligence community.

Both recommendations were accepted, Abidjan being the first target. It was codenamed "Jasmine". Within hours, Frost contacted NSA's Patrick O'Brien and set the wheels in motion to get the equipment ready for shipment to Africa. The same two operators who had been in Caracas were again sent down to College Park where the Abidjan "environment" was simulated for them in the "live room".

As for "key-words", since they expected to intercept a lot of French communications, anything that had to do with the Quebec separatist movement was high on the list; the name René Lévesque was one of them. CSE also knew the frequency such sensitive communications were likely to be carried on.

From a technical point of view, "Jasmine" was rather uneventful, except that the copper-mesh tent was beginning to be a problem. Holes had developed in it, it was as hot as a Turkish bath, and it was not an easy thing to hide. The "Pilgrim" people were starting to wish there was a way to do without it. They also had to do some destructive work in the "Pilgrim" room at the embassy: a hole had to be dug through the ceiling for the antenna cables. There were also windows in the room. Before the CSE operators arrived, the embassy technician had been told to shut the curtains for two or three hours a day. Gradually, they worked up to shutting them all the time for the duration of the operation, to hide the equipment. It was a calculated risk they simply had to take.

For the first time, the intercept went on for sixteen hours a day, to coincide both with European and American working hours, instead of being limited to the normal local business period. They split the two eight-hour shifts between the operators so that the equipment was manned practically all the time, although it was sometimes on automatic while the CSE agent lived his cover, pretending to be just a technician and testing bogus equipment. They still didn't do any weekend work, however.

They were able to get into the PTT, car phones, ambulances, taxis, police, and the microwave towers that were the main communication link for the whole West African coast. They got a lot of banking transaction information and government communications. But Abidjan, after a six-week survey, was another Caracas from an intelligence point of view. Technologically perfect, with tons of information; but as for intelligence, zilch. Not even a hint of anything to do with Quebec or even Canada, even though they got a CSE analyst very familiar with the "French problem" to sift through the material.

The collected material was sent down to NSA as usual and, much later, Frost was to find out that the Americans had discovered something they liked in the Abidjan intercept. He never knew what but suspected it had to do with the banking transactions.

When they shut down in Abidjan, Frost had to make a decision. Economically and time-wise, it would make more sense to ship the equipment directly from Abidjan to Rabat, the next survey site, codenamed "Iris." But was the risk of blowing the cover too great? He consulted the GCHQ people and they agreed that, although it might seem like a waste of time and money, the best way was to bring everything back home first, and send it to Morocco through the usual diplomatic route.

Once more, Patrick O'Brien prepared the College Park "live room", this time to reproduce the Rabat environment. "No problem," said the NSA man. "You guys are doing great. Get your confidence up so you can do Beijing."

This time, along with their best agent, Alan Foley, they sent a new man by the name of Richard Robson, whom Frost knew from his Inuvik and Alert days. After Vanier, Jamaica, Caracas and Abidjan, they figured that at least one of the two operators who had done all the work deserved a break and Tom Murray was saved from Morocco.

By the time they got to Rabat, CSE had upgraded the quality of its equipment considerably and was now getting into pulse-modulated systems. A lot of the work was being done by an Ottawa electronics contractor. CSE was starting to customize its own equipment to suit Canadian needs, though to a lesser degree than NSA did for U.S. needs at College Park. CSE was also going to try new types of desktop antennas developed by NSA.

An item that would become a crucial part of any "Pilgrim" intercept site was now used for the first time. It looked like just a black box, not much bigger than a briefcase about six inches high, but it contained an intricate set of computer circuits that produced something close to a miracle. It had been developed by an NSA engineer and given the name of "Oratory". It was in fact a key-word selection computer. On one side you programmed your list of keywords, and out they would come on the other. What "Oratory" did with fantastic efficiency was eliminate a lot of useless traffic and endless, often useless analysis — everything CSE had suffered from in Caracas and Abidjan. It didn't matter if the intercept was voice, fax, or teletype, "Oratory" selected only what CSE wanted to see or hear. And you could change its program at any time if new keywords came to mind.

In July 1994, NSA was still denying it had such a capability when the issue was raised in the U.S. Congress. James Banford's *The Puzzle Palace* describes the equipment but not its code name.

"Oratory" was "Tempest-proof", it was small, virtually indestructible and easy to repair: all you had to do was open the lid and replace the defective board. It had been developed by a very young computer wizard who had originally worked for NASA, an eccentric hippie-type, in jeans, T-shirt and sneakers, who worked with circuit boards with the ease of a plumber fixing a leaking faucet and was dedicated to his job to the point of often bunking over at College Park overnight.

Mike Frost couldn't say enough about "Oratory" or the engineer who created it. Because for CSE, it was truly a godsend. It worked so well in Rabat, in fact, that at first the operators reported back to CSE: "We're just not getting anything." They were told to check if a given light on "Oratory" was on. If it was, the device was operational. If they weren't getting anything, it just meant the magic box was eliminating a lot of meaningless traffic — in other words doing the work of CSE analysts. It also almost eliminated the need for an operator, since "Oratory" would turn on the recorders only when its program "heard" a key-word. They even tested it by feeding it obvious key-words that were bound to be heard and, sure enough, "Oratory" would spit them out as soon as it intercepted them.

In that sense, Rabat was a ground-breaking operation for "Pilgrim". Technically, once again, no problem. Well, maybe a small calculated mishap: they had to break one of the windows of the embassy when they realized that the lead content in the glass was interfering with the antennas that had been positioned to "shine" through the window. Since Rabat was an "island site" the CSE agents believed they could get away with it without causing too much commotion.

On the intelligence side of things "Oratory" captured many communications between France and Quebec relating to the question of separation. Frost does not know the details of that information, only that it was forwarded to the proper Canadian authorities. He is also convinced that, much as he and Bowman agreed with the survey sites selected, someone in high places had picked West Africa specifically for the intercept of Quebec-France communications. When it comes to CSE, the ultimate authority is the Prime Minister. In this case it was Pierre Trudeau, the separatists' nemesis. It is not at all far-fetched to assume that at least verbal briefings of CSE's intelligence findings were given to the leader of the country.

There were also PLO communications. Yasser Arafat's name, for instance, was on every key-word list. NSA was happy about that.

CSE had to close down Rabat earlier than they would have wished. External Affairs had warned them beforehand that an employee of the embassy was not to be trusted while "Pilgrim" was going on. She was sent on vacation at the start of the survey, but CSE had a deal with External that they would leave as soon as the employee was due to return. They stuck to it.

By now, though, they were ready to go truly behind enemy lines. Bucharest, Romania, and the tyrant who ruled it, Nicolae Ceausescu, were about to be "Pilgrimed". The operation was code-named "Hollyhock".

SEVEN
TAKING ON DRACULA

"OH YES . . . ONE MORE THING. Make sure you go with a suitcase full of Kent cigarettes."

"With what?" asked a totally befuddled Mike Frost who thought his hearing or attention span were failing.

"Kent cigarettes," repeated NSA's Patrick O'Brien.

"Why on God's earth would I do that? Don't they sell cigarettes in Romania?"

O'Brien chuckled and explained: "They're hard currency over there. Better than the American dollar. You can buy anything with them. Meals, booze, taxis, hookers, hotels, chewing gum, name it . . ."

Still Frost thought he was pulling his leg. "Kent? Not Marlboros or Camels or . . .?"

"No, no. Kent cigarettes. Trust me."

Frost felt like quizzing O'Brien more; he craved to know whether the NSA man had ever himself been to Bucharest. But he knew better than to ask. The Americans will share knowledge about espionage techniques when it serves their purpose. They simply won't tell you everything, especially when it comes to what a specific agent, be it O'Brien or another, did or is doing "in the field".

He also got another rather weird piece of advice from the U.S. top embassy-collection man. "Oh," O'Brien said, "the night you get to your hotel [the Sheraton, where Frost was staying while surveying the Canadian embassy site for a 'Pilgrim' operation], you will probably find one or two 40-watt lightbulbs. But that's it. Just ask the front desk for some 60-watt lightbulbs and they'll fix you up, no problem."

Frost wasn't too sure what the smirk on O'Brien's face meant. Later he would find out that the NSA man was both playing a practical joke on him and also letting him know, in no uncertain terms, that, when it came to Romania, he knew what he was talking about.

Frost and CSE were finally doing something they felt would be truly meaningful. Not that they thought they hadn't done good work before. But "Hollyhock" was their first "dangerous" mission: going behind the Iron Curtain, in the midst of what was still very much the Cold War. Both the Americans and the British were elated at the decision, and the Canadians felt they had something to prove.

The choice of Bucharest had come after much consultation, especially within CSE. They did not want to put their men in jeopardy, for starters. They had been told that, as far as the "spy game" went, the Romanians generally played by the unwritten rules: in other words, they knew the other side was doing it to them, but that was fine as long as they could pull the same trick abroad and be sure the authorities would turn and look the other way. All Iron Curtain countries operated this way. Because they knew that if they did something, say, to the Americans in Moscow, there would be retaliation in Washington. Just as in 1979, when, Canada having expelled three Soviet "spies" from the embassy in Ottawa, the then U.S.S.R. did the same to the Canadian military attaché in Moscow.

But Romania was then being tyrannized by a communist leader who, the world would find out later, was closer to a modern version of Count Dracula. The CSE agents and External Affairs people did not know the extent of the atrocities he was committing, but they did know he had a despotic way of solving problems, ruled by fear and total surveillance of the population, and that you couldn't absolutely count on him not to retaliate hard against Canada should he find out it was in on the espionage network when it wasn't supposed to be. He might just interpret that as being outside "the rules".

Who knows how this man later proved to be a homicidal maniac might have reacted then?

The most dicey point, though, was that it not be known in the opposing intelligence community that Canada was in on the game as an active third player. They especially didn't want the Soviets to know, since there was no doubt in their minds that some day, somehow, they would be returning to Moscow. They so badly wanted to accomplish the survey operation without getting caught that every minute detail of the operation was viewed and reviewed, over and over again.

As for political and bureaucratic implications, CSE figured it had the mandate to survey eight sites from Allan Gotlieb, and that was good enough. Besides, there was little doubt in CSE chief Peter Hunt's mind that the Prime Minister would be verbally briefed. If objections were going to be raised, they would come, and quickly.

From a strict intelligence point of view, the "Pilgrim" people had Bucharest at the top of the list. They knew NSA and GCHQ had sites there. But, geographically, because the Canadian embassy was in a different part of the Romanian capital, CSE thought they had a good chance of collecting unique intercept. This could do wonders for them in terms of intelligence-sharing with their allies. It would become currency for the Canadians who knew that, generous as their CANUKUS partners were, they were withholding crucial information from their own collection operations. If Canada came up with something its partners didn't have but dearly wanted, it could expect something good in return that it wouldn't even have known about otherwise.

As for Mike Frost, he simply wanted to be the one to do the pre-survey. Maybe it had a bit to do with the Moscow disappointment of a decade earlier. But there was more to it than that: he simply thought he was the best man to do the job and it was in his nature not to let others take on such a risk. He wanted to accept full responsibility should things go wrong. Bowman and Hunt had no problem with that. In fact, they fully agreed there was nobody better or more dedicated.

The toughest part was trying to explain it to his wife Carole, while abiding by the rules that prevented him from telling her what it was really all about. He already felt terribly guilty about his pre-survey in West Africa, when she hadn't contacted him even though she had contracted pneumonia. He did not want a repetition. Nothing, not even "Pilgrim", was worth his wife's and his family's health and welfare, though the thought did cross his mind that he had probably never made that clear to them.

Even now Carole's concerns would not stop him from getting on that plane to Bucharest. But he had to let her know how much he cared, though in his usually secretive manner. He told her one night at the dinner table: "I have to go to an Iron Curtain country . . . Romania, Bucharest."

"Oh . . ."

"But don't worry about it. I won't be gone too long and it's not really a dangerous place."

She didn't say anything, but he did see the flash of grief go through her eyes. Carole had years of training in not asking too many questions, so she didn't ask for an explanation.

He added: "For God's sake, though, if anything like the last time happens to you or the kids, don't hesitate to use the procedure and call."

She said she would. But Mike couldn't be sure about that. His wife was a tough woman who had learned to survive on her own. At that point it hit him just how much he was leading two lives: one as a caring husband and father, the other as a spy who had been and would be sent again on what were always perilous missions. He couldn't share this crucial part of himself with those he loved the most. He found it strange that this had never dawned on him before. He had always gone about doing "his duty", in the military and at CSE, and expected Carole fully to understand. Perhaps he had just realized, after 24 years in the business, that this game was for keeps. It was a painful realization of what he had become: a secret agent; a man who could share neither pain, nor glory, except within the limited circles of his intelligence "friends", a man who couldn't even share his anguish with his family.

For Romania the "Pilgrim" operators went out of their way to make sure they wouldn't miss any angles. The trips back and forth to NSA and GCHQ had been many. Frost and Bowman wanted a perfect operation — if there was such a thing — and they had already learned from experience that it is usually the most innocuous things that go wrong, in the most innocuous circumstances.

First on the list of concerns was the cover Frost was going to use. Would it wash? Would going in with a diplomatic passport (the problem of prying it out of External Affairs was out of the way by then) and claiming to be in the Canadian embassy to upgrade the communications centre be accepted? NSA and GCHQ had assured Frost and Bowman that they were bound to be harassed by the Romanian secret police, but had also stressed the odds were no physical harm would follow. The Romanians' methods — as Frost was about to find out by himself — were different. Not that subtle, but perhaps more efficient. In the light of this and after much debate, the "cover" story came to seem, to a certain extent, a useless worry. What NSA and GCHQ had told them was that whoever or whatever they posed as, they would be tailed, bugged and shaken up psychologically; but in all probability, their mirage would hold.

"Just don't let them get to you," said NSA's O'Brien. Easy to say; harder to accomplish.

Another important thing they learned about "Pilgriming" in Romania was that the electrical power would be a daily problem. "It can go, from one minute to the other, from 40, to 50, to 60 Hertz. . . . That's normal," said O'Brien. But it would play havoc with electronic equipment of the kind the Canadians were using — which was basically the same as the Americans' with just a few "domestic" variations. NSA pointed out that they shouldn't take the strange power surges and shortages as a trick or as a sign that they had been busted by the Romanian secret police. It was simply part of life in Ceausescu land.

Then came the question of how to get the equipment over there. NSA's solution was not an option for Canada. The Americans said they just used a Hercules airplane, put their stuff in crates and trucked it to their embassy, period. Easier said than done for Canada: the last thing CSE wanted was to have the whole project put on hold simply because they made the politicians nervous. And requesting the use of an Armed Forces Hercules would inevitably have raised eyebrows, if not tempers. CSE had no money or mandate to do this kind of grandiose thing. In bureaucratic Ottawa, it would have delayed this crucial operation by weeks, months, maybe years.

Anyhow, Frost and Bowman thought the British way a lot smarter. "We ship it in little pieces," said the GCHQ people who had, CSE knew, gone into places for intercept purposes where NSA couldn't. So that's the course Frost and Bowman chose: patiently sending the equipment over, piece by piece, in diplomatic bags.

By this time CSE's operation depended heavily on "Oratory", the magic box that eliminated so much useless "traffic" and concentrated on the meaningful targets. They got a list of "key-words" to feed into the computer. They made up their own and asked their American and British allies to do the same.

Of course, anything resembling the word "Ceausescu" and any of his relatives or close political, military or bureaucratic associates was on there. There was, however, one name that surprised and puzzled the Canadians, and made them wonder what the Americans were up to. But, as the "game" goes, they didn't ask any questions and just included it in the list for "Oratory". The name was that of Nadia Comaneci — the Olympic gymnastics sensation of Montreal's 1976 Olympics, the first athlete in the history of the Olympic games ever to register a "10"-score from the judges. The world would find out years later that Nadia was being raped and abused as "a mistress" almost daily by Ceausescu's son, Nicu. Nadia's mother, Alexandrina Comaneci, would claim in February 1990 that Nicu Ceausescu had repeatedly beaten and tortured her daughter during a five-year "relationship". "I would like to hang him by his tongue and watch him die," she was quoted as saying.

In the fall of 1982, the Americans knew this — or at least were fully aware that the Olympic superstar had a unique inside view into the higher circles of the Romanian government. Nadia revealed her ordeal with Ceausescu's abusive son to the world in 1989 when she escaped from Romania — more than likely with the help of intelligence people from the U.S., Britain and Canada. She defected just months before the so-called Christmas Revolution that saw the Romanian people over-throw the monster who had been terrorizing them. Nicolae Ceausescu's execution, and that of his wife Elena, by a firing squad that didn't even wait for the order to fire, was caught on video for all the world to see in late 1989. As for Nadia Comaneci, she first went to the United States as a safe haven, but quickly settled in Montreal, Canada, where she had known the greatest moments in her life.

High on Canada's own "key-word" list was the Canadian CANDU reactor — since Canada was negotiating at the time a highly publicized nuclear reactor sale with Romania. The sale never amount-ed to much — certainly not as much as the Canadian government had hoped. Mind you, for CSE a brand-new nuclear power station would have come in handy at the time of the operation to solve the power problem. CANDU alone met the criterion of "Canadian interest" that CSE had to demonstrate for a "Pilgrim" operation. It was probably why few questions were asked from higher-ups who could have thrown a wrench in the machinery when it was revealed to External Affairs and the Prime Minister's office that CSE was going to tackle "Dracula".

The ambassador, Peter M. Roberts, who was later to become Canada's diplomatic representative in Moscow, was bought back to the country on some bogus excuse to be told what was going to hap-pen. He wasn't fazed one bit. He had been in Romania long enough to know that something had to be done to improve lives of the people in that sad country.

Frost's stomach was churning as he prepared to board the British Airways flight to Paris and then Bucharest. The magnitude of what he was about to do crashed down on him. He was going to a lawless country where a ruthless dictator made the rules by the day. And he was going as a spy. Had he lost his mind? This "duty" thing, was it that important? Clearly it was.

Off he went, with his spy briefcase, a flight bag and a suit-bag, and, yes, a dufflebag full of cartons of Kent cigarettes. He had about twenty or thirty of the cartons. He had deliberately driven about sixty miles south of the Canadian capital, across the St. Lawrence River to Massena, to do his Kent cigarette shopping. The Romanians would not question what they were used to as "hard currency", but they might just look twice at an unfamiliar pack of Kents purchased in Canada, which would have a special label on the package indicating they were imported goods. That was the kind of small thing that could give him away.

The flight from Ottawa to Romania was pretty uneventful. It was the calm before the storm.

Bucharest, on landing, was everything it promised — or that Frost feared it — to be. Rainy, gloomy fall weather, everything you would expect but were afraid to ask about Ceausescu land. Frost's first apprehension, though, was that he had to surrender his diplomatic passport. This was standard procedure in Romania. He and Bowman had discussed it at length and he had said many times how much he hated the idea. But he had also concluded that: "If I don't give them the passport, then they'll know I'm not just an ordinary diplomat. . . ."

To aggravate him further, he had learned from his briefings that he also had to provide two extra passport pictures to be turned over to Ceausescu's police. That was a major bummer, but NSA and GCHQ had convinced him he simply had no choice: he would have to give the passport and the two photos to Romanian customs or forget about ever crossing the border. It's not exactly the sort of action a budding international spy wants to take: having his mug officially in the hands and the files of a communist country, possibly plastered on the walls of their secret police, on a dart board or something worse. But any other behaviour would arouse suspicion as to whether he was a real diplomat or not.

Reluctantly, Frost went to CSE's official photographer to have his pictures taken. They were handed to him in an envelope that he never bothered to check before his departure. He didn't particularly care to see them. As he left the aircraft at Bucharest airport, Frost was still milling all of this through his mind. His rebellious nature told him to fight the procedure, but there he was standing in line about to go through customs, and he knew his tie was caught in the fan belt: he would have to go through without screaming too much.

Then "luck" happened. As he held his precious briefcase in one hand and his passport and pictures in the other, he happened to glance at the photos taken by the CSE photographer. He was then three passengers away from the Romanian customs agent, who had a clear view of him. For some reason he will never know, he flipped the photos to look at the back. And there it was, stamped for Nicolae to know: "Property of the Communications Security Establishment, Defence Department, Canada."

To say that terror struck him is an understatement. He wanted to die. He might as well hand himself over in handcuffs. "Think quick, Mike! Your life may be on the line here!" In a flash of reason or total insanity, he put the two passport pictures in his mouth, chewed them up quickly and swallowed. He doesn't even want to remember what they tasted like — only that he didn't even have cognac to wash them down, and that, somehow, the customs agent didn't notice what he had done.

Now he had another problem — apart from a resentful stomach. He still had to get inside Romania without his mandatory pictures. And he had been told time and again this was impossible. By this time Frost was just hoping they would reject him and he would quickly be on a plane back to Canada, where he would show up at CSE, bang his fist on a desk, and scream: "You guys screwed up and I had to eat photographs! I guess you'll just have to send in another agent." In practice, once his turn came, Frost was confronted by two — as opposed to the usual one — customs officers. One was holding a hand on his shoulder, while the other had his diplomatic passport in his hand. Frost was hanging on for dear life to his briefcase, doing his best to play the total innocent.

"You can't gain access to Romania," said one of the guards with a fierce, disdainful glare.

"Fine," answered Frost, "but give me back my passport, because I'm not going back to Canada without it!"

That was the "tough" part of his act. He also played it smooth. He told the Romanians it was his first time there and that, somehow, somebody in Canada must have forgotten that he had to provide the two extra pictures.

"I'm only here for a short time to meet with the ambassador," he said, figuring only a "name-dropping" strategy would work.

"The ambassador? Is he meeting you?"

"No. But his chauffeur is."

What happened in the backrooms of Bucharest airport when one of the guards left to check out Frost's story, he doesn't know. How long the ordeal lasted, he doesn't remember. Doesn't want to. He was in a near state of shock.

When the guard returned, he simply said, sternly: "All right, you may go." Like an automaton Frost went through the airport to where the embassy driver anxiously awaited his arrival. The fact that the car was being driven by a Romanian national probably had a lot to do with the Romanians finally letting him through. Besides, they knew that they could keep watch on him. And they did.

As the rain spilled down, Frost wasn't sure if he was relieved or not to be finally on his way. He couldn't help but think of how it would be so nice to just relax with a good meal and some wine in a British Airways jet. Besides, what did the Romanians have in mind when they let him through? Perhaps he would never get out? What hit him was how dark the place was. There were houses, apartment blocks, sure, but everywhere he looked there seemed to be little or no lighting inside. And he thought to himself: "It's not even bedtime yet. . . ."

Even the Sheraton Hotel, when he finally arrived, seemed to be a closed establishment — by Canadian standards — since you could barely see a lit room from the outside. Frost wondered if the front desk was still functioning but it was, and he figured he still had time to unpack and have a nice quiet dinner.

When he walked into his room, however, Patrick O'Brien's words came back to haunt him. Was O'Brien ever right about the 40-watt lightbulbs! It was almost with a sense of proud confidence that Frost stopped by the front desk on his way back down to politely demand better lighting.

"No problem, sir," said the hotel employee, "it will be taken care of by the time you get back to your room."

Off went Frost to the dining-room for a well-deserved dinner. Whatever he ordered, he's not sure what he got. He knows there was cabbage, and some form of meat — whether it was pork, chicken or fish he will never know — and beets. He was so hungry and tired, he gulped it down anyway. Despite his daze, though, he still couldn't wait to test the Kent cigarettes theory. So after he finished eating — or swallowing — he left a couple of packs on the table.

"Is everything all right, sir?" asked the waiter.

"Fine," said Frost.

He never got a bill for his meal. Not then, nor on his hotel bill when he left.

"This O'Brien really knows what he's talking about," he thought admiringly. He went up to his room, ready for a well-deserved night's sleep. Lo and behold, his lighting had been altered. In the place of the two 40-watt bulbs were two candles sitting on something that looked like a dresser. That was it.

"Patrick, you sonofabitch!" he hissed though his teeth. He'd been had, and he couldn't help but think of O'Brien, in his NSA office, probably rolling on the floor with laughter.

His final trial was a messy encounter with Romanian toilet paper: something like tiny sheets of waxpaper about half the size of what he was used to in Canada.

Frost went back downstairs to the front desk. By now he had figured out that the employees were probably Romanian secret police anyway.

"Gentlemen," he said, "you win. Could I have my 40-watt lightbulbs back, please?"

And with a straight face the deskman shot back: "Sir, is that not sufficient?"

"No thanks. I'd like the bulbs back."

Somehow, he got lucky. He was given one 40-watt and one priceless 60-watt bulb. Maybe it was the Kent cigarettes. . . .

He had been told by O'Brien to stay on his toes. "Because the secret police will be watching you. Your room will probably be bugged too."

Just about every day, Frost would return from his work at the embassy to find his room had been tampered with in strange ways. There would be cigarette butts in the toilet bowl. He didn't smoke. Furniture, lamps, had been moved around. Drawers had been left open. It was a little eerie. But if others had survived it, he would too. After all, he was there for his country, and setting foot in Romania had made him feel more patriotic than ever.

It was his practice on such trips to order his breakfast from room service. In Romania what he got on his plate was supposed to be toast. But it had come out halfway between warm bread and the real thing. He would have loved coffee, but could only get tea. They served him something they called "butter", but it was more like lard. One morning, out of total frustration, he yelled at the empty walls: "Even orange juice would be better than this shit!"

The very next day, on his room-service tray, was a glass of orange juice. And he remembered another piece of NSA advice: "If you want to test if you're being bugged, just say something out loud."

Then came the "hot water" trick. Frost had made the crucial mistake of lodging an official complaint with the hotel management that he couldn't get hot water in his shower when he needed it.

"Look," he said, "I get in the shower for fifteen seconds and it turns cold. Could you do something about the hot water, please?"

"No problem, sir."

By then he should have known those three words meant the exact opposite. The next day all he had was hot water — which felt like washing yourself in a microwave oven. On another day, it would go from hot to cold, hot to cold, hot to cold.

He finally figured out what the NSA and GCHQ people had meant: the Romanian secret police were trying to harass him to the point where he would lose his cool and say or do something, anything, they could use against him. He also understood what kind of regime he was confronting: one where the authorities had total control over everyone and everything. Totalitarianism was no longer an abstract word. It dawned on him that the stern, sad faces he kept seeing on the streets of the Romanian capital were the visages of tyrannized and terrified people.

The first morning he had been driven to the embassy he had seen an apparently endless line-up of people on a main street. Every day after that, the scene repeated itself, for block after block. Frost finally asked his Romanian chauffeur: "What are they lining up for?"

"They don't know," answered the man.

What he meant was that when they finally reached the end of the line, the people of Bucharest, who were simply looking to buy something to eat, had no idea what would be available. The driver added: "My wife is there. . . . Yesterday, she got cabbage. The day before she got beets. Today, she's hoping to get some eggs."

Total sadness. Even in the hotel bar, Frost couldn't hear anybody laughing, no matter how hard he tried his dry sense of humour on them. And this constant look of fear they all had in their eyes, as if everything they did and said was being watched.

That was closer to truth than fiction. On the night of his tumultuous arrival, Frost remembered more wise words from Patrick O'Brien: "If you go to the dining-room they'll probably sit you at the second table on the left, next to the window. That table is bugged."

But the *maître d'* hadn't done as predicted, and Frost had wondered if O'Brien wasn't engaging in some slight paranoia. One evening, though, he invited a member of the Canadian embassy staff to dine at the Sheraton — not for the food, but for company and conversation. He was led directly to the table O'Brien had pointed out to him. And the place was half-empty. "Patrick, you sonofabitch!" he thought, this time with respect.

All this had the effect that repressive action has on people like Mike Frost. It made him more determined. By this point, he really wanted to defeat Ceausescu. To use a Hollywood cliché: They made one mistake. They got him mad.

Frost had already paid a "courtesy" visit to the ambassador at the Canadian chancellery at 36, Nicolae Torga Street. Peter Roberts had been careful about the words he used and was very discreet. But he had said: "We are very grateful you're here . . . we'd like to have you home for dinner, my wife and I, some night." It made the CSE envoy feel welcomed — finally.

Frost already knew, from External Affairs briefings, that there was a good chance the top floor of the embassy was made-to-measure for a "Pilgrim" operation. In an era of "Participaction" that had infected Canada, the diplomats had decided to turn it into a small gymnasium — that nobody was using. Frost's assessment was quick and painless: "the gym" was the place to do it. There was plenty of space for the copper-mesh "Tempest-proof" tent and the room was air-conditioned and isolated from the rest of the embassy staff. The embassy was also surrounded by a nine-foot-high fence and far from the road where jamming or listening devices could be used by the Romanians. Because of the perimeter provided by the fence, he had more than the 150 feet required to make sure radiations from the electronic gizmos would not be picked up. The antennas could go in the attic, no problem. It was, as in Morocco, an "island site".

There was something troublesome about the roof, though. Whatever it was made of didn't seem like anything the Canadian was accustomed to. It looked like pieces of heavy slate — rock — and moss had grown all over it. He wasn't sure the "Pilgrim" antennas would pierce that armour. And, of course, he already had to deal with the uniquely Romanian power-surge problem. Frost had to find some way to be sure that signals would cut through the roof. The slate would have to be analysed by CSE experts before any decision could be made to place the antennas where they belonged. And yet he couldn't see a better or even another place to put the antennas that were essential to the intercept and, as always, had to be well disguised.

Frost had also learned through the Rabat operation that "shining" antennas through windows was not a good idea — mainly because the lead content of the glass can attenuate radio waves, but also because it is easy for the "other side" to figure out what you're doing and where you're aiming your antennas if they suddenly pick up something different about a given window — like curtains that suddenly appear and are constantly kept closed. Moreover, if you had to break the window, as the CSE agents had done back in Morocco, then you were stuck with using the local economy to get a replacement. In Romania that was simply too risky.

They could have built bogus air pumps on the roof itself to camouflage the listening devices. But in this case the roof wasn't flat enough. No, the attic was by far the best option — if it wasn't for that cursed slate. The last thing he wanted was a repeat of the "Stephanie" mess, where the CSE agents had had to dig their way through a Moscow attic. And he knew how it's always the smallest things that go wrong. He still didn't know if those two passport pictures had made it through his intestine.

At some point in his three-week pre-survey, he figured he had no choice but to risk it. He took the ambassador out for a walk.

"Sir, I need your permission to go back to the chancellery tonight. I've got some work to do that can't be done during the day."

Roberts didn't argue. He gave both Frost and the embassy technician, who had been cleared and briefed for "Pilgrim", the keys and codes to the building. He also wished him luck.

Frost's main concern in concealing this stunt was not so much the Romanian secret police. By then, he knew they would be watching his every move, whatever he did. However, what he had to do would definitely raise the suspicions of other embassy staffers. CSE policy on that was clear: only a selected few, plus the ambassador, could know. Yes, there would certainly be questions raised if they saw him climb out of a top-floor window and onto the roof — for Frost saw no other way to retrieve a piece of the slate but to go out there himself and pry one loose.

It was another gloomy Bucharest autumn night when he and the technician drove back to the embassy for a little acrobatics. Once inside, they went up to the third floor. Frost had earlier picked out a dormer window from which he could climb onto the slate roof, while being relatively shielded from view. Even if the secret police spotted him, he figured it would fit his cover as somebody who was there to improve the satellite communications.

There is one problem with roofs. They never look as steep as they really are until you actually climb out on them. When he looked out the window, Frost realized that what he was about to take a walk on looked more like a moss slide than a rock garden. He was scared — but he was not one to turn and run once he'd made a decision. He needed that slate shingle. As carefully as he could — if one can talk of prudence in such a daredevil act — he crawled out and pulled on a piece. As he grabbed, it came loose and he felt like shouting: "I did it!" Then came a slight variation in the plan. When he finally pried the shingle off, and was holding it in his hands, his feet suddenly went off under him. Mike Frost was going down, from three storeys high.

"Mother of God! Now what?" flashed through his terror-stricken mind as he uselessly tried to hang on and went into a free fall.

All he remembers from the dive is that he landed in some bushes and that his whole body hurt. But he had hung on for dear life to that piece of slate. From the third floor he could hear the Canadian technician screaming hysterically: "Are you all right? Are you all right? . . . Mike!" The horrified witness expected the worst.

Lying in the bushes, checking his limbs to make sure every-thing was still in working order, Frost said to himself: "There you are, Mike, trying to be low profile, and you go and do this!"

The technician came running frantically into the embassy yard, panting and clearly fearing he'd find a dead man.

"I'm all right," lied Frost. "Just bring me back inside the embassy so I can clean myself off."

He was hurting like hell. But when the slate was put in a diplomatic bag to be checked at CSE, he was proud of his job. The engineers at CSE soaked it in water for several days to check if rain — since there seemed to be a lot of that in Romania — would alter its composition and block the antenna signals. It didn't.

Frost felt relieved he had done the job well. The attic was indeed the perfect location. He made a recommendation to himself, however, to use a rope or a net the next time he performed a circus act.

That was not the end of the risks Frost took in Romania. As he looks back on it, the following adventure was a pretty stupid thing to do. But the food, if not the secret police, at the Sheraton had got to him. Having dinner at the ambassador's residence — where nothing seemed to be missing, from lobster to steak — had helped. One day he just asked Peter Roberts if there was any place, anywhere he could eat properly in Ceausescu land.

"Sure," said Roberts, "there's an excellent restaurant on the out-skirts of town . . . and they have a great floor show. It's kind of costly, but just leave cigarettes on the table and there won't be a problem."

Frost had come to believe Kents could truly buy anything in that country. And they did wonders for his government "per diem". He took a cab out to the restaurant that night, on his own. It was a huge place, looking like an arena. And the floor show consisted of "gypsies" dancing in traditional costumes. For perhaps the first time since he'd been in Bucharest, Frost felt good, almost at home. Even the food was edible. The cognac and vodka were flowing, the Kent cigarettes paid for everything, he was having a marvellous time.

By the end of the night, he was on top of the world. To the point where he probably forgot which country he was in and why. Nothing was wrong any more. No harm would come to him. Why had he been so paranoid anyway?

So, as he left the place, feeling like a million dollars, Frost decided he was going to take a walk. Yes, a walk in the Romanian countryside. For once, the weather was right, the night and the stars were bright, and the road was lined with beautiful trees that looked like poplars or sycamores. Somehow, in his groggy mind, he imagined he could just hail a cab when he felt like going back to his hotel. In the woods outside Bucharest.

He walked. And walked. Then it hit him. "What on earth am I doing out here?" He was lost. He had no idea where he was, didn't know his way back to the restaurant and couldn't exactly knock on a door and ask someone in English to, please, phone him a taxi.

As these thoughts were going through his now troubled brain, suddenly, from behind, a black car pulled up with two men in dark suits sitting in the front seat. In incredibly good English they asked him: "Where are you going, sir?"

Frost said: "I'm trying to get back to the Sheraton Hotel in downtown Bucharest. I had dinner at that restaurant and, frankly, I'm lost. I don't know how to get back to my hotel."

"No problem, sir," said the dark-suited man in the passenger seat. "Just jump in the back of the car and we will take you to your hotel."

He was so amazed at this stroke of what he thought was "luck" that he just hopped in. Within seconds, though, fear struck. He thought: "You don't know who these two guys are. You're sitting in the back of a car going God knows where, in the black of night, you're really into shit now! They may never see you again." He didn't know whether to jump out of the car, just sit there, or try to make foolish conversation with these two mysterious English-speaking strangers who had just seemed to appear out of the Romanian night. He decided to do nothing. He would glance out the window once in a while to see if there were any recognizable buildings, while thoughts of Carole, his kids, his life, the operation he might have jeopardized, went racing through his head.

Before he knew it, he was at the Sheraton Hotel.

"Here you are," said one of the strangers. "This is where you live. . . . We would just advise you not to walk in the Romanian countryside at night."

He thanked them very much, thanked God, and went straight up to his room for a stiff drink. Still, the instincts were there: he did have enough wits left about him to look at their licence plate.

The next morning, at the embassy, the ambassador couldn't wait to ask him how he had enjoyed his dinner.

"Well, I'd like to talk to you about that," said Frost. As procedure required, they went for a walk and he related the whole story to Roberts. When he was finished, the ambassador simply asked him to repeat the licence-plate number.

"Bah," said Roberts. "Don't worry. Those are the guys tailing you!"

Funny and normal as the ambassador seemed to think the incident was, Frost couldn't help but reflect on the irony of being there to conduct an espionage operation and being driven back to his hotel by the agents watching him. Did they know what he was up to? Probably not. Despite the passport-picture meal, the roof fall and the idiotic walk in the night, CSE was just about to get Ceausescu.

Before flying back to Canada, Frost took the extra step of going "sightseeing". The embassy driver drove him around the city to what he thought were interesting sites for a tourist. In fact, what Frost was looking for was the American and British operations — to try to figure out what their antennas were aimed at. He also wanted to spot as many microwave towers as possible. He didn't take a camera, although that was tempting. He remembers seeing three fibreglass "huts" on the top of the American embassy, a dead give-away to somebody like Frost. From what he saw, NSA had to have a massive operation there. Conversely, he couldn't see anything at the British embassy. If they had some intercept going on, it was well concealed.

After this last survey, Frost and the ambassador went for another of their walks. Frost told Roberts what his findings were and added: "I will recommend that we mount a 'Pilgrim' operation here for a duration of four to eight weeks. Would you agree with that?"

"No problem at all," Roberts answered. "I will send a memo to my staff saying communications technicians are coming, they will be Defence Department personnel and the top floor will be off-limits to the staff."

Then the ambassador did something unexpected.

"Want to check if we're being tailed?" he asked.

"Uh . . . yeah, sure. Are you tailed?"

"Yeah. I'm always tailed."

"Okay . . ."

"Well, on the count of three," said the ambassador, "let's do a 180° turn and we'll see what's behind us."

Sure enough, about a block behind them was this one lone man in a dark suit following them. Frost knew the tail couldn't have heard the conversation and that he couldn't have mounted any kind of listening device to do so. For one thing, they were facing the wrong way. The experience wasn't wasted on Frost, though. "Pilgrim" should reconsider its cover stories. It was entirely possible that seeing somebody of his theoretically low status walk around with the ambassador would give away his real importance to a trained counter-espionage agent. He would have to discuss that with Bowman and the others when he got back to Canada. Their agents had no choice but sometimes to be visible with the ambassador. If the "other side" did its homework, they would immediately smell a rat. There was a weak link there, and the first suspicious people would be the embassy staffers — who knew protocol.

The flight back was as uneventful as the one in. Back in Ottawa, Frost took a good night's sleep and the next morning, with Frank Bowman, was in Peter Hunt's office. Hunt was always anxious to know about his findings. The decision to hit Bucharest was automatic.

Two crack CSE agents were chosen for the "Hollyhock" mission and sent down to College Park, where the NSA engineers replayed for them the Bucharest "environment". The decision was also made, on Frost's recommendation, not to use the "Tempest-proof" tent, which was an awful, steamy, smelly place to work in. He believed the risk was worth taking because of the distance separating the third floor of the Canadian embassy from the street. And they wouldn't have to ship it in a diplomatic bag.

CSE sent a lot of equipment through External Affairs. It took several months, but there was no problem getting it through. All an X-ray could see was boxes inside the bags. And in any case the cover was that this was to upgrade satellite communications between Canada and the Romanian capital. The "Pilgrim" team was not surprised to discover that each and every diplomatic bag sent to Romania concealing electronic equipment had indeed been X-rayed (they had taken the precaution of putting film negatives in each of them to see how the Romanians operated).

For the first time since the beginning of "Pilgrim", CSE sent their own encoding equipment, so the operators had the opportunity to send something back to Ottawa quickly if they spotted an emergency. They had found out through experience that, although they could pick up a lot of information from foreign countries, it would often be of no intelligence value once they processed it. By the time it had got back to Ottawa, it was already printed in the newspapers. "Pilgrim" would have little reason for even existing if it couldn't beat the press. That would give the politicians the perfect reason to kill the whole project. But these were still, technically speaking, trial runs. Up until Bucharest every intercept had been sent back on tape, or paper copy, in diplomatic bags. The operation had to become more time-sensitive. Sending encoding equipment was the first step in what would be a longer road to reach that goal.

They couldn't do it the way NSA and GCHQ agents did. The Americans and the British would report directly back to their agencies from the intercept site, through their satellite links. CSE had to develop a Canadian method, mainly because they had to go through External Affairs to protect their cover and keep other countries believing that Canada was not part of the espionage game. There could be no obvious link to CSE. They also had neither the expertise nor the equipment — especially the satellites — to do otherwise.

The decision was also made to leave the equipment on 24 hours a day, seven days a week. With the power-surge problems in Romania, it didn't much matter anyway. Nobody over there knew what was going on with the electricity. The only important thing was to turn it on gradually, two or three pieces a day. Then just let it run. This was the first "24-7" operation. The equipment wasn't actually manned around the clock, but it was left on automatic pilot, functioning just as effectively.

Technically speaking, the Bucharest caper was perfect. Although the power surges played hell with the technology, Frost was prepared for that: every single piece of machinery had been duplicated, while some new parts were regularly sent through diplomatic bags from Ottawa. The only piece of equipment left unaffected by the electrical problems was "Oratory" — which made the CSE people even more amazed at the high performance level of this unique piece of American engineering. As long as that functioned, the rest of the problems could be more easily solved. And CSE had also taken the precaution of sending two "Oratorys". They had been shipped slightly differently: taken entirely apart, and with the more sensitive circuit boards hand-carried through Romanian customs. "Oratory" was too advanced for the Americans to let the communists have even a peek at it.

From an intelligence point of view, Romania was a huge score for CSE. From Day One, the CSE agents were shocked not only at the amount of traffic they intercepted but at the volume of solid inside information they were getting from Ceausescu's people. They intercepted an endless stream of government communications, by car phone especially, between high-level members of the Romanian government. That told them, years before Ceausescu's fall, what Mike Frost couldn't pry out of the Romanian people themselves in casual conversations: Nicolae Ceausescu was not popular with his people, but the ministers of his own cabinet hated him even more. They seemed to disagree with his policies almost unanimously, but felt they could do nothing about it. In retrospect, this offers a unique perspective on how his dramatic fall came about. The conversations collected were extremely sensitive, top secret even, and made it clear that Ceausescu's own entourage was bent on getting the bastard, his wife, his son and his brother Lt.-General Nicolae Andruta Ceausescu. While awaiting trial, after the fall of the regime, Andruta was quoted as saying he was "happier in prison" than under the regime of his brother.

Were these unique intercepts by "Pilgrim" people eventually used by CSE, NSA or GCHQ to provoke the dramatic fall of the regime — as blackmail material, for instance? Frost doesn't know. He only knows that the information was available to do exactly that.

It was also the first time CSE decided not to share everything with their partners from NSA. They were getting good at their job and conscious that their first duty was to the Canadian government — no matter how much they had been pushed into it by the Americans. A lot of the intelligence gathered had to do with the nuclear reactor sales between Canada and Romania. CSE was really beginning to give its political leaders their money's worth. And they were still only at the survey level. That would be crucial come budget time.

In fact, money was becoming a problem for "Pilgrim". Success in Bucharest made it clear that CSE lacked the processing capabilities in translation, analysis and decoding to mount a useful permanent operation. They had to get more people and a budget to buy new equipment. It made no sense that the traffic intercepted in Romania took a year to process in its entirety. If "Pilgrim" was to work, they needed a budget. They were already a far cry from the two desks they had started out with twelve years before.

Bucharest also provided another lesson. Like the Americans and the British, they would need not only collectors and technicians on site but analysts, linguists and decoders. The odds were CSE could never justify to its own government sending that many people. Also the cover stories would probably fall apart, since this was not Canada's way abroad. Frost and Bowman were eventually to solve that problem by training their best collectors as analysts, decoders and translators. In other words, don't send more bodies — just take one body and improve on the original version.

CSE was so happy with the "Hollyhock" operation, they didn't want to shut it down. But Allan Gotlieb had given authorization only to *survey* eight sites. The "Pilgrim" people were tempted to tell Gotlieb this had to be a "long survey", but decided it was better to stick to the original script and not play with dynamite. They also didn't have the liberty of simply purchasing even more equipment to do the rest of their surveys. Frost, Bowman and Hunt had to move on. They got their operators back safely. The operators' main complaint was about the Sheraton Hotel and the food. But the warm congratulations they got on their return helped their digestion. The equipment was shipped out over a six-month period without a glitch. Success felt mighty good. The "Pilgrim" team knew they were real players in the game now, and they were there to stay.

EIGHT

"Daisy" — Target: Sikh Terrorism

Mike Frost and Frank Bowman kept their poker faces, but they were as stunned as a gambler who has just got an improbable inside straight.

"We were wondering if you could go into India and take a look at the Sikh problem."

The comment came from an External Affairs "Pilgrim" operative. It was unusual in more ways than one. First, External people didn't usually make demands of the CSE agents. They had a unique talent for putting obstacles in their way, and still secretly wished they had been tasked with embassy collection themselves. But they would seldom suggest anything specific. They mostly provided logistical support and information on the targeted countries. Second, to be honest, Frost and Bowman weren't too sure what the "Sikh problem" was, and certainly had no clue that it was a priority for the Canadian government. So far, most suggestions for intercept had come either from their end or from NSA. All of a sudden, out of left field, in the spring of 1982, here was an External pin-striper casually asking if they could mount a special operation.

"The 'Sikh problem'?" asked Frost.

"Well, we have had a request from Immigration. . . . The minister is concerned about Sikh activity in the Toronto area. They're giving him a hard time."

The then Minister of Immigration was none other than Lloyd Axworthy, who was to be handed the powerful Human Resources ministry in 1993 by Prime Minister Jean Chrétien. Axworthy had been in the news in the summer of 1981 for having to expel from Canada about a thousand Indian immigrants, mostly Sikhs, who had applied for refugee status. "We suspect from the information we have from India that the claims are not genuine and will be rejected," an External Affairs spokesman had commented at the time.

Still, the "Sikhs" or anything associated with them weren't even on any of the "key-word" lists CSE had used up to that point. The "Cold War" was still on, and the CSE agents were looking at targets behind the Iron Curtain, at Cuba — although reluctantly — and there was always that standing order from NSA to "get their ass into Beijing". Never mind the Middle East and the OPEC cartel. And these guys wanted them to chase down Sikhs!

Bowman and Frost kept their composure in front of their External counterparts, but once they got out of the meeting it was, as usual, the outspoken Mike who blasted out: "What the fuck is that all about?"

"Dunno," said Bowman in his always even tone. "But if they want us to do it, why not?"

In fact the External "suggestion", which Frost is sure came directly from Immigration, who were working in conjunction with CSIS and the RCMP on such matters, was a major compliment paid to the "Pilgrim" team. The Bucharest and Rabat capers had paid off to the point where high-level people in government were now starting to "depend" on CSE, rather than treat them like a bunch of over-eager amateurish spy buffs who liked to trek around the world with electronic gizmos. Overnight, "Pilgrim" was needed. And, in the end, Frost and Bowman didn't really care why. After all, their job was "technically" just to "collect" the information. They didn't have to be given a reason for it.

Still, they did rely on one of their most trusted mentors before launching into the operation. They went down to NSA to meet with Patrick O'Brien.

"Patrick," said Bowman, "we've been asked to do embassy collection on the Sikhs. . . . What do you think?"

Neither he nor Frost expected the enthusiastic response.

"That's great!" O'Brien said. "We're a little concerned about them ourselves. . . . There's a region in California that's got the greatest concentration of Sikhs in North America. Almost all of them are all right. But they do have terrorist activities going on in the Punjab. . . . We suspect some of their people down here are helping them out."

The NSA man's endorsement was good enough for the "Pilgrim" team to take this on not only seriously but with a vengeance. Something was definitely going down that they had never been made aware of. While Sikh terrorism still hadn't exactly shaken the world, spy agencies like NSA were already concerned about the potential for trouble in a new "theatre of operations". Canada, and the rest of the planet, was going to find out just how serious it was in a devastating manner just three years later. There was one other important factor in CSE's decision to go full tilt on this one. Even though there was an interest in the Sikh terrorist movement within the intelligence community, the information they had on it was very sparse. There were too many other angles to cover elsewhere in the world. If the Canadians wanted to take up the task of tracking them down, it would be a bonus for everybody.

For one of the rare times, O'Brien actually confirmed NSA had "a site" in New Delhi, India's capital city. "Perhaps you guys should do your intercept from somewhere else within the country," he suggested.

"Sorry," said Bowman, "but our policy is to do collection only from our embassy. We strictly refuse to use another location and the only place we can operate from in India is New Delhi."

"Fine," conceded O'Brien. "Chances are you'll get stuff we're not getting anyway . . . you know how these things go."

At this point, not even a pre-survey had been done on Canada's New Delhi embassy. It wasn't even on the list of targets being considered as possible priorities. "Pilgrim" was still not up to the "eight sites" Allan Gotlieb had allowed to be surveyed. But they were getting there, after Caracas, Abidjan, Rabat and Bucharest — and also Brasilia and San José (Costa Rica) where Frank Bowman had pre-surveyed successfully and recommended surveys be held. (Both operations took place, but Frost was never involved in them.)

Bowman decided to pre-survey the New Delhi site in mid-summer 1982. He came back with a highly positive report. The High Commissioner was fully on side. There was room in the embassy and its roof also had a huge sun-shield that was in fact another roof, open on the sides, about six to eight feet higher. Not only would it be easy to put antennas up there but Bowman believed CSE could go as far as installing a permanent hut to hide the equipment. Also, like Bucharest and Rabat, New Delhi was an "island site" surrounded by a fence.

India was considered a "soft target", and the timing for the operation couldn't have been better. The Indian government itself had let it be known at about the same time that they would be conducting surveillance on Sikh activities outside their own country. In other words, they were openly admitting to espionage for their own security reasons. Chances were, even if they found out what the Canadians were up to, the Indian authorities would not only look the other way but secretly applaud it.

CSE's survey of New Delhi began in March 1983. Two veteran operators, Alan Foley and Tom Murray, were sent in with the usual cover of being there for National Defence to upgrade satellite communications, after a visit to the College Park "live room" with a list of signals to intercept. The equipment, which like everything electronic kept being upgraded, was sent ahead in the usual manner, through red diplomatic bags.

Already, even before the survey started, the "Pilgrim" team was considering New Delhi as its first "permanent site" — which meant they would go on as long as they didn't get caught or jammed or there was no more intelligence requirement. India's capital had gone from nowhere to the top of the pack in less than a year, which gives an idea of how strong the political and bureaucratic will was behind this project. It would become even stronger.

When their eight-week survey was completed, the CSE operators came back and had produced superior results. Not only was it a technological success but the amount of Sikh communications intercepted was staggering.

"We knew what they were up to in the Punjab, we knew what they were up to around the world," remembers Frost. "It was so good, the Immigration Department kept saying: 'We want more, we want more!'"

At that point it became evident that New Delhi was CSE's best crack at getting approval for a permanent site, which is what they had been looking for all along. Because it was fine and dandy to do surveys, but if it all petered out after the "eight sites" there was always that fear that the government would simply give up on the project. However, when they recommended making the Indian capital the first real "Pilgrim" operation, nobody at CSE expected the response to come as quickly as it did. After all, they had been accustomed to exactly the opposite when it came to dealing with the rest of the bureaucracy. Within days, word came down from Allan Gotlieb to go ahead.

"You're not going to believe this," Bowman told Frost.

"What? They turned us down?"

"No. They've actually approved New Delhi as a permanent site."

"You're kidding! They couldn't do it that fast."

"That's not all. We don't even have a budget for this thing. And they just told us to buy what we had to buy and do what we had to do."

"Hey, let's go ahead and do it before they change their minds."

Frost doesn't know whether the decision was made unilaterally by the Under-Secretary of State for External Affairs, or by his minister, Allan MacEachen, or Prime Minister Pierre Trudeau himself. The best guess is that everybody was at least made aware of it and that Gotlieb knew he'd have no problem convincing any "higher-up" of the necessity for Canada's first long-term espionage operation abroad in peacetime. The "Pilgrim" people also came to wonder if the Indian government itself was not in on it. After all, they wanted the

Sikh terrorists watched and caught at any cost. That too might explain why the green light was given while their own foot was still on the brake.

Frost and Bowman felt like they had made it to the big leagues. A little more than a decade after the token "Stephanie" effort, they had turned a whole government around to their way of thinking and doing things. And they had accomplished it with basically the same people in power, both politically and bureaucratically — with the nine-month exception of the short-lived Joe Clark government that had produced more stalling than anything else — as in the early beginnings of "Pilgrim".

With this moral victory, though, came a host of problems that, once again, forced Frost and Bowman to look at the minutest details of the operation. This was not just a "hit and run" any more, so there were problems they had never had to face before. The agents they were going to send overseas were to be there, with their families, for periods of up to three years.

One special problem, which when you talk about espionage sounds rather bizarre, was the union. The CSE employees who would become operators for "Pilgrim" were members of the Public Service Alliance of Canada (PSAC). This was as crazily Canadian as problems can get. NSA and GCHQ didn't have to face these problems since their personnel were not unionized. But Frost and Bowman couldn't just pretend the union and its collective agreement didn't exist. They agonized over it. What were they to do? Could they trust a union leader to keep a secret of such magnitude, one they themselves were trying to hide from other employees of "The Farm". In the end, Frost asked Bowman a question he already knew the answer to: "Do we have a choice?"

"Nope. We're stuck with this one. We just have to cover our ass."

"The last thing we want is to get them upset if something happens to one of their members. . . . They could start saying things they're not supposed to say," added Frost.

So the two "Pilgrim" men called in the union representative to brief him on the situation. It seemed, at the time, like trying to untie the Gordian Knot, because there were a lot of small, bothersome rules to be broken here, and the CSE spies were terrified that the union would react in a way that would blow their whole operation out of the water. They were basically, among other things, asking the PSAC rep to agree to break the collective agreement for the sake of espionage.

First and foremost was the danger of having the whole embassy-collection caper become the subject of gossip within the whole federal bureaucracy. It would then be only a matter of time before it got to the outside and the media. But, strangely enough, the most troublesome aspects of the deal with the union concerned the salaries and perks that "Pilgrim" operators were entitled to.

When they walked out of the meeting with the PSAC man, Frost and Bowman looked at each other with some disbelief. The meeting had been incredibly docile. He had agreed to their terms — with a few conditions that they didn't see as a problem. The agreement was that the operators to be sent to New Delhi were to sign a form giving up some perks and protection they were entitled to. The union rep was asked to sign a form of indoctrination himself. But neither Frost nor Bowman ever enquired as to whether he reported any of this to his superiors at the PSAC headquarters. They had already decided the only way to go was to cross their fingers and hope the rep would understand the gravity of the situation.

The second major problem was the wives. Frost and Bowman had been going through their marriages faking their real lives. They had reluctantly "trained" their spouses not to ask too many questions, and lived on the hope that their spouses would understand. This was different. Much as they liked to believe that New Delhi was relatively safe for their agents, everybody in the espionage world knows that you're only a step away from disaster wherever you are operating. Frost and Bowman had consulted both NSA and GCHQ people on this touchy issue. The Americans' policy was never to tell the wives or the families — supposedly to protect them. As the theory went, if they were ever caught by "the enemy" the family members could truthfully say they didn't know anything. Over the following years, however, Frost came to believe that this was a bogus excuse. In a totalitarian country, such ignorance would not protect a wife or children from harassment, torture or even assassination. CSE went rather with the British approach: You tell the wives as much as you have to.

After running a security clearance on the spouses of the prospective New Delhi operators, the wives were brought into CSE, sat down in a classroom and told what their husbands were about to embark on and what they had been up to for the last few years. The women sat there with their mouths open in astonishment throughout this incredible lecture about the men they had been sleeping with. They were told of the conditions they would have to accept. To Frost's great relief, none of them raised any major objection; indeed they gave their full support to the operation. One did say, quite understandably given the sacrifices she had already been asked to make over the years, "My husband and I worked hard to get where we are. . . . It's hard for me to accept that for two or three years we will have to live under conditions that are lower than what we deserve." But Frost said, "Well, you either accept it, or he doesn't go." She did. The spouses of "Pilgrim" operators were then asked, as usual, to sign forms of indoctrination.

Once again, when it came to solving these problems, the biggest stumbling block for CSE was the mandarins at External Affairs. The recurring issue was directly related to the "cover" used by "Pilgrim" operators. If they were "officially" sent over to India as communications centre operators, they were considered support staff. All of them, however, had, according to the bureaucratic hierarchy, the rank of officers, which meant they were entitled to bigger cars, better housing and even better schooling for their children while on diplomatic assignment. It didn't matter how hard the CSE guys tried to explain that they would risk detection if they pretended to be support staff but were still seen profiting from superior perks, the

External people simply wouldn't accept it. Why? Because they were afraid that, should it be known that these "officers" were accepting "inferior" conditions, those perks would be taken away from their own high-ranking diplomats. It sounds petty and, yes, stupid. But that's the way it is in Ottawa. Frost and Bowman simply dug in their heels with the now classic line: "If you don't accept this, we don't go!" But they couldn't believe the headaches External caused them over this. Eventually they won out. But Frost is convinced this remains an on-going problem between "Pilgrim" and External.

One of the trickiest problems to resolve — which directly involved the union — was the pay scale. The CSE operators had salaries way above the norm for communications centre support staff. Normally their paycheques would have been issued directly through the New Delhi embassy personnel office. But that would have been a dead give-away to the rest of the embassy staffers that these new guys, who had arrived with tons of electronic gear and were placing weird antennas on the roof, were not what they pretended to be. The CSE union rep insisted that the agents be given the choice: either they would have the balance of their salaries deposited in an account in Canada or it would be directly wired to a bank in New Delhi since they were entitled to it.

Frost didn't like the second idea at all, but felt he had little choice. After all, this was their money, and they were asking enough sacrifices of them as it was without depriving them of what long years of hard work — and tougher work ahead — entitled them to. What this meant, though, was that CSE had to create a special clerk position, in Ottawa, to handle exclusively the cases of their "Pilgrim" people in India. To his relief, none of the operators asked for money to be deposited in India. They were of course not too subtly swayed in that decision by the "gold-at-the-end-of-the-rainbow" trick — when they came back to Canada, they'd have nicely padded bank accounts waiting for them. And this was still in the days of high interest rates for saving accounts. They were also compensated for the difference in "per diem" rates that foreign diplomats are allowed. Still, it bothers Mike Frost even today that Canadians have no idea of the sacrifices "Pilgrim" agents and their families made. As he says: "I don't even think CSE ever thanked them for it!"

He remembers getting a message back from a New Delhi operator that particularly touched him. The man was complaining that his children couldn't even use the embassy pool at the same hours high-level diplomats' kids were allowed to swim in it. "Talk about apartheid!" says Frost. "Maybe they've changed it now, but that's the way it was when 'Daisy' went under way. And that's the way we had to play it."

So although the "Pilgrim" team now had the technical and logistical problems of carrying out an operation down pat, they had to face problems that immensely complicated their task due to what they believed to be ridiculous eccentricities on the part of protocol-conscious External Affairs people. They ended up with a "Daisy sub-committee" just to solve these problems. "The list just went on and on," remembers Frost. "We'd solve ten and there would be ten more. . . . But we solved all of them to the best of our ability."

The "Pilgrim" team wanted to be fair to the people who were going to carry the load. One of the things that had been stressed to CSE by both NSA and GCHQ is that the last thing you wanted was to have "unhappy operators" on site.

"You've got to have happy operators, you've got to have happy wives. If you don't, you're going to have trouble," NSA's O'Brien told them. "If they're not happy, they're going to crack. Because they're not living a double life for two or three weeks. They're over there for two or three years."

Frost and Bowman held what can only be qualified as a "rigged" competition to hire their operators for the New Delhi permanent posting. They already knew who they wanted. All they had to do was make the job definition so tight that only that one person could fit it. This is done all the time within the bureaucracy, hypocritical as it may seem. But when it came to picking "spies", there could be no room for mistakes. One of the operators for New Delhi actually had to be yanked out of the Navy, where he had achieved an honourable, even comfortable career. He just happened, though, to be one of the men who had been sent on the first embassy-collection mission of "Stephanie", back in the early seventies. Frost and Bowman had decided on hiring three operators for "Daisy": two on site, and a back-up in Canada should one have to be replaced. The second man chosen came from within CSE — although, like many of them, he was ex-military himself. So did the third.

Next, Frost and Bowman had to deal with the double-triple life syndrome. How could they take CSE employees out of "The Farm" and have them simply disappear for a couple of years? CSE had to come to an agreement with External Affairs that these people would be, in bureaucratic terms, "seconded" to their department for an undetermined period of time. In other words, as far as CSE employees were concerned, these operators were on an exchange program with External Affairs. At External, however, they weren't seconded from CSE, but from National Defence. Although Frost has no doubt that CSE employees knew something was up, the "Pilgrim" people had no choice but to refuse to confirm it. That was the best they could do. After all, they didn't have a College Park. And when the operators who were "seconded" to External finally came back to Canada after their turn of duty, they spent a few months at External to "rehabilitate" themselves for going back to work at the espionage shop — and perhaps in the meantime have their New Delhi suntans fade a little. "Can you imagine the strain we put on these people?" asks Frost. "To remember all those lies, for so long . . ."

The agents chosen for the Indian caper were not the same ones who had been doing the surveys for "Pilgrim" up to that point. New agents were required because, by then, embassy collection had taken on a life of its own within CSE. They had to keep on looking for other sites and they wanted to keep their most experienced people available in Ottawa ready to go on new surveys. The new agents had to be trained almost from zero for the mission, a job that was taken on by Frost himself. They were not asked, however, to learn the language. Because there were so many Sikh dialects, it was virtually impossible to send people over, within reasonable time, and expect them to add that aspect of the job to their competence. Besides, English is more often than not the working language in India. The New Delhi team went down to the College Park "live room" for intensive training that lasted at least three weeks. They also spent another week at NSA headquarters in Fort Meade being thoroughly briefed on Sikh terrorist activities.

One moral problem that bothers Frost is whether they should have told the other embassy staffers in New Delhi about the presence of intercept operators in the chancellery. Was it right to keep them in the dark when you were targeting a terrorist operation which could react in the most unpredictable way? NSA didn't tell its people, neither did GCHQ. But when you are an American or British diplomat, you rather suspect that somewhere in the embassy there is somebody doing espionage work. Canadians, by and large, have no clue this is going on when they are assigned to seemingly innocuous foreign postings.

"Morally, I think it's wrong," says Frost now. "But then again you're in the espionage business and that's not all that ethical anyway."

Frost struggled with the concept, but to this day feels he would have made the same decision. The importance of the mission was greater than the possibility of terrible consequences — which, in the case of New Delhi, was relatively small.

Then came the matter of the electronic equipment to be used. CSE needed a whole new set of toys — including the antenna "hut" they planned to put on top of their embassy in India, the prototype of which still sits on the roof of the main CSE building in Ottawa today. Back in 1983 the "hut", about the size of a garden shed, cost approximately $15,000. Among other things, it had to be air-conditioned and have its own power supply because there were rotors inside to move the antennas around. The "hut" also contained pre-amplifiers and multicouplers, and in the heat of India, this kind of equipment would have burnt out in no time. All in all, though, compared to the administrative problems, the technical issues were relatively easy.

As had become the practice, the pieces of equipment were shipped to External Affairs piece by piece. Strangely enough, though, the "Pilgrim" operators opted once again for the "Caracas" solution, and sent all two tons of it in crated diplomatic containers, in one shipment. Which makes one wonder again whether the Indian government wasn't in total agreement with the operation in the first place. Two External Affairs couriers were sent along with the electronic gear on its long trek halfway across the globe. The "Pilgrim" team thought it wasn't fair for just one courier to be responsible for keeping the "luggage" in his line of sight through the whole lengthy ordeal. Frost also figured it fit perfectly with "the cover" to do it openly. As he told Bowman: "Hey, we've told the Indian government we are upgrading our communications. If we don't ship anything over there, they'll wonder what's going on." But they did hide what the equipment actually was, because then the intent would have been crystal-clear. "Oratory", the magic box provided freely by NSA, was taken apart and some of its crucial circuits were hand-carried into India by CSE agents with diplomatic passports.

The most amazing aspect of the whole operation was that, despite all the problems involved, it took them less than a year from the time they got the go-ahead from Allan Gotlieb in the spring of 1983 until they were up and running in early 1984. That included the hiring and training of new agents, the purchase of new equipment, solving the hassles with External Affairs, and another minor occurrence: a change from a Liberal to a Tory government in the fall of 1984.

"From the time we got the green light from Gotlieb, we didn't give a shit who was running the government," says Frost with a laugh. "We were up and running. And there was a lot of pressure from External. They were telling us: 'Just get this thing up and going.' "

"Pilgrim" was provided once again with an endless list of "key-words" to insert into "Oratory". Two of the most important targets were a "Dr. Jagjit S. Chauhan" and Kuldip Singh Samra. The latter was considered one of the leading Sikh activists in Canada, while calls from the doctor could be intercepted in New Delhi. Frost remembers these two in particular because "Oratory" subsequently spit out their names constantly, together with all their communications. In Samra's case, they were picking up his communications from Toronto to India — which, as he looks back on it now, makes Frost wonder if they weren't in fact spying on a Canadian citizen. "It's where you get it from that counts, I suppose," he says now. In fact, though, in the spy game it's "what" you get that counts. When you're under the spell of the game, you come to a point where ethics do not seem to matter as much as results.

Dr. Chauhan moved around the world a lot. But CSE was tracking his movements and feeding his communications back to External Affairs and Immigration in Canada, not to mention that NSA could pick up on Sikh communications just about anywhere in the world with the push of a few "Oratory" buttons.

CSE was aware of many Sikh plans, thanks to the "Daisy" operation. Once you know a suspected terrorist's movements, you can at least keep an eye on him or her, if not stop their action altogether. "Pilgrim" made it possible for Canadian officials to know, for instance, of planned public demonstrations in advance. It also provided Canadian Immigration ahead of time with lists of Sikhs who desperately wanted to be accepted into Canada at a time when Canada was being flooded with requests from the Indian religious minority group, most of them claiming to be political refugees. "Pilgrim" could not necessarily provide the RCMP or any other agency with specific plans for, say, terrorist attacks. Such strategies are not normally communicated over the phone. But, as Frost points out, movements of terrorists can be just as significant. And through the intercept they knew all about, for instance, airline reservations.

None of this prevented the greatest Sikh terrorist coup of the decade on June 23, 1985, when an Air India Boeing 747 with 329 people on board, flying from Toronto to London, exploded over the North Atlantic. A radical Sikh group claimed responsibility for the bomb that brought down the jet, leaving no survivors. A second bomb, this one planted on another Air India aircraft in Vancouver, went off in Tokyo, after the plane had landed, killing two baggage handlers; nearly 400 people, 374 passengers and sixteen crew members, escaped death by a matter of 30 minutes.

What is interesting about the investigation that followed, however, is that within hours the Canadian RCMP had a list of suspects for the killing. Their names were all "key-words" for the "Daisy" operation. Stories were then mysteriously leaked to the media about the fact that Sikh terrorists were being trained in the United States. That information came from NSA and the CIA, through CSE. Although, to this day, no conviction has been obtained against the suspected perpetrators of the bombing over the Atlantic, the RCMP still keeps the file open should they ever surface on their territory.

Two years later, in 1987, six Sikhs living in Canada were accused of planning a terrorist attack and brought to trial. The case was thrown out of court because the RCMP's evidence was based mainly on wiretapped evidence, which the Court decided violated the Canadian Charter of Rights and Freedoms. The six men were living in Hamilton, Ontario. The Crown did try to reopen the case two years later, but again it was rejected for the same reasons. Most of the wiretaps that initiated the case probably came not from the RCMP, but from CSE and NSA. As previously stated, in the espionage game the last thing you identify is the source of the information. "Daisy" had been fully operational for four years and, to the best of Frost's knowledge, still is today.

In 1985, the "Pilgrim" team got another "special" request from External Affairs for the New Delhi team. At one of their meetings an External representative told Frost: "The Minister would like you to look into some economic intelligence. . . . We have a Canadian company bidding on a pipeline to be built in India for $2.5 billion, and we'd like to get as much information on what's going on as possible." The Secretary of State for External Affairs was then Joe Clark.

Frost also remembers "Daisy" intercepting a speech to be given to the United Nations by a foreign official, days before it happened. "I learned about it over lunch, when somebody high up in CSE told me: 'By the way, you guys are really paying your way. We really got something hot. We just got copy of a speech to be delivered at the UN that nobody knows about.' " Information was relayed back to Ottawa and directly to the Canadian representative at the UN, former Ontario NDP leader Stephen Lewis. His rebuttal of the speech was well prepared, although he was never told where the speech had suddenly appeared from.

"Daisy" became so productive that the CSE processing lab Frost had been tasked to upgrade was working on material emanating from India for up to four hours a day. In those four hours the lab processed 64 hours' worth of intercept, covering more than 200 channels.

There were minor glitches. Kids got sick and the wife of one operator came home. One of the agents also had to be called back when he got into financial difficulties. Instead of sending him the extra money he had stashed in the bank of Ottawa — from his real salary — CSE opted to bring him back to Canada.

"Frank Bowman and I knew he was entitled to his money," remembers Frost, "but we were terrified that it would blow his cover to send a huge cheque over to New Delhi. . . . We decided to terminate his posting. I like to think he was relieved by the decision, because it solved his financial problems."

This story illustrates how, in the spy's world, normal everyday problems can become enormous since, when they happen, you have to put a whole espionage machine in motion to solve them. And these people are posted abroad for two to three years while living a cover that condemns them and their families to a lower status of living.

"They were happy to do their jobs," says Frost. "But they were under constant stress. . . . In the embassy you have to act like a member of the support staff. At the same time, you have to earn your salary as a CSE operator. That is your primary purpose. And you have to remember at all times what your role is. If you're supposed to be an expert in communications, you have to be able to discuss communications with your peers from other embassies should you bump into them at a cocktail party. At the same time, you have to produce intercept. Basically you have to remember who you lied to and what the lie was. You have to be suspicious of everybody. Making friends is very difficult, because you don't trust anybody. You ask yourself: 'Why are they friendly? Why are they asking me these questions?' It's not easy. You can never let your guard down."

That's why Frost believes one of their best decisions was to let the "Pilgrim" wives know what their husbands were really up to. He admits he was a little jealous of that himself, because he had never had the luxury of sharing anything he did with his own wife, Carole.

"There were times when I really wanted to share my successes with her and say normal things a husband might say, like: 'Boy, did I do a good job today!' Sometimes I wanted to share my failures, my disappointments. I could never do that. . . . Yeah, at times I was jealous that these operators could go home, lie in bed at night with the ceiling fan on —in case of electronic bugs — and discuss their day at the office."

A standard part of External Affairs training when being posted abroad is teaching diplomats how to converse in their home. Basically you have to make sure the television, a fan or an air conditioner is running and "talk softly". "Pilgrim" operators were not asked to avoid discussing matters of some sensitivity with their wives because Frost and Bowman believed that to be unreasonable and unrealistic. But they were briefed on the necessary precautions for both spies and diplomats, such as playing tapes that sound like a cocktail party is being held. "They are just God-awful tapes to listen to," says Frost. "It's just hours and hours of background noise. People talking gibberish, toilets flushing, glasses clinking. . . . They're the most aggravating things you've ever heard."

"Daisy" did encounter one rather unusual problem: the High Commissioner. Not that the man was against the mission. Quite the opposite. A classic spy buff, he was so enthusiastic about it that he kept going up to the "Pilgrim" operators' room to ask them: "What have you got, boys?" Indeed this became so much of a pain that CSE had to intervene from Ottawa to let him know that it wasn't a smart thing to do if he didn't want to blow the agents' cover. High

Commissioners and ambassadors don't visit communications centres every day. But they are also not used to or amused at being told what they can and cannot do within their chancellery — which gives an idea of the clout CSE, and especially the "Pilgrim" team, had acquired since the days of "Stephanie".

After "Daisy" and by mid-1987 CSE got approval to continue with the survey program with no limit on the number of sites to be targeted. They also got the green light to set up more permanent sites, with no finite number on how many they could establish. If there was a need for it and it was possible within normal security requirements, then CSE was to go ahead.

"Pilgrim" still seemed to have a limitless budget and had now been handed a gift like Jack and his Beanstalk. The operation would clearly require more and more human and financial resources. After all the heartaches, the headaches, the mistakes, the money spent, the intelligence gathered, "Pilgrim" had become by the mid-eighties the most successful electronics espionage operation ever mounted by Canada.

Following the success of New Delhi, the "Pilgrim" people also started to feel something that would drastically change their attitude: they were not just Uncle Sam's "gofers" any more. They could hold their own with the best at NSA and GCHQ. CSE started "telling" NSA what it intended to do, instead of "asking" the Americans about it. "If they liked it, good; if they didn't, too bad," says Frost.

The Americans were still pressuring the Canadians to "get into Beijing," but Beijing was not necessarily that high on CSE's list of priorities at the time, and it was still considered very risky. By now the "Pilgrim" people felt they didn't have to pay so much attention to the Americans' demands. They were also withholding information that they believed to be more profitable for Canada. For instance, they shared none of the "economic" intercept — they knew full well the Americans didn't share theirs.

Frost came to believe that "Pilgrim" had achieved the perfect blend between the GCHQ type of operation and NSA's bulldozer approach. Had "Pilgrim" failed, CSE would have been cut off from foreign intelligence and left with its "official" role as a rather inoffensive intercept network, concerned solely with counter-espionage at home and listening posts on the edge of the ocean.

As we shall see, the "surveys" are going on to this day. But for now, let us take a step back from "Pilgrim" and look at the spy game as it has developed in the modern world. Mike Frost had a unique insight into what the Americans in particular were up to.

NINE
"DAMN YANKEES!"

MIKE FROST HAD ALWAYS been intrigued by what he considered to be Patrick O'Brien's "trophy rack". It was in his office at College Park, the secret NSA "special collections" installation located in the northeastern area of Washington, D.C. The display was behind O'Brien's desk, and, although Frost had often wondered about the strange things he saw there, he had never dared ask questions about it.

By this time, however, he had been down to College Park so many times that he and O'Brien had practically become friends — as much as "spies" can trust each other, which is not your run-of-the-mill friendship.

There were two things that had really caught Frost's eye. The first one was a stuffed pigeon. Why would an NSA special agent have the "mummy" of such a common bird enshrined there as if it was King Tut? This wasn't exactly a bald eagle or a pterodactyl skeleton, just a pigeon. On one of Frost's visits to College Park for a brainstorming session, when there was a lull in the conversation between Frost and O'Brien, the CSE man couldn't hold back his curiosity.

"Patrick, what's that stuffed pigeon doing on your trophy rack?"

"Oh, there's a long story behind that pigeon."

"I'd like to hear it."

He half expected a cold stare meaning "Don't you know better than to ask such questions?" But instead O'Brien smiled broadly, and went on to tell a tale that shows just how far the Americans are willing to go when they want to succeed in an intercept operation.

"Well," O'Brien began, "there was a 'target' we couldn't get to, we couldn't get close enough to bug."

Then the NSA man clammed up.

"Oh, come on, Patrick, you can't just whet my appetite like that and not tell me what it's all about!"

Again O'Brien smiled.

"It was the Soviet embassy [in Washington, D.C.]," he said. "It's an island site, surrounded by a fence with a perimeter too big for us to intercept. There was one specific office, on the top floor, we desperately wanted to get into. And, for all the great equipment we had, there seemed to be no way to do it."

But NSA doesn't give up that easily.

"We scouted it. We took pictures. Looked at it over and over again. . . . One day, while we were looking at the photographs of the office window, one of our guys noticed that there were these pigeons sitting on the window ledge. We looked at more pictures, and there were the pigeons again. We figured out they were nesting beneath the eaves, on the roof. So, one of our engineers came up with a brilliant solution: 'Why don't we bug a pigeon?'

"At first we just laughed at it. But the more we thought about it, the more we figured maybe this wasn't such a bad idea after all."

NSA agents finally set out to attract the pigeons with corn seed and draw them into a trap. They caught three they believed were regular visitors to the Soviet embassy's window ledge. A small "bug" was inserted in the pigeons' chests, while they were under anesthesia, with a tiny antenna running down one of the wings. Once they regained their composure, the birds (who must have felt like people who claim to have been abducted by UFOs) were set free near the Soviet embassy, in the hope they would return to their preferred spot on the window ledge.

"It was summertime," went on O'Brien. "And the window was left open most of the time. We got incredibly good results from it. We were actually able to hear."

"Oh, come on, Patrick! You're putting me on!"

"No. I'm dead serious. And after the operation was all over, we caught the pigeons to remove the bugs and I decided to have one stuffed and kept as a memento."

O'Brien invited his sceptical Canadian friend to look over the pigeon. Once it was stuffed, they had put the bug back into the chest and the little antenna down the wing to give full meaning to the "trophy" from what NSA considered one of its most imaginative coups. Frost could see the electronic device with its small circuit boards, and the antenna. Initially he was sure O'Brien had been pulling his leg, but now he came to the conclusion, in the face of the stuffed pigeon with its electronic trappings, that it had to be absolutely true. Why else would one of NSA's top spies keep it there?

Frost was taken aback by how the Americans would, in the end, go to any lengths to get what they wanted. Their strategy was always the same: if you look long enough, you'll find a hole in the enemy's net that you can slip through. You take photographs and more photographs. You send your satellites — your outer space "birds" — over the site to take more pictures. Then you sit around a table and study them until somebody comes up with a plan. In this case, a brilliant solution. If it means bugging a bird, you can find a way to do it.

In the course of the same conversation, Frost thought he might as well try for an explanation of the second curious item — a "twig" that O'Brien seemed to hold just as dear as his bird.

"What's that stick?" asked Frost, pointing to the three-foot-long branch.

"That's not a stick," answered O'Brien proudly. "That's a piece of fibreglass."

He picked it up and handed it over. It was a fibreglass replica of an ordinary, broken tree branch, about half an inch in diameter. Inside were, once again, wires and circuit boards.

"What was that used for?" asked a bemused Frost.

"Well, we couldn't get near the Chinese embassy in D.C. They too had a big fence around their building. We tried to put a bug in there, but we couldn't. . . ."

"Well, what the hell did you use this branch for?"

"Same procedure. . . . We took pictures. We watched and watched and watched, day after day. Finally we noticed that the ambassador, who obviously thought his office was bugged, would come out and sit on the garden bench every morning and have long conversations with his top staff or any high-ranking visitors. We noticed a tree very close to the bench. So our first instinct was to bug the tree, but it was too risky. We couldn't get near enough. Again, one of our engineers came up with the idea of making a fake tree branch, putting a bug in it, and air-dropping it near the ambassador's preferred bench."

"You mean you actually planted the branch in their gardens?" asked an incredulous Frost.

"Well, we waited for a very high windstorm. . . . After the storm was over, lo and behold, there was 'our' branch sitting next to the bench."

O'Brien never explained how NSA managed to get it there. The most logical explanation would have been an air-drop from something that looked like a traffic helicopter. Then again, maybe a commando just went over the wall in the middle of the night.

"Not only did we put it there," said O'Brien, "but it worked. It sat there for a while, until a gardener finally raked it up and threw it away. . . . Then we just dropped another one and another one every time the need arose."

The "twig" in O'Brien's office was in fact retrieved from the garbage of the Chinese embassy.

"All I can tell you, Mike, is that it worked. We got some good stuff from the Chinese ambassador."

The branch was so well designed that there was no way anybody could mistake it for a bug. If you were to break it, it would crack. You would have to take it all apart to find the wiring — and you would have to be very suspicious in the first place.

O'Brien had other interesting items on his prized shelves. There were crystal objects, mugs, Royal Doulton porcelain roses, dried floral arrangements, even a small totem pole. All of these objects had "bugs" inside them and had been used as plants in the offices of people from whom NSA wanted information, or as gifts to foreign dignitaries. One of them seemed quite out of the ordinary, even a little out of taste, to Frost. It was an icon of the Virgin Mary holding Baby Jesus in her arms, painted on a one-inch-thick piece of wood. The painting, however, was hollow, and contained a listening device. How deceitful could "the game" get when you would use the Virgin Mary to get an espionage target? How many of these "gifts" were handed out by the Americans to unsuspecting foreign visitors? "Just typical Yankee shit," thought Frost. "The American way. Not only do they do it, but then they boast about it!"

CSE, for all its secretiveness, was not in that line of business. As for the British, Frost figures that if they ever went to such extravagant lengths to get what they needed, none of their top agents would be so assertive as to have a trophy shelf glorifying their exploits.

Frost took due note, however. In Bucharest he was given a painting by the Canadian ambassador. It was a gift from an official in the Ceausescu government, but Peter Roberts didn't particularly like it and Frost did. "Here, it's yours," said the ambassador. When he came back to Canada, Frost mentioned the painting to CSE Security chief Victor Szakowski, who had it checked for "bugs" right away. There were none.

All of the gadgets on O'Brien's trophy rack came directly from College Park. They didn't mass-produce them. Each one was designed for a specific target — and bugs do have a shelf-life. Like satellites, they eventually stop functioning. The smaller they are, the more you can conceal or disguise them within the object of choice, the better. If there is a way to plant a minuscule microphone in such a fashion that, even if the object breaks apart, it probably won't be discovered, then the Americans will find a way to do it. And as Frost points out, "The pigeon and the branch happened some ten years ago. . . . So you can just imagine what they're up to today." NSA and CIA agents would sit down with their engineers and try to figure out the best methods. If someone liked icons, they would make an icon; if they liked porcelain, they would get a Doulton rose; if they were Chinese, they'd get a branch — not an olive one.

After a conversation like this, Frost and O'Brien would often go to the NSA employees' favourite restaurant, Henkel's, for lunch, about a ten-minute drive away. A lot of classified information was exchanged over Henkel's famous shaved ham or turkey sandwiches and draught beer. This sort of openness was a bit out of the ordinary, but in fact, as Frost describes it, all the people you could see around the restaurant had chains around their necks: they had slipped their NSA ID cards into their shirt pockets. "I never saw anyone but NSA people in there."

For all their flashy and cocky behaviour, Frost did envy the Americans their seemingly endless resources of money and equipment, and even more so their enthusiasm at accomplishing something good for their country.

"You'll never find a CSE employee coming to work in the morning at 5:00 a.m. and staying till 9:00 p.m. and sometimes sleeping in his office overnight," he admits. "At NSA, they were totally dedicated. You'd find this sort of thing constantly. Especially at College Park. Even the highest levels of authority would put in countless hours of work. I had a lot of admiration for that."

Frost remembers a husband and wife who worked as a "team" of NSA agents. Sometimes they would be sent together to the same foreign country, sometimes they would be split up. But they were totally immersed in their jobs.

College Park, in particular, was a fascinating place. First of all because, if you weren't actually brought there, you would never guess it was the centre of the highest technological espionage operation in the U.S. — perhaps the world. It wasn't at all like NSA headquarters, which blazons its name on a highway street sign. College Park actually looks like a strip mall when you first reach it. It is located in a relatively sparsely populated area near Washington, D.C., not too far from Laurel, Maryland, where Frost always overnighted when going down to NSA.

The first time Mike Frost was driven to the secret NSA-CIA installation, he went in through a restaurant that was part of the "strip mall". "We walked through the restaurant and then went through a door at the back," he remembers. The second time he entered after going through a dry-cleaning store. In other words, not only did the American espionage agencies have their covert operations installations hidden there, but they also owned, operated and manned all the little dinky businesses in the fake shopping-centre.

You couldn't get to College Park, especially as a visitor from a foreign country, if they didn't know exactly who you were. You had to be driven there by an NSA or a CIA agent. What really struck Frost was how well the installations were camouflaged. To a trained eye like his, there was absolutely nothing like antennas or ray domes that could give it away. "I'm sure the people living in the area didn't know what was going on in their own backyard."

Once there, you couldn't help but be overwhelmed by the feeling that here lay the real power in the intelligence-gathering universe. The person who ran College Park had enormous clout. One of the telephones on his desk was a direct link to the White House. It was, in Frost's mind, at the very least at Chief-of-Staff level if not direct to the President himself. Patrick O'Brien, although he had to go back and forth between the NSA headquarters in Fort Meade and his real base of operations, was in a certain way more powerful than the official director of NSA himself, if only because when he wanted something done, he didn't have to go through the bureaucratic motions other people at NSA had to deal with. The same went for O'Brien's successor from the CIA, Charles Clark. The directorship of College Park alternates every four years between the two spy agencies. Just the fact that NSA and the CIA accept an alternating directorship and the sharing of equipment and human resources within one facility gives an idea of how truly powerful and effective the "strip mall" is. In fact it may just be what makes American counter-espionage and covert operations work, because without it the two giants would probably be constantly involved in self-destructive turf warfare.

Frost's best description of College Park is "organized bedlam". It is not the usual sanatorium-clean atmosphere you would expect to find in a top-secret installation. Wires everywhere, jerry-rigged gizmos everywhere, computers all over the place, some people buzzing around in three-piece suits and others in jeans and T-shirts. You could tell this was where things actually got done — there was little protocol and a lot of action.

It is a difficult place for Frost to describe, because its entrails are a maze of corridors and rooms — many of which had signs on them prohibiting access. "It's just a fantastic place. It's a series of little compartments, all working independently on various projects, all of them covert operations." None of the signs on the doors gave away the purpose of the locked room or what was going on inside. It was also impossible to figure out how many people actually work there. Unlike NSA headquarters, it doesn't have a gigantic parking lot to give it away. And the faces Frost saw there, with the exception of the top-level officials, seemed to change a lot from one visit to the next. Several people travel back and forth between there and NSA's or the CIA's main installations. Many are agents, working out in the field, on the move all the time.

All Frost could feel was the true power of College Park. "Patrick O'Brien would tell me: 'Mike, if you need this piece of equipment, or to send your people to a given location, or if you have any special request, we can do it.' " As we have seen, he could tell CSE with utter self-confidence that he would "move the birds" (satellites) over any site where CSE wanted to mount an operation. And he would deliver. College Park kept providing CSE with a seemingly endless stream of "Oratorys" whenever they requested them. If Frost had gone to NSA headquarters, he would have had to deal with a bureaucracy, the "we'll-send-it-up-the-line" syndrome. "College Park, and the people who ran it, were the exact opposite. Patrick would make the decision and that was the end of that." You would walk out of his office feeling that anything could be done if you just asked for it. After all, this is where the "tasking" of all American spy satellites comes from. The physical control of the orbiting surveillance satellites is controlled from another location — probably Houston. But the choice of targets comes directly from College Park.

The two American espionage agencies each have their respective satellites, known by the code names of Talent (CIA) and Keyhole (NSA). They are technically "parked" over the Equator, but can be quickly moved in any direction when needed. These satellites are not small round objects, but what amounts to space stations half the size of a football field, equipped with highly sensitive listening devices and super-cameras capable of reading the licence plate off a car from outer space. They do not have a very long lifespan — half a year or so — and new ones have to be launched on a regular basis. But Frost swears they are every bit as precise and efficient as the reports that have filtered out over the years. For NSA to give Canada practically free access to their use shows how insistent the Americans were about getting CSE into the international espionage game. If only because every time you move a space platform of that size, you burn fuel and reduce its lifespan.

College Park had its own travel department, a seemingly bottomless budget, and (something that really impressed Frost) a lot of foreign currency available to their people right there in the building's special bank. If they needed francs, marks or rubles, they had enough stashed away to provide their agents with cash on the spot — plus, of course, American currency.

College Park is also, as mentioned before, the ultimate testing and engineering centre for any espionage equipment. "Oratory" came out of College Park. In the mid-eighties, they were experimenting with a "digital recognition" system, something that sounds as if it comes right out of a *Star Trek* episode. Instead of using the magnetic strip on an ID card to allow access to a restricted area, College Park engineers had developed a machine that could actually read fingerprints. The person demanding access would put his or her hand on what looked like an x-ray plate, where the fingerprints would be digitally scanned. If they didn't match, the door would remain shut. The device was still in the experimental stage, but was already working, to Frost's total amazement.

"They were very proud of that," he says. "And this was ten years ago. They've probably progressed to voice recognition by now. They must be literally talking to their computers." The Americans have had the capability to identify people by the way they speak, for intercept purposes, since the late seventies. And they have been steadily improving on that "voice recognition" system. Given that ability, and given that they were successful in the mid-eighties in developing a technology that would open doors with a fingerprint scan, the chances are that College Park can now do the same thing with the sound of a security-cleared person's voice. Sounds like *Star Trek*? It is. But the future is here now.

Finally there was, of course, the "live room", so crucial for the preparation of "Pilgrim" agents. As far as Frost knows, there was only one "live room" at College Park. The room was about 30 feet square, but was full of various types of equipment NSA and CIA agents used around the world. It was the basic training ground for covert intercept operators. If NSA had a certain kind of equipment being used in Moscow or a different gadget in Bucharest, it was also there.

Another feature of College Park is that it is located within the "no-fly zone" that prevents any aircraft from flying over the White House.

I was asking Patrick one day if they couldn't be spied on from an airplane or a helicopter. He said: 'Don't worry about it. They can't fly over this place; we're too close to the White House.' " That, in Frost's mind, is one of the main reasons for the location of the ultra-secret site.

One day when Frost was down at College Park just before the operation in New Delhi, O'Brien had yet another surprise in store for him.

Out of the blue, the NSA man said: "How would you like to see how the CIA do their training?"

Frost had just shared with O'Brien that he had recently been made responsible for the training of the operators who would be sent on the three-year mission.

"The CIA does some training of operators in various fields," O'Brien continued. "Would you like to visit their school and see if you can learn something?"

This was like tempting a horse with a sugar cube. But Frost tried to restrain his enthusiasm.

"Well, if you think it might be beneficial."

"I don't know," shot back O'Brien. "In fact, I don't even know if I can get you in: they have a very strict policy of allowing no foreigners into the CIA school at all. But if I can, would you like to go?"

"Sure, I'd love to."

About two or three weeks later Frost heard from Peter Vaughn, who had replaced Stew Woolner as the Canadian liaison man with NSA — the CANSLO.

"Patrick says he can get you into the CIA school in Virginia. He says maybe I should visit it too before you do. . . . Do you have any objections?"

"Go right ahead."

Vaughn made a courtesy visit to the secret training school, the first Canadian ever to be allowed in there. But his trip was limited to a talk and a cursory tour with the commanding officer.

Frost's own visit came in the spring of 1983. He flew down to Washington once again and stayed in Laurel, Maryland, as he always did, because it is second nature for a spy to ensure that his movements don't appear to be unusual. You never know who's watching. The next day he was picked up at his hotel by a CIA staff car. As they drove across the Potomac and into Virginia, the driver knew where he was going, but Frost had no clue and wasn't told of his exact destination. He remembers travelling through the rolling hills of Virginia, but he didn't pay too much attention to which road they were taking — a built-in "you can't say what you don't know" reflex.

The school was about a two-hour drive from Laurel. It was in the middle of next-to-nowhere, in the countryside, surrounded by lots of farmland and grandiose mansions of Southern plantation style, spaced far apart. It was obviously a "money-area". These were not struggling farmers' fields. There were a lot of stone walls and high fences, and when they pulled up to a particular wrought-iron gate, they could have been at somebody's private home for all Frost knew.

The chauffeur muttered something into the voice box at the entrance, and the gates swung open automatically. They went along a narrow, winding driveway up a hill. The leaves had just started to come out, but the trees were still relatively bare. When Frost looked up he could see that just about every tree had a video camera on it. He could see nothing else, however, until they reached the top of the hill. The house that stood there looked like any other stately mansion he'd seen in the countryside. It was quite big by itself, but didn't look like a major training school for American spies. As he walked up to the house, however, on the backside of the hill he saw a collection of spacious "barns", outbuildings, and one huge cinder-block building surrounded by a barbed-wire fence. There were a few cars parked here and there, a few people walking around, and a dog. "I couldn't believe this was a CIA base. It didn't look like a farm — but it also didn't look like it couldn't be."

The odds are pretty good that this was part of the CIA's Camp Peary training facility, located near Williamsburg. Frost was here to see whether any of the agency's methods could be used to train his own operators for "Daisy", and also to see their "charm school". This was the classroom where American agents were trained in how to behave at, for instance, embassy cocktail parties: how to get people to say things they don't want to say without them realizing they are actually providing intelligence. "They teach you how to go to dinner parties and hold your fork and your knife correctly so you look like you belong in the diplomatic corps . . . all that sort of thing."

Frost was ushered into the main house, then into the office of the chief of operations. After coffee with the man, he was handed over to the chief training operator for CIA "special operations". Limited as his tour was, Frost was actually the first Canadian to see the facilities, since Peter Vaughn had only met with the director and then left. There were buildings he was not taken to. Only those that might relate to the "Daisy" operation were open to him: the training facility; the processing lab; the area where they manufacture huts to hide antennas from view; and the "charm school" — where his "tour director" commented: "This is where we turn a sow's ear into a purse."

Frost remembers seeing a classroom with a lot of books. Most CIA agents are college graduates whose education has been paid for by the agency. But if you have to turn a person straight out of university into, say, a gardener, it requires some basic training. CSE, by the way, also recruits extensively starting at the high-school level. It was not uncommon to have a rookie hired at "The Farm" who would then be sent to university for two or three years to learn a special trade. If a student showed interest, a preliminary security check was done and they were brought into CSE headquarters and given just enough to whet their appetite. They were told, for instance, that should they decide to attend university, it would be a good idea to take such and such a course. In the recruiting field, the Americans, as in everything else, were even more systematic and certainly didn't mind throwing money at it, much as they do for sports scholarships. Also, whereas CSE was largely unknown in Canada, it was a lot easier to get "patriotic" young Americans to study hard in the hope of working for the prestigious CIA or NSA. CSE recruiters could never allude to their covert role, especially on the international scene, but any young American student knew that being drafted by one of the two agencies meant an "exciting" life as a spy.

Frost found the Virginia establishment just as action-oriented as College Park, but also a lot more "James Bondish". After all, this was the CIA, the stuff of countless spy novels. It fitted the part. At College Park people walked around in jeans and running shoes. The people Frost saw at the CIA training ground looked like a movie cast: white shirts with the sleeves rolled up; dark glasses, sometimes up on their forehead, sometimes covering their eyes.

He walked into a lecture on radiowave propagation in the training facility, then was taken to the processing lab where the CIA agent told him: "This is where we teach our people the proper way to mount bugs, either in a room or on a person."

From the moment he arrived, Frost had the uneasy feeling he wasn't all that welcome. He didn't feel at home as he did at College Park.

"They were polite, but they weren't as open. They treated me with caution. If I asked questions, their answers were never detailed — much like a politician's. I felt this guy had been told what to do and he would do it, but he wasn't too happy about having me snooping around. Let's face it, I was the first Canadian to be given a detailed tour of the facilities where CIA agents are trained, the first to be taken right inside to see how they operate. I got the feeling they didn't like it too much, if only because they weren't used to it and it went against their policy. . . . After a while, I just stopped asking questions. I sensed it was making him uncomfortable and he was tightening up. So I just let him talk."

Frost did, however, manage to go into quite some detail with the training instructor about "cover" stories, the problem he believes "Pilgrim" hasn't really solved to this day.

"We have only this one 'cover' story," said Frost. "And it's causing us headaches. We don't have a plan B."

"Oh, we don't work on just one 'cover'," said the CIA man who opened up more on this subject that he did on others. "We use anything to fit the location. From officer to chauffeur, to clerk, to gardener. . . . In some cases we train the ambassador himself."

Frost tried to hide his astonishment at finding out the CIA actually had American ambassadors trained as spies. That would never fly with External Affairs. When Frost tried to pursue the issue, the American probably sensed Frost was a little too eager to learn or realized he had just let one slip. He merely said: "Well, you know, every cocktail party is a source for intelligence, and ambassadors always have their ears open."

If "special collection" was the stuff of College Park, Frost saw this CIA school as the centre of the "special ops" team. The agents being trained there appeared to be used for hit-and-run missions.

The CIA agent did ask Frost one question that took him aback: "Are you guys going to get into land-line tapping?"

"Well, land-line tapping is not easy," said Frost.

"If you want to know anything about it, just let us know."

But when Frost asked for more details, he once again got an evasive answer.

"You guys do it?" he asked.

"You guys want to get into it?" was the reply.

This time Frost didn't answer. But he was puzzled by the question, if only because he was fully aware of how difficult land-line tapping is to accomplish. He and Bowman had already come to the conclusion, after many discussions, that land-line tapping was not worth the risk or the effort. Land lines, whether underground or above ground, are difficult to tap because you physically have to get to the cable itself, whereas microwave towers can be intercepted from a distance. Once you reach the cable, it has to be sliced open, and another cable spliced into it running to a remote listening post — much like attaching a new pipe into an existing water distributing system. In electronic terms the "resistance" of the line increases, just as your water pressure will decrease should somebody turn on a connecting tap while you're taking a shower. That increase in resistance can be picked up both at the receiving and the transmitting end of the line. That's assuming you don't get caught cutting into the cable in the first place. So CSE had decided to tap into land lines only when they switched to microwave or satellite communications.

Frost's visit to the CIA's processing lab was particularly productive. He surveyed a lot of equipment there that he believed could be useful to CSE, and learned that the Americans dealt in large part with a company by the name of Microtel. CSE was later on to buy a lot of electronic gear from Microtel.

At Frost's request, he returned to the CIA training school about a month or so later, with one of his most trusted operators, Alan Foley. He wanted to re-examine the lab facilities to see how they wired things up and how they trained their operators to do it. He was also grooming Foley to become the training instructor for "Pilgrim" so that he could unload part of his mounting responsibilities. He spent half a day there. He then asked if he could leave the door open to come back again. "Sure, by all means," the chief of the base told him. But when he asked to be admitted one more time, in late 1983, the request was denied. "I was told that the CIA had said that having foreigners into their training facility was probably not the best thing to do." No reason was ever given. Did the CIA feel they had already given away too much information? Perhaps. More likely, though, they were worried that, should such visits become routine, the Canadians would eventually learn things the CIA didn't want anybody, anywhere in the world, to know. As Frost says: "They do have a 'no-foreign dissemination' policy for their intelligence and they stick to it."

Frost wasn't all that surprised by the CIA's decision. Both times he had visited the Virginia site, he had felt the authorities were showing him round because they were ordered to, not because they wanted to. They treated him as a stranger, rather than a member of the family.

He saw from his brief visits, however, how the CIA would take a person and train him or her in a very specialized field. This was drastically different from CSE, which, for reasons of human and financial resources, had to go entirely the other way and broaden the training of its agents. "Where the CIA would take and train fifteen people to do fifteen specific jobs, at CSE we had to take one to handle those fifteen jobs."

He also got valuable information on equipment, especially a Microtel spectrum analyser that was state-of-the-art in those days. He recalls the price as close to U.S. $80,000. CSE bought three of them.

Just before he left "The Farm", CSE contracted out for even more of them, because they intended to make great use of the device. A spectrum analyser looks a lot like a heartbeat monitor in a hospital. What it gives you, though, is a visual presentation of all radio activity within a tuned frequency spectrum.

Finally, he also saw some strange-looking antennas in Virginia, antennas with which he, as an expert, was totally unfamiliar. It would be years before he spotted something just as bizarre, but in a more familiar setting. The Americans were spying on Canada. Frost knew this from his CSE days. But what he was to discover, four years after retiring, was that they appear to have found new ways to do it.

The American embassy in the Canadian capital, Ottawa, is located on a prime piece of real estate. It occupies a solemn turn-of-the-century building at 100 Wellington Street on the corner of Metcalfe Street. It is right across from the Parliament Buildings, and less than 500 yards away, with an unobstructed view, from the Prime Minister's main office in the Langevin building. Strangely enough, the United States Information Agency has its offices a couple of doors down the street in, of all places, the third floor of the National Press Building that houses Canada's National Press Club and the bureaux of media outlets from across Canada, including a large contingent of the CBC.

If Canada was a "hostile" nation, you probably couldn't ask for a better location to put an embassy-collection site. Although, in a "hostile" country, the Americans would be under close surveillance if they ever got their chancellery so near to the source of power in the first place — an unlikely occurrence in, say, communist or former communist countries.

Patrick O'Brien always said to the CSE agents: "The rule of thumb in embassy collection is to get your antennas as high as you can and have your intercept room as close to your antennas as possible." Another thing the NSA man told his Canadian allies was: "When you're really stuck, you use heat pumps and air vents to hide your antennas and rotors."

He taught this to Mike Frost at College Park. CSE took it into account for the "Daisy" operation, but in the event didn't use it, though they may be using that solution in another foreign capital today. For the Americans, however, it was part of standard procedure for embassy collection. Frost was actually shown, at College Park, the type of air vents and heat pumps that NSA would use.

Once Frost first became aware that embassy collection even existed, it didn't take him and his colleagues long to figure out, after a few NSA-College Park briefings, that the Americans were intercepting Canadian government communications too. "It would be naive, first of all, once you know that they spy on other friendly nations like Mexico, to think they don't do it to Canada," says Frost, who is firmly convinced NSA will collect information covertly anywhere in the world if they can do so. "Their philosophy is that you never know what, where or when you're going to get something that's crucial to you. . . . In fact, that philosophy is the *raison d'être* of embassy collection and intercept in general. The Americans don't care who they commit espionage against, on the principle that they may get something that's useful to their country. They routinely collect foreign intelligence against everybody." On the economic front, a British Channel Four documentary about the huge U.S. installation at Menwith Hill in Yorkshire, England, recently claimed that intercept of interest to U.S. business is forwarded to the Office of Intelligence Liaison in the U.S. Department of Commerce.

That the U.S. is spying on Canada is more than just guesswork or wild speculation on Frost's part. In his CSE days he and his "Pilgrim" colleagues would often refer to the white plastic hut that was sitting on the roof of the Americans' Wellington Street embassy. None of them had any doubt that this hut housed antennas for intercept purposes, since NSA had taught them how to build such a "shed". Indeed it looked much like the one Canada used in the New Delhi operation.

If CSE knew, why didn't they try to "jam" the Americans? The answer lies in the way "the game" is played. Even if you are convinced that an allied nation — even one with whom you are sharing intelligence and espionage expertise — is spying on you, the standard practice is simply to look the other way. As Frost puts it: "We simply couldn't take any 'aggressive' action against an allied country — especially the Americans." Deliberate and effective "jamming", which basically means rendering the intercept devices totally useless by purposely flooding them with airwaves, is considered practically an act of war in the espionage world. On the receiving end it means that you have not only been uncovered but are being attacked. "By jamming them, we would be telling them that we knew. . . . Jamming is reserved for the 'bad guys'. They could easily have made our lives difficult, especially in the early days of 'Pilgrim' when we depended so much on their expertise and equipment."

But what was the solution? Surely CSE couldn't sit idly by while knowing that high-level Canadian government communications could be intercepted by the Americans? In fact, what they were doing was "jamming" themselves — in other words, scrambling any sensitive communication they thought could be picked up by anybody listening in. This is actually part of CSE's "overt" role: to protect government communications from foreign interference.

A good example of this are the meetings of cabinet ministers held on an almost weekly basis in Parliament's Centre Block. Since there is French-English interpretation provided in the room where the ministers sit, and everything is recorded anyway for the record by "indoctrinated" government communications technicians from the Privy Council, the Prime Minister and members of his or her cabinet speak into microphones. It is not impossible, with today's more advanced electronic equipment, to pick that up. That is why every time a cabinet meeting is held, CSE operators set up scrambling equipment and also listening devices in an adjoining room that can tell them if anybody is trying to listen in. This approach is easy to explain to an allied country. Canada can claim it is really worried about eavesdropping by the Soviets or the Chinese or — as overly paranoid government Security people often suspect — the media. (In fact the media, despite all their electronic gizmos, do not have the capability or the expertise to do this.)

Just about any amateur spy buff can intercept cellular phone discussions if they know or luck into the frequency being used and make enough trips to Radio Shack to buy the basic gear. American spies are, of course, far more advanced in their methods and capabilities. If they could not get inside Parliament's cabinet room itself, an ideal set of targets would naturally be the stream of ministerial limousines arriving and leaving the building, since they are all equipped with car phones. Brian Mulroney, as Prime Minister, was especially wary of such intercept. Not necessarily from the Americans, but from anybody. He would staunchly refuse to carry on a long or serious conversation on his car phone, and would always ask the other caller to tell him where he or she was so that he could phone back from a "secure" telephone minutes later. He had obviously been thoroughly briefed on the intercept world, and believed everything he had been told. There is a strong possibility that this belief of his stemmed from what CSE itself was providing him in foreign, and even domestic, intelligence, gathered from the airwaves.

For all Canadians know, the Americans may know more about what is going on inside the Canadian government, at the highest levels of power, than Canadians do. All it takes is for one minister to say something like "Bah! They can't be intercepting me now," and they can fluke into something that is important to them, and possibly ruinous to Canada.

Mike Frost is firmly convinced that in 1994, from their Wellington Street embassy, the Americans were conducting an all-out intercept operation. "If we were to mount some kind of operation against that site, on the fifth floor of the embassy, I'm sure we would pick up some radiation from electronic equipment." For this book, he mounted his own "survey" of the roof of the building in May 1994. What he found up on the roof was not the white plastic hut any more, but, as we shall see, some strange-looking "air vents" and "heat pumps" and an even more out-of-place grey box.

He carried out his "survey" by posing as a colleague of mine. (I am a familiar name and figure on Parliament Hill.) Frost showed up at the Victoria Building, which houses mainly senators' offices just next to the American chancellery, with his "photographer" — in fact his son Danny. Somehow, perhaps because of his CSE training, Frost managed to convince the Senate guards at the entrance that he needed access to the roof of the Victoria to take pictures of Parliament Hill. Without even having to give out his name, Frost managed to get his son onto the roof with a zoom-equipped camera.

What Frost saw once the negatives were developed led him to a firm conclusion: "It became obvious to me that the Americans were doing to us what they said we should do to others; what they had taught *us* to do!"

The photographs clearly showed the suspicious-looking "air vents" and "heat pumps", one vent covered in what looks like fibreglass. Another photograph showed the mysterious grey box that, in his view, didn't belong on any roof.

"If I had been doing a survey, say overseas, and had seen these pictures, there would be no doubt in my mind that there was an intercept site there," says Frost. "That is what I would have written in my report."

Danny Frost's photograph reproduced in the photo section on page 8 shows the "air vent" at the front west corner of the roof, right up against a small cement ledge, facing north, toward the Parliament Buildings. About 30 feet behind it, again right up against the ledge, this time on the south side, is an even bigger "air vent". As far as Frost knows, they were not there during his CSE days. Both are located over the top of windows that have bars on them and curtains that are constantly kept closed. It's important to remember O'Brien's advice: put your antennas as close to your intercept room as possible, and as high as possible. On the east side of the building, on the same floor, the windows facing the Langevin Block, where the Canadian Prime Minister's office is located, are also barred and the curtains closed.

The first question a CSE-trained operator like Frost would ask — knowing full well the answer — is why would they put bars on fifth-floor windows? The Americans would probably claim they do it for protection against terrorist attacks. But some windows on the fifth floor and other windows on lower floors don't have such protection. Frost's guess is rather that they would not want firemen, for instance, bursting into a room full of electronic gear should a fire occur in the building. The Americans would rather have it burn. Closing curtains, as previously explained, is standard procedure to conceal an embassy-collection site. That in itself, in any foreign country, would raise suspicions.

The two "devices" — for lack of a better word — on the embassy roof are very different and don't appear to be linked, which in itself is a strange way to set up a heating or cooling system.

"First of all, why would you put boxes like these up against the edge of the roof facing out if they were air vents? Wouldn't you put them somewhere else, out of sight, in the middle somewhere?" The "air vent" at the front of the roof is open on three of its four sides, and entirely enclosed at the back.

"This front 'air vent' has a strange-looking something inside it," says Frost. "I'm not sure what it is, but it appears to be a horn antenna and it seems to be facing toward the Parliament Buildings. The wiring of it is all wrong for AC electricity. It is left exposed to the elements and is all twisted up. No professional electrician would do a job like that for AC. So it has to be hiding electronics of some sort. Then why is it closed on one side and open on the other three? It doesn't make sense. . . . And what is that little shelf of metal sticking out from the east side of it, like a small roof? It has to be protecting something, because there would be no reason for it in a heating or cooling system. It's the kind of thing NSA would use to hide a VHF or UHF antenna with a very small rotor in it. . . . That's about all you could get inside it. It's very similar to the stuff they showed me at College Park." Radiowaves of that type will go through concrete very easily, so neither the cement vent nor the wall of the roof would weaken the signal.

The "air vent" at the backside of the roof is bigger and consists of not one, but two, totally enclosed boxes, joined together by what looks like an air duct. There is also exposed wiring around it.

"These things are obviously jerry-rigged," affirms Frost. "My speculation is that this 'air vent' contains antennas for ultra-high and super-high frequencies. To transport those frequencies from the antenna to the receiver you have to use a 'waveguide', which looks like a hollow tube, the size of a plumbing pipe.

"There's no doubt in my mind that the Americans have taken the hut down and put these things up there because they now have smaller, more sophisticated equipment that can be more easily concealed. It can't be seen from the road as the white shed could. And if I had to report on it, I would write that the target of their intercept is the Canadian government's communications."

Frost is even more adamant about his findings because in just about every other window of the American embassy sits a run-of-the-mill air conditioner. Which means there is no central air-cooling system in that building. "If those are legitimate air vents on the roof, they are used to help cool the two rooms immediately below. And, if they are, that's because there is electronic equipment in there." But he really doesn't believe in that possibility. The two side-by-side "heat pumps" on the front left corner of the roof may, in fact, be used to cool the room directly below; however, they may also contain intercept antennas.

As for the mysterious grey box his son caught on another photograph, it is, once again, up against the wall of a lower roof, a sort of fake balcony, on the same side as the "air vents". Frost couldn't figure out what it was, but felt sure it didn't belong there. It looks like a small, three-foot-square tin box, with no apparent purpose. Frost's instincts told him it had everything to do with embassy collection, and was probably something new the people at College Park had come up with.

CSE would never discuss this sort of thing, even jokingly, with their American counterparts. And they would certainly never raise a protest against it. Because, in the espionage world, there comes a time when "the game" is wide open and supposed allies find themselves mounting intercept coups against each other. It is a strange concept to the ordinary citizen, but one that is routinely accepted within the spying community. It then becomes a question of who can do it best.

CSE wasn't too bad at it. In fact, they came to be pretty good, even against the mighty Yanks. In the early eighties, they scored a big one.

TEN
FRIEND OR FOE?

IN A UNIVERSE WHERE YOUR ultimate goal is to commit a perfect crime, there are times when the line between right and wrong, the definition of who is an ally and who is the enemy, becomes very blurry. Such is the espionage game. After all, most spies, no matter what country they originate from and what they dedicate their lives to, would say they spy out of patriotic duty. That seems to overcome any "moral" or "ethical" consideration whenever a decision is taken to proceed with an operation that, were it put up for public scrutiny and debate, would certainly generate controversy, if not outrage.

General Norman Schwarzkopf, when asked about some questionable tactics used by his soldiers to defeat the Iraqis in "Desert Storm", said that "war is not a pretty thing". In the same way, espionage is not a very clean business. But, as in battle, spies know that by and large everybody plays by the same rules — or rather a rulebook that is subject to amendment but only if there is no way the other party can contest, or preferably ever find out about, how you cheated. For cheating is certainly the nature of the beast. And that makes it easy to begin to believe that anything you can do to perform your "duty" is perfectly acceptable.

CSE never had any doubt that, co-operative as they were (for their own reasons), the Americans were also conducting intercept operations in Ottawa against the government CSE was set up to protect. At the same time, they never did anything to discourage them other than the usual scrambling attempts.

But, as in any game, in the espionage or the sporting world, there always seems to come "payback time". You can call it luck. But every athlete will tell you that luck comes only after a lot of hard work. You just have to run with the ball when it appears to land magically in your hands, and keep your wits about you as you plan what you're going to do with it.

In 1981, CSE got "lucky" and smart. And the "target" was the United States government.

It seemed to fall out of the sky, like a meteorite. CSE and the Canadian government were simply fortunate that it hit the communications security operator like a bolt of lightning. What he intercepted, by fluke or flair, on that fateful day, would come to rank right at the top of the CSE book of records and contribute greatly to CSE's credibility, perceived efficiency and proven necessity in the eyes of its political and bureaucratic masters.

The ComSec people, as they are known at CSE and in other government departments, were mounting what could be described as a rather routine operation on Parliament Hill some time in the spring or early summer of 1981. The CSE operators drove one of the two white vans filled with tons of electronic gear to the Hill, to check for "compromising radiation". In other words, they were there to find out if any signals coming from the seat of power in Canada were emanating outside the walls to a point where they could easily be picked up by foreign interceptors. They were also trying to find out if anybody was attempting to tap in from the outside.

"The ComSec people parked their truck on Parliament Hill, as they often do when they check for radiation . . . as they did, for instance, when we were checking ourselves during the 'Vanier dry run' at the beginning of 'Pilgrim'," recalls Frost. While they were going about their habitual business, they happened to pick up a car-phone conversation between two people. "This is not abnormal in itself," says Frost. "We listened to zillions of car-phone conversations. Why they happened to stick to this one, I have no idea. . . . If I had to guess, I'd say that they picked up a non-Canadian accent, or the subject just interested them, or they were just nosey. But they happened to stop their receiver on the frequency that was being used by that car phone." The recorders were running in the CSE van. That was standard procedure. The recorders never went off until the van's duty was up.

What they had stumbled onto was a conversation between an official at the American embassy and the American ambassador to Canada, most probably the new Reagan-appointed ambassador Paul Robinson, who was in his car. The two men were discussing an upcoming wheat deal between the United States and China in which Canada was a dangerous competitor.

If ever a medal of honour is given to a spy for economic espionage on behalf of Canada, perhaps it should go to this anonymous CSE ComSec operator who chose to stay on the frequency and record the whole conversation. As Frost points out: "He wasn't even an intercept guy! But he had enough smarts to know this was important . . . probably because of the amounts of money being spoken about."

He could easily have turned the dial, or just walked away from what he heard, pretending he had no idea what it meant. Who would have known? But a few days after the fluke intercept, the operator walked into Frank Bowman's office. Why did he go to see Bowman? Well, much as the "Pilgrim" people tried to keep their operation secret within "The Farm" itself, many people knew Bowman and Frost were doing unusual things. The ComSec operator didn't know what to do with the priceless tape. But he had an idea that Frank Bowman might solve the puzzle for him, or at the very least be a man onto whom he could unload the responsibility.

"The guy just walked into Frank's office, handed him the tape and said: 'You might want to listen to this,' " recalls Frost. It didn't take long for Bowman to figure out what he had. Urgently, he called in a transcriber. Bowman went right from there up the proper channels. Frost sums up the reaction: "Jesus Christ, if Frank and I had bent down on Sparks Street they [their bosses] would have come to kiss our ass!" What were they so ecstatic about? Well, what the CSE van on a routine mission had tripped over was the American government's detailed plan for negotiations on the huge wheat deal with China.

Frost, who listened to the original tape, remembers the ambassador asking the other unknown official, who was obviously extremely knowledgeable in the field: "What is our bottom line on this?" It was a rather lengthy exchange, and the anonymous American expert referred to the other man throughout as "Mr. Ambassador".

Frost describes the experience of listening to the intercept as "orgasmic". Beating "Uncle Sam" at his own game was something they had never expected to happen with such devastating results. "Politicians and people in government are strange when it comes to car phones," says Frost. "Even when they are told by CSE, NSA, GCHQ or the KGB that people are listening, somehow they don't seem to believe it. . . . It's a bizarre kind of denial. But it's exactly the attitude spying agencies bank on."

The American official who was being quizzed by the ambassador went into great detail about what the U.S. was prepared to offer to the Chinese and what their lowest bidding price would be. In other words, they had given Canada, their chief competitors, their entire game plan. All this in a car-phone conversation that, had the stars, the moon and planets not been perfectly aligned, would never have been intercepted.

"I was both elated and pissed off," admits Frost. "Here we were, at 'Pilgrim', going out of our way to pick up intelligence, sending people to Moscow for the two-year 'Stephanie' operation, and coming up empty. And, there, out of left field, without even trying, without planning it, without targeting anybody, without any special effort, these guys come up with something better than we could ever have dreamed of! It was like walking down the sidewalk and suddenly looking down to find the Hope Diamond!"

The net result of the intelligence provided by CSE to their government — and you can be assured it went up the line very quickly — was that in May 1982 the Canadian Wheat Board signed a long-term agreement with China worth about $2.5 billion at current prices. The Chinese contracted to purchase between 10.5 and 12.6 million metric tons of Canadian wheat over a three-year period: 3.85 million tons annually. This deal was in fact a renewal of a previous agreement that was to expire on July 31, 1982.

The Americans were not happy. The following month they made it known publicly that they didn't like Canada muscling in on their business with another wheat-buying nation, the then Soviet Union.

In the following year, 1983, Canada once again angered its Southern Giant by invading its traditional wheat market of Mexico with sales of $50 million. Frost has no direct knowledge of what took place in this instance, as far as CSE intercept was concerned. But he did hear that, once again, "something good" had been "collected" from the airwaves on the Americans' intentions and their "bottom line". This later intercept may have been more deliberate, although Frost says that if CSE ever specifically targeted U.S. communications to obtain this kind of information in his day, he wasn't told about it.

It is necessary to remember, however, that CSE, like NSA, is extremely compartmentalized in its operations. The "Pilgrim" people did not discuss what they were up to with colleagues not involved in the project. The same was true of other CSE employees working on various projects. It is not far-fetched to speculate that, after the first score with China, perhaps orders came down that CSE should pay close attention to what the Yanks were up to in specific situations — when a foreign official visited Ottawa on a mission dealing with the Free Trade deal, for instance. All it takes is for somebody in a position of power to give the word and the "Farm" employees will simply go out and do the job. "It's possible that we're doing it now," says Frost. "Remember, in those days we were just getting our feet wet in the area of microwave, i.e. super- and ultra-high radiowave frequencies, and we were still relying a lot on NSA and GCHQ. CSE evolved a lot in the following decade in that field and it hasn't stopped, I'm sure." There is no doubt that, should CSE wish to mount an operation against the Americans or anybody else, they could do it with a lot more expertise and superior equipment than they did back then. And CSE knows that NSA is spying against Canada.

"Right now," Frost says in 1994, "I'm sure the Americans are very concerned about what the Chrétien government is doing about overfishing. They would love to intercept anything on the subject that could be of use to them."

The wheat-deal intercept was crucial to the continued existence and expansion of CSE. Every time CSE's budget came up for review, the example worth $2.5 billion to Canada farmers was brought up. In times of government restraint and reductions in the staff of the public service, CSE kept getting more money and more people, as well as a brand-new $30-million addition to its main building. The Auditor-General has cautiously stayed away from prying into the CSE's management of its finances — a courtesy he doesn't give other government departments. As an official from his department in charge of overseeing the Defence Department told me in 1994: "No, we're not going to look into CSE. Whatever we could find there, I'm not sure we could tell anybody about it." (Though in Britain recently, as referred to in the preface, the whole intelligence community, including MI5, MI6 and GCHQ, has recently come under scrutiny, including financial scrutiny, by a new Parliamentary Intelligence Security Committee.)

Little as they had to do with the "Chinese caper", Frost and Bowman were "strutting around like roosters for months" after it happened. Only about 30 to 40 people within "The Farm" would have known about it. The information was not broadcast throughout CSE. First, it was an intercept against the Americans and the last thing they wanted was to let the Yanks know about it. To this day Frost doesn't think they ever found out. Second, it had been done by ComSec people, who were not supposed to do this sort of thing and whose role is the "overt" reason for CSE's continuing existence. If they were caught doing something they were not supposed to do, it could cause trouble if it leaked too far within the bureaucracy or to the outside world. But the people who mattered knew. And that could only help CSE and the "Pilgrim" project. Frost could point to it himself and say: "See the kind of stuff we could get."

They didn't feel guilty for one second about possibly betraying a friendly country that was literally giving them the means to achieve such ends, through training at College Park, expertise and expensive top-secret equipment of the "Oratory" type. After all, as Frost knew, they had done dirty work for the Americans before.

The intercept against the ambassador wasn't the first time espionage had been committed against a U.S. citizen by Canadian government operators. In one extraordinary case Canada actually did it on American soil . . . but on orders from NSA. The target was believed to be engaging in very "un-American" activities. What NSA asked Canada to do, though, did not conform to what American idealists would consider the democratic way.

But it appears all's fair if the referee is looking the other way. It may seem incredible to ordinary Canadians that this happened not in wartime, but in the mid-seventies. The story is nevertheless a prime example of how spying agencies try to bend not only their own rules of engagement but the law of the land itself when they need to do so. "Bending the law" is, in fact, a weak term. "Breaking it" would be more accurate. Otherwise, why would NSA have asked the Canadians to do it for them?

In 1975 Mike Frost had just come out of the "Stephanie" caper. He was working in CSE's section N1A, monitoring KGB and GRU communications directed to North America. As we saw in Chapter Four, if you intercepted communications, via satellite or otherwise, between the Soviet Union and North America, and managed to pinpoint the target of this information, the chances were you had found a KGB or a GRU spy.

The request from NSA came in the fall of 1975. Frost and his N1A colleagues had been doing a lot of work with the American agency's "A Group" that dealt with East Bloc counter-espionage. The "Watergate" scandal was still fresh on the minds of every American, and NSA had become a little gun-shy about crossing the line that could put them "above the law", a damning charge against treasured American civil rights that had forced President Richard Nixon to resign just a year before.

One day Frost was called to the office of his section head, Steven Blackburn, to give his advice on something that had just been sent up the line from NSA.

"We've had this request from A Group," said Blackburn. "It's a special request. They want to know if we could help them determine if and from whom specifically HF emission bursts emanating in Maryland and going back to Moscow are coming from . . ."

"HF transmission bursts?" said Frost, whose expertise always clicked in on technical matters. "The want to know if the guy's KGB?"

"Yeah . . . that's what I understand," said Blackburn. "But they'd like us to do the intercept for them."

"On American soil?" asked Frost stoically.

"Yeah . . . They'll pay our way and everything. They just don't want do it themselves."

"Why not?"

"Well, with this Watergate thing and everything. . . . They didn't really say so, but I think they want to be in a position to say publicly that they didn't do it should they ever be asked."

"Why?"

"Because it's directed against an American citizen."

"Who they suspect to be a Soviet spy?"

"I guess so . . ."

It really didn't faze Frost that much. After all, he was in the business of catching Soviet agents, no matter what their citizenship was. Doing it on foreign soil was not that big a deal to him. It was all for the right cause, no? And the "Cold War" was still very much on in those days.

In this specific case a coded message, intercepted by NSA, was regularly being sent to the Chesapeake Bay area and someone was talking to the suspected agent on HF using one-time-pad and regular "hand-speed" Morse — in other words, signals a trained person can take down with a pencil and pad in hand. It is next to impossible to determine who the message is directed to, if the intercept operators don't know who is answering back. Technically, anybody on the frequency could listen and not know what it was all about.

In this case there had been "burst transmissions" (see Chapter Four) from the area to Moscow and NSA thought they knew who they were coming from. The problem with this individual was that he was an American citizen whom NSA suspected of transmitting from his home. Had he been doing it from, say, a government office, they wouldn't have needed the Canadians and could have claimed "national security" with full justification. What the American agency had to determine was not only whether the "burst transmissions" were emanating from his house but whether he was present when they were. "The people at NSA did not want to conduct any kind of aggressive intercept against this American citizen, in his home," recalls Frost. "They wanted to be able to deny any involvement in the future." Paradoxically, though, all they asked CSE for was manpower. They were willing to foot the bill with American government funds and provide all their own equipment. It seemed they gave little thought to what explanation they would use should the Canadians — like the "Cubans" in Watergate — get caught with their equipment, in their vehicle, driven by their chauffeur and having their hotel and meal bills paid for by the American people.

"All they asked us to do, basically, was to provide a body to turn on the equipment. They knew where they wanted us to go, they knew the frequency they wanted to check, they knew the timing of the 'burst transmissions'."

It gets curiouser and curiouser. Because, after the request came to CSE and went up the totem pole, CSE's response was that they didn't want to be caught doing it either. That didn't mean they couldn't find another scapegoat, however. CSE went to the Canadian Forces intercept base in Leitrim, in Gloucester Township south of Ottawa, for the answer. This is where Frost and many other CSE employees had come from — a prime recruiting ground for Canadian spies. There were two intercept operators there who were known to be very dedicated to their counter-espionage jobs. One was supervisor of the section monitoring KGB communications, the other was supervisor of the section spying on GRU communications. They were known for their strong conviction of being on the "good side" as opposed to the "evil" one, and they would do just about anything to ruin the Soviets' day.

"They were very much the 'Yes, sir!' kind of guys, who wouldn't question orders," says Frost. "They were very trustworthy. They weren't CSE-trained. So you could ask them to mow the lawn, but tell them not to mess with the garden. Actually, when it comes right down to it, all they were being asked to do was to push an 'On' button at the right time in the right place."

The two men were brought into CSE and asked if they "wouldn't mind" going down to Washington, D.C., on "a special project" for a week or two. They were given a cursory briefing on what was expected of them. They were sent down to NSA, where they were given a more detailed briefing. Clearance was given by the Canadian military authorities to go ahead. How far up the political ladder did it go? Frost doesn't know. "I would suspect CSE didn't go very high up for approval," he speculates. "It was a very short, in-house, one-time thing: get in, get out and NSA will be grateful. CSE was aware but not involved. It didn't cost us any money. The men got good training, we got good PR; that would have been the reasoning of those who gave the green light. Besides, we had covered our ass. We'd just blame the military. . . . In fact, we were glad to be asked to do something important for NSA. Up to that point, it had seemed as if it was always the other way around."

The two Canadians were sent down to the Chesapeake Bay area to conduct a counter-espionage operation on American soil for and at the expense of the American taxpayers for the sole reason that

NSA wanted to pull a "Pontius Pilate" and wash their hands from it should they have to. The "official" reason for the trip, as far as Ottawa's bureaucracy was concerned, was that they were going down to NSA for "technical discussions". That was standard for CSE. In the years to follow, as more and more Canadian CSE employees travelled to the U.S. on government business, the CSE ID card became so well known to customs officers at the Washington, D.C., airports that it was, as Frost points out, "better than a passport".

The Leitrim operators were given everything they needed, including a driver. After two weeks of monitoring the American citizen's home, the Canadian team was able to establish that the HF burst transmissions were indeed coming from the house, and that he was present whenever they were sent. They caught him twice in the span of two weeks.

"The tapes and conclusions were turned over to NSA and we never heard about it after that," says Frost. "Feedback on an operation of this kind is rarely given freely. Unless specifically requested, NSA won't provide it. And in the end, the last thing you want to know, curious as you may be, is the result of your action. You just do your hit and get out. You don't want to know so much that you yourself start to be seen as too nosey and become a liability."

Translation: at a time in the mid-seventies when they were getting free intelligence from the Americans, including Talent-Keyhole satellite intercept the general public was barely aware of, the last thing CSE wanted was to raise eyebrows among their American allies by asking too many embarrassing questions.

Frost never knew who the targeted American citizen was, or what happened to him after their involvement. He sensed that NSA was already almost 100 per cent sure he was a Soviet spy. They just needed uncontestable evidence. "The Soviets had a sort of vacationing-resort area in Chesapeake for their diplomats working in the U.S.," says Frost. "I understand this man had been spotted several times going there for parties and other functions." NSA just wanted the Canadians to put the dots on the "i"s and the crosses on the "t"s.

Frost doesn't know if this was a common occurrence at CSE, but he suspects it wasn't, because his own section chief had to check with upper management who, in the end, decided to "contract" the job out to the military. "NSA was really spooked by 'Watergate' at the time," says Frost. "I'm sure it had everything to do with that and I doubt that such requests were made at any time before or have been made since. On the other hand, we did get into embassy collection after they threatened to cut us off. So I guess that was another way of getting Canada to do things their way."

Years later CSE would be asked to perform an even dicier task for an ally. But this time it was across "the Pond" for British GCHQ. What they did for their friends in 1983 not only crossed the line of legality but involved Canada's intercept centre in the political affairs of a foreign country.

In February 1983, just as the "Pilgrim" people were eagerly making preparations to get "Daisy" off the ground, a very special request came down the pipe.

It was unusual for two reasons. First, the agency asking for help was GCHQ. Second, it implied very sensitive intercept that amounted to meddling in not only Great Britain's national politics but very partisan politics at that.

Mike Frost was up to his neck in the details of the New Delhi project when Frank Bowman asked to talk to him about something a little different, not to say totally off-the-wall. "BRLO went in to see the chief," Bowman began. BRLO (pronounced affectionately BRILO) was the familiar name "The Farm" gave to the British Senior Liaison Officer (like CANSLO with NSA). "The chief" was the head of CSE. "BRILO asked him if we wouldn't mind mounting a special operation, two or three weeks max, in London, paid for by the Brits."

"Sure," said Frost. "Why not? Three weeks all paid for in London sounds great!"

"Yeah," answered Bowman. "Somebody in 'Pilgrim' will do it." Somehow he didn't seem too eager to divulge any details. But

Frost did ask: "Well, what's the mission?" There was a pause on Bowman's part. Then he went on to say what he didn't quite seem to have a grasp on it himself.

"Well, it seems as if Margaret Thatcher [then British Prime Minister] thinks two of the ministers in her cabinet are not 'on side'. . . . She wants to find out if they are."

"So?"

"So GCHQ has asked whether, if we were given the frequencies to look for and the time-frame to do the intercept, we could assist the British Prime Minister in her intelligence-gathering on her ministers."

"She wants to spy on her own ministers?"

"That's the way I understand it. . . . GCHQ feels it cannot, in all honesty, mount an operation against its own ministers. Just too risky. But they don't want to turn off the Prime Minister either. But if *we* do it, they can safely say they didn't if anybody asks." Sounds familiar?

This is another prime example of how warped the "cheating game" can get. Sure, the British intelligence people could say, no word of a lie, that they hadn't done it themselves. They had simply asked the Canadians to perform the unethical duty for them. And they would, of course, forget to say that they paid for the Canadian's stay in an always expensive London hotel and his *per diem* in British tax-payers' pounds.

Even though Bowman did share the GCHQ request with his "Pilgrim" people, there was really never any hesitation in his mind. "He had said 'yes' right away," recalls Frost. "At the time there was no moral issue involved for any of us. We never stopped to question the morality of doing what amounted to dirty tricks for a partisan politician, for her very personal reasons, in a foreign land. After all, we weren't spying on Canadians . . . that time anyway."

In 1983 Thatcher was coming to the end of her first mandate and planning an election for June of the same year. She had also just proceeded in January with a cabinet shuffle that involved the "depar-ture" of two ministers and the appointment of three new ones. Did

Bowman and Frost know exactly what Margaret Thatcher was looking for? "I'm not sure she knew herself!" says Frost. "She was a bit paranoid, you know. I think she was simply looking to see if she could find anything at all: What are these guys talking about? Are they ganging up against me? She obviously suspected these men of being against her and was looking for conclusive evidence." A little more than seven years later, an increasingly paranoid and extremely bitter Thatcher would eventually submit her resignation after mounting pressure from her own caucus and several of her own ministers.

"The moral issue wasn't raised," says Frost. "We listened so routinely to private conversations we were not supposed to hear that I guess we had become immune to that kind of soul-searching. The other prime reason for going ahead eagerly was the total lack of danger. Who was going to catch us? The guys who did the catching were the ones asking us to do it.

"In the end, we just thought it would be a fun thing to do. Hey, three weeks in downtown London, all expenses paid. We knew Thatcher was up to no good, but we didn't care. Why would we?"

Their only brief hesitation concerned the logistics. Could they do it technically, and did they have the time with New Delhi coming up fast? But it turned out that "Pilgrim" had several practical reasons for agreeing to the request. The first one was that it came from GCHQ. They had done a lot for NSA, but for all the help they had had from the Brits over the years, they had given very little in return. It was seen simply as returning many favours. The other reason was that Bowman was already scheduled to travel to GCHQ in March 1983 to do some preliminary work on "Daisy". Since he had decided to do the operation himself — Bowman didn't enjoy travelling much, but he loved London — he would just leave a few weeks early and perform a little caper for his British friends, who would undoubtedly be grateful.

Finally, the "Pilgrim" operators were eager to test a new piece of advanced equipment they had just purchased from Microtel. It was a receiver that could be carried in a briefcase. CSE had also developed a very small antenna, about the size of a cigar box, and were also working on small cassette-type recorders for narrow-band intercept. This caper would give "Pilgrim" a perfect opportunity to test all this equipment.

The only problem with the Microtel briefcase receiver was that there was no spectrum analyser, which meant no visual representation of the activity on the RF band. Without a spectrum analyser you have to know specifically what frequency to go to. However, "BRLO had already provided us with that, so it didn't matter so much."

Bowman flew over and set up an intercept post right inside Canada's Macdonald House. The intercept was done during normal business hours, but was extended at both ends, so that the ministers could be caught either on their way to work or on the road back home. Bowman started early and he stayed late. He had to hide his operation from the embassy staff, but given the size of Canada's diplomatic corps in Great Britain — some 400 people — he was just another face in a crowd. All he needed was a private room, where he wouldn't be suddenly interrupted by an intruder. The question of cover wasn't even discussed. Just another "technical visit" to GCHQ.

Bowman just walked into his assigned office with his briefcase and walked out with it to his hotel. He also did part of his intercept from the hotel room itself, although he didn't like to because it was British territory as opposed to the Canadian High Commission. The equipment worked fine and Bowman captured a lot of conversations. "He got quite a bit of stuff," says Frost. "A number of tapes."

On completion of his mission, Bowman was told he would be met at GCHQ, in the Cotswolds, by a person to whom he was to hand over the tapes. When he arrived, he met with the Canadian liaison officer there and said there was somebody else he had to see. The agent showed up right away and Bowman simply gave him what he had. Bowman never made copies of the material. That would have been "unethical".

Frost couldn't help being curious, on Bowman's return, as to whether he had heard anything out of the ordinary. Bowman was a man of few words at the best of times.

"It was interesting," he said laconically. "I don't know if she got what she was looking for. . . . But some of it was very interesting." Then he added: "To be honest, Mike, I might as well have been copying Hindu . . . fucking . . . stani because I can't understand these English accents anyway!" It may have been his way of telling Frost, "Don't ask me any more questions, please." Once again, it was just another job well done. Don't talk about it once it's over.

The story does raise questions, however, about the bizarre intercepts that came to light almost a decade later involving the Royal Family. Damning tapes of Prince Charles and Princess Diana, for instance. The rumour at the time was that GCHQ had made them and leaked them to the media. The chances are, says Frost, that they were done by NSA or even CSE people, for whatever reasons, on whoever's orders. "Because in my day, which wasn't that long ago, the British didn't want to touch that sort of stuff. . . . So if anybody got up in the British Parliament to ask about it, they could say: 'No, it wasn't us.' " They might be lying, of course, or at the very least getting themselves off the hook on a technicality.

The Thatcher episode certainly shows that GCHQ, like NSA, found ways to put itself above the law and did not hesitate to get directly involved in helping a specific politician for her personal political benefit. It also shows that, in given circumstances, Canada was not hesitant about spying on its friends. But as with the espionage on American soil some eight years earlier, the decision to proceed with the London caper was probably not put forward for approval to many people up the bureaucratic ladder. It was something CSE figured they would get away with easily, so checking with the higher-ups would only complicate things unnecessarily.

There were other instances, however, when orders did come down from the Canadian authorities to spy on a friendly nation, even on a Canadian province.

The targets were none other than France and Quebec.

Frost first learned about what is known within the spy community as "third-party" intercept when he was monitoring the Soviet's "Gorizont" system in the period between his "Stephanie" and his NIA work. This was a "tropo-scatter" system of communications the Russians were installing for their Arctic communications. The airwaves in such a network are bounced off the troposphere from a transmitting tower and bounced back to a specific receiving post — as opposed to HF waves that are sent to the ionosphere and travel around the world. Frost, who already had extensive experience in monitoring Soviet Arctic communications, had been picked for the job shortly after "Stephanie" was shut down.

It was then that he learned in a very innocuous way about "third-party" intercept. One day he got to the office to find a pile of copied transcripts sitting on his desk.

"Where on earth did all this stuff come from?"

"Oh, that's 'third party'," answered a CSE colleague.

"It's what?"

" 'Third party'," answered the man, who seemed genuinely surprised at Frost's puzzlement.

"What do you mean, 'third party'?"

"Well, we buy intercept, primarily from the Scandinavian countries . . ."

"What do you mean we 'buy' it?"

"Well, it's much cheaper for us just to buy the raw traffic from them instead of doing it ourselves. They have it, they collect it and they sell it to us."

"How do we task them?"

"No real tasking is being done by CSE. They just give us what they have. As far as I know, they have a blanket mandate to intercept communications, they give us hard copy in bulk and we pay them for it."

Norway was the major supplier by far, but some of the intercept also came from the Swedes and the Danes. The Scandinavians understandably had their own "overt" intercept network, being so close to the Soviet border. And most of their collection was targeting

Soviet communications. Basically they would just sell it by the box-ful to a friendly buyer. It wasn't at that period very time-sensitive material. Most of it was outdated, but when you were working on a long-term project like "Gorizont", some of it could be useful.

A few years later Frost's ears perked up again on the question of "third-party" intercept when he was told that the Norwegians had received a very specific request from CSE — one that was to that day unprecedented as far as Frost knows. "We asked the Norwegians — and probably the other two Scandinavian countries — if there was any way they could provide intercept of French communications," says Frost. "What we were targeting were communications between France and Quebec." This was, as he recalls, shortly after the election of separatist Parti Québécois premier René Lévesque, who had promised a referendum on the separation of Quebec from Canada for the year 1980. "The Trudeau government wanted to know anything they could about what was going on between the two countries."

Relations between the federal Canadian government and France had been extremely tense since 1967. That was when the grandiose President of France, Charles de Gaulle, had shouted his famous *"Vive le Québec libre!"* from the balcony of Montreal's City Hall while on an official visit to Canada. Canada's Prime Minister Lester B. Pearson had quickly cancelled de Gaulle's planned visit to Ottawa, accusing him of having meddled in Canada's internal politics, since he seemed to have openly backed the separatist cause. Shortly after, René Lévesque became the first credible separatist leader in the province, after splitting from the federalist Liberal Party. This caused great concern in Ottawa, which until then had viewed the separatist threat as relatively marginal. In October 1970 Canada was also plunged into what is known as the October Crisis, after the terrorist FLQ (*Front de Libération du Québec*) kidnapped the British envoy to Montreal, James Cross, and assassinated the provincial government minister Pierre Laporte.

Prime Minister Pierre Trudeau took the extraordinary step, still highly controversial, of declaring the War Measures Act, which gave sweeping powers to the police and the army to arrest anybody suspected of being an FLQ terrorist or sympathizer. More than 400 people were thrown in jail without a warrant or a trial.

In 1973, on Lévesque's second attempt to win power in Quebec, his Parti Québécois was soundly routed, largely because many people in the province were still reeling from the shock of the October Crisis. Three years later, however, the story was drastically different. On November 15th, Lévesque turfed a scandal-ridden Liberal Party led by Robert Bourassa out of power and created great uncertainty for Canada's future as a united country.

Frost learned about the Norwegians' intercept of France-Quebec communications at the beginning of Lévesque's years in power. "All I know is that they kept doing it for us and we got a lot of stuff, mainly telexes as I recall."

A staunch federalist and patriotic Canadian, Frost hesitated before revealing this, but has come to feel the people of Quebec and Canada have a right to know. "For us, we were doing it to preserve federalism," he says. But he admits that "although technically we were intercepting French communications, in fact we were also spying on Canadians because the targets were Quebecers." He's not sure, today, that was the right thing to do. After all, these were not KGB spies from a totalitarian regime — just people who were presenting a different political and constitutional option and who had been elected democratically. But at the time he felt CSE was only trying to keep the country united.

The Canadian authorities were obviously looking to see whether the French government of Giscard d'Éstaing, which was known to be at least privately sympathetic to the cause of separation, and Quebec's secessionist leaders were planning anything specific against Ottawa. Such orders could have come only from the highest political level. From November 1976 on the Trudeau government was engaged in an all-out effort to defeat the upcoming referendum — which they did — and they used every means at their disposal to do so, clearly including their espionage establishment. Mind you, it was none other than Lévesque's Finance Minister, Jacques Parizeau, who himself became leader of the Parti Québécois in 1986, who boasted publicly in the seventies of having "a network of spies" for the separatist cause within the federal bureaucracy. Perhaps this was only fair game. CSE's means and resources for espionage, however, were far superior.

As far as Frost knows, this effort to spy on France-Quebec communications carried on throughout his remaining years at CSE, even though the separatists lost the 1980 referendum and were eventually defeated in the 1985 provincial election by Bourassa's federalist Liberals. As this book goes to press, however, they have just returned to power with Parizeau at the helm, promising to hold yet another referendum and to declare independence.

Frost knows of the existence of a "French Problem" section at CSE headquarters. He has no details as to what transpired or transpires behind the door of the room, but he knows the people working there deal solely with the question of Quebec separation.

He also remembers how External Affairs was very insistent on "Pilgrim" putting one major world capital on its list of potential survey sites: Paris. "They really wanted us to get into Paris. They were not all that happy with the third-party intercept, which again was too dated to be useful in a timely fashion. However, while I was there, we never even did a pre-survey of Paris. For three reasons: Politically, we knew it was dynamite. Technically, we didn't think we could do it. Physically, the embassy was too cramped to house an intercept site."

He had been warned about the technical difficulties involved in a Paris intercept by NSA's Patrick O'Brien. "I remember him raising his eyebrows and telling me that we'd better take a lot of equipment and a lot of good people over there, because the communications environment in Paris is extremely complicated."

On the other hand, Frost points out that "Pilgrim" did survey Rabat, for the same reasons, and captured France-Quebec communications from that site. "For all I know, they may very well be in Paris today. External really wanted to go there and I guess if they wanted it badly enough, they could find room for it and CSE would get the equipment to do it."

Friend or foe? Sometimes it seems to depend on the hour of the day or the weather. The basic rule is: Don't ask too many questions, especially of your own conscience.

ELEVEN
"SPHINX" —
BACK IN THE U.S.S.R.

IN EARLY 1987 CANADA'S two close "friends" in the espionage world came knocking on CSE's door asking for a huge favour. The request led to perhaps the most prestigious and ego-boosting operation "Pilgrim" was ever asked to do. The Americans and the British were, literally, "in a jam". Something really strange, and extremely annoying, had happened in Moscow. Frost first learned about it through his usual source of information, Frank Bowman:

"The Americans and the Brits have come to us to solve an urgent problem."

"What's that?"

"Well, for some reason, 'Broadside' and 'Tryst' have both become inoperative." As previously explained, "Broadside" was the American embassy-collection site in the Soviet capital, "Tryst" the British one.

"How so?"

"The Soviets have been jamming them."

"Jamming them?" Frost was surprised. He had never had any illusions that the KGB and the GRU were not fully aware the U.S. and Britain were up to no good from within their embassies. But he had always assumed that, between superpowers, this was part of the game. They let you try to listen to them, while expecting you to let them try to listen to you.

"What brought this on?"

"Dunno," said Bowman. "Maybe the Soviets decided enough was enough. Maybe they're retaliating for something the Yanks did. Maybe they're hiding something big. Maybe they're just being pesky. But it's been going on for months, maybe a year. NSA told me they tried everything to get around it, but there's no way. The Soviets are pretty good at what they do once they decide on doing it."

"It's that bad?"

"They're simply not getting anything any more. No intercept, no intelligence at all. . . . They figure they can't let it go on, with everything that's happening over there, this Gorbachev guy and whatever he's really up to, *perestroika*, *glasnost* and all that; the place could blow any minute and they wouldn't know about it."

"And what do they want from us?"

"Nothing much," said Bowman with a smile. "They just want us to go in and replace both of them."

"You mean they want us to go into Moscow, put up an embassy-collection site and hopefully give them back the intelligence they once shared with each other?"

"Yep. What do you think?"

"I think that's fantastic!"

"I figured you'd say that."

"But this one is going to be extremely sensitive. Not only do we not want to get caught, but it would be a real feather in CSE's cap if we were to do it successfully and not get jammed."

"Right."

"Let's do it, Frank."

"Okey-doke."

What had taken place in Moscow over the previous year, as Frost was to find out later from College Park people, was that the Soviets had first showed up near the two embassies with a ComSec van. They had assuredly picked up some kind of radiation from the American and British sites and had started "jamming" them occasionally. Very quickly, though, it had turned into a permanent operation.

"Jamming" is done in cases like this from a close location. There was no problem of access in totalitarian Russia. You use very directional antennas directed at the building you are targeting and the frequencies you believe they are trying to intercept, and simply flood the place with noise. The trick for the "jammers" is to avoid jamming themselves. So they must use enough power to block the intercept, but not too much to disrupt their own communications. This was relatively easy for the Soviets since, if they didn't know exactly what frequencies the Americans and the British were tuned onto, they certainly knew which of their own frequencies they didn't want them to hear.

"Broadside" and "Tryst" had tried several ways around it, turning the equipment off and on at odd times. But the Soviets had them pegged so well that as soon as their electronic gear went on, the jamming would start. And it would stop almost automatically whenever they turned their gear off. It was in total frustration and with an admission of utter defeat that they turned to the Canadians. Maybe the now seasoned "Pilgrim" people could achieve success where they had met only with failure.

This was a major vote of confidence in "Pilgrim". Could CSE climb that cliff? They were certainly willing, but their main concern was to do it as cautiously as possible. They simply didn't want to get caught. They never had been before, of course. But this time the game was to be played against the most potent adversary from the "other side".

The operation was codenamed "Sphinx". The first thing Bowman and Frost decided was that they had to change their normal *modus operandi* for a "Pilgrim" operation. The KGB were just too good. The chances were the KGB had files on the two of them, and indeed on most CSE employees who had travelled abroad, whatever covers they had used. Which meant the first thing they couldn't do was send in their own regular people to do a pre-survey or survey of any kind. At least technically, CSE wanted to be seen as being totally uninvolved.

They still opted to recruit intercept operators within the Defence Department and send them to External Affairs to be trained as embassy communications centre operators. All were either Russian speakers already or had intensive training in Russian before the posting. CSE decided not to try to hide the fact that these new staff in the Moscow embassy came from the military, because they were worried the Soviets might pick up on even the slightest deception, for example if they already knew that one of the agents being sent was a member of Canada's Armed Forces. But once again the cover would be that they would be in the embassy as communications technicians testing new equipment to improve communications between Moscow and Ottawa. "We made up all sorts of phoney excuses — increasing the capacity of the phone lines, the satellite links, anything we could think of. But they all made sense, they all fit the cover of them being Comcen operators."

They certainly needed many excuses and this must have been seen by the Soviets as a major upgrading of the communications in the Canadian chancellery because CSE had decided it needed a total of five new staffers in Moscow to achieve what the Americans and the British were hoping they would. One supervisor and four operators were picked, none of them having any previous link with CSE. It was an unusual move for Canada to increase its personnel by such a number. Within CSE itself, extraordinary precautions were taken to limit dissemination — there was always the concern of a "mole" lurking somewhere in the bowels of "The Farm". Very few people ever knew of the existence of "Sphinx". It became a secret even more guarded than "Pilgrim" itself. Within External Affairs and the Moscow embassy it was announced that these five new staffers were coming on board. Another bogus excuse used to convince the Soviets was that Canada was getting ready to improve its communications in light of the undeniable fact that they were also preparing to move the embassy to a better, bigger site.

In another variation, the "Pilgrim" team didn't adhere to the usual tactic of meeting with the ambassador to brief him and ask for his permission. That was deemed too risky, whether done on the streets of the Soviet capital or in Ottawa. Instead it was the Moscow military attaché, a Lt.-Colonel, who was asked to go to West Germany, which was not that unusual a journey given that Canada was a NATO country. He was the one who received the CSE briefing and relayed it back later to the top Canadian diplomat in Moscow, who for a short time just happened to be Peter Roberts. Frost still remembered Roberts fondly from the "Bucharest caper" and knew "Pilgrim" would be welcome there.

No objections were raised. However, the cover story did cause some problems within the embassy at one point. "Some of the staffers who had been told communications would be improved so that they could carry more capacity wanted extra access to send this and that to Canada," laughs Frost. "Of course, we couldn't accommodate them because the story wasn't true. We just told them we were still at the testing stage."

Careful and secretive as they had been in all previous "Pilgrim" operations, Frost and his team became really paranoid about this one. "I remember that, whenever we travelled to External Affairs for anything that had to do with 'Sphinx', we would always check if we were being tailed. It came close to being ridiculous."

There was also the problem of having to send the five operators down to NSA — something else the Soviets might pick up on if they then saw the same people pop up in Moscow. CSE made them fill in paperwork that enrolled them on a top-rated "Directional Finding" course given by NSA to which Canadian military personnel were regularly being sent. The hope was that the Soviets would see nothing out of the ordinary in these five people attending it. In fact, the "Sphinx" operators spent most of their time in the Washington, D.C., area in College Park's "live room" — familiarizing themselves with the Moscow electronic environment that the Americans knew like the palm of their hand, but couldn't read any more.

The question of what to tell the wives of the men involved became another headache. The policy adopted for New Delhi was in

Frost's mind the right one, and had worked well. He remembered O'Brien's warning that they had to have happy operators, which meant happy wives. Somehow, though, the paranoia got to the "Pilgrim" team on this issue too. After several discussions, they decided not to tell the spouses of the spies what their husbands would really be doing in the Soviet Union. "We just couldn't take the chance of having one of them let slip something she might think insignificant at an embassy cocktail party," says Frost. "The KGB was just too good. They were trained to get information out of people, just as we were, just as the Americans were at their CIA 'Charm School'."

Another major change in procedure was that the four operators and their supervisor were sent in ahead of the equipment and pretended to be doing work in the ComCenter of the embassy for a month or so. It was usually the other way around: get the gear there, make sure it was secure and then send in the shock troops. The equipment followed the usual diplomatic bag route through External Affairs and was sent piece by piece, rather than in a bulk shipment as had been done for Caracas and "Daisy".

The most amazing thing is that, with all the difficulties involved, the "Pilgrim" operation was up and running within four months of the first request from NSA and GCHQ. They went to a "24-7" procedure, which meant, as we have seen, that after being turned up gradually at first, the equipment was left on 24 hours a day, seven days a week. It was manned, however, only during normal working hours, five days a week, so as not to blow the operators' cover. By that time, the equipment had become so sophisticated that operating it by remote was easy.

The supervisor of the "Sphinx" team also had an option that wasn't freely given to "Pilgrim" operators: he could report any intercept he might think was urgently needed by CSE and its allies. That would be done in a "triple-encoded" message through an External Affairs channel to a "Pilgrim"-cleared employee. It was then relayed immediately to CSE and just about as quickly to NSA.

The operation was a success. The Canadians were not jammed, at least up until the day Frost left "Pilgrim", about two years after "Sphinx" started. Which means that from summer 1987 to summer 1989 it was Canada that was providing the two most powerful Western nations with the intelligence that had been so crucial to them and, in fact, to the whole Western Alliance. They intercepted all the frequencies "Broadside" and "Tryst" had been copying before: KGB and GRU communications, government communications, police — everything that mattered.

"We were ecstatic; the Americans and the British were ecstatic," says Frost. "Mind you, NSA kept telling us: expect to get jammed any day. . . . But at least up to summer 1989 we never did . . . Did the Soviets not suspect it at all, since it was coming from Canada? Did they figure we were up to something but not have the expertise or equipment to cause much harm? I don't know. But they took no aggressive action against us."

It is therefore quite probable that, when a group of radical Communists tried to overthrow Gorbachev by holding him and his family hostage for 72 hours in August 1992, the intelligence provided to the world actually emanated from "Pilgrim" and CSE. On the list of "key-words" inserted in the "Sphinx" "Oratory" from Day One were the names of several of the defendants who would later face charges of high treason and conspiracy: former KGB chief Vladimir Kryuchkov; former Prime Minister Valentin Pavlov; former Defence Minister Dmitri Yazov; former Vice-President Gennady Yanayev; and former Interior Minister Boris Pubo, who committed suicide after the failed coup.

Boris Yeltsin's name was also part of the "key-word" list, as was, of course, Gorbachev's.

Prime Minister Brian Mulroney made at least one visit to the Soviet Union while Frost is positive "Sphinx" was still up and running, in the fall of 1989. If CSE followed its prescribed policy, though, the intercept was turned off during the visit. Frost had strongly disagreed with that policy, since he believed the Canadians should be listening even more closely to protect their country's leader. But, politically, the decision was taken that the Prime Minister had to be in a position where no operation of the kind was going on while he was in the foreign land concerned.

"Sphinx", much as it was asked as a favour, really showed NSA and GCHQ that they weren't dealing with minor leaguers any more. No doubt it has increased not only CSE's prestige and respect in the espionage field but also its clout.

To Mike Frost, for whom the Soviets had always been his prime target, it was the ultimate accomplishment, even though sadly his career was coming to an abrupt and premature end.

TWELVE

WHAT NOW?

IN THE COURSE OF WRITING THIS BOOK, Mike Frost happened to bump into an old "Pilgrim" colleague from External Affairs. Casually he asked him what he was up to.

"Oh, still the same old shit," he answered.

Frost also dropped by a restaurant favoured by CSE employees in Billings Bridge Plaza in Ottawa and struck up a conversation with an employee of "The Farm", asking how "so-and-so" was doing.

"Still up to the same thing," she said.

Four years after Frost's forced retirement, "Pilgrim" is very much alive and has probably taken over a major part of CSE's activities, certainly on the covert side. It may even have overtaken the CSE's overt operations in size and importance. Frost can offer only educated speculation as to where the "Pilgrim" team is striking these days. But his informed guesses come from conversations that took place only four years ago, and relate to what he knows were "Pilgrim" intentions at the time. He cannot see why the plans would have changed.

"I see no reason why we wouldn't still be in New Delhi," he says. "And I see no reason why we should not still be in Moscow, unless they managed to jam 'Sphinx' and we couldn't get around the jamming. 'Sphinx' was a relatively cheap operation, so they are most likely still there.

"Caracas? It wouldn't surprise me at all if we've mounted some kind of semi-permanent operation there. . . . We didn't get any solid intelligence out of our survey there, but we did get a lot of intercept. Given the targets they are probably aiming at today, Caracas would be a logical site. The embassy had a lot of room and, technically, the operation went extremely well.

"Bucharest? Maybe. That was one of our most successful collections of intelligence. No reason we shouldn't try to find out what has been going on since Ceausescu's fall.

"Beijing? I'd be very surprised if we didn't finally bow to pressure from NSA. If only to say: 'We are going to go in and have a look.' "

Beijing had been Patrick O'Brien's first choice back in 1977 and throughout the years that followed, whenever there were contacts between NSA and "Pilgrim" people, the Americans would ask: "When are you going into Beijing?" The pressure was such that a potential "Pilgrim" operation in Beijing was given a cover name: "Badger". The reason for the Americans' insistence was that in Beijing embassies are grouped together within a diplomatic compound. There was a crucial microwave tower located within earshot of an intercept, but the Chinese had erected buildings in front of it lined up in such a way that neither the Americans nor the British or the Australians could seize its signals. Frost still remembers O'Brien drawing a diagram on a white board with a black marker to show the Canadians the positions of the buildings and the embassies in the compound. The Canadian embassy (the old one at least — they have now built a brand-new complex) was the only one that had a shot at the microwave tower, both visually and electronically (see diagram, p. 255). "It was considered by the Americans to be a great hole in their intelligence," says Frost.

A "Pilgrim" operation in China would mean, of course, that CSE would have had to drastically improve its capacity to deal with Chinese intelligence in its Ottawa processing lab, since they would never send "Pilgrim" material directly to NSA without analysing it first. (Think of the "wheat deal" discussed in Chapter Ten.)

Frost is also pretty sure "Pilgrim" is in Paris, because, in that case, the insistence came from External Affairs. "It's almost a given

FIGURE E

BEIJING

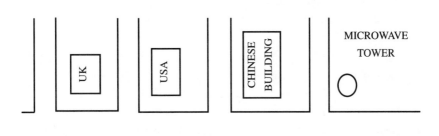

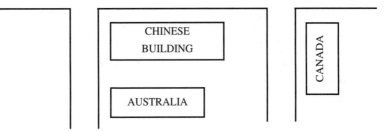

COMPOUND IS NOT EXACTLY AS SHOWN

(DIAGRAM BY DAVID FROST)

that we are there," he says. "There wasn't room to put a piece of cigarette paper in that embassy, but I would think that somehow External Affairs found room for us. They would have moved people out, or doubled them up or made their jobs redundant. . . . Given the political situation in Canada now, with the separatist threat so great and Lucien Bouchard travelling over there to meet with top French officials, it seems highly probable to me that we have an operation there."

In spring 1994 the separatist Bloc Québécois, led by Bouchard, held 54 seats in the Canadian House of Commons and was the Official Opposition, despite being the first secessionist party from Quebec ever to elect even one member to the federal Parliament.

The ambassador in Paris, on the other hand, was Benoît Bouchard, a former faithful minister of Tory Prime Minister Brian Mulroney, a man who, like many Mulroney loyalists, saw Lucien Bouchard, also a former minister and personal friend of Mulroney, as a traitor. Would Benoît co-operate in a caper to perhaps foil Lucien's plans?

The only problem with Paris, as we have seen, is its complex electronic environment. "To penetrate it would have taken a lot of resources and equipment. It would be terribly, terribly difficult to conquer."

Another "Pilgrim" site Frost believes likely is Belgrade in what is now Serbia. "Even though it may have been just a temporary thing, I suspect we went there either ahead of time or with our peace-keepers, to support our troops."

As for other possible sites, Frost acknowledges that he is purposely omitting speculation about certain locations where he believes agents could be in danger, should their presence become known.

Speculation about "hot spots" like Belgrade is based on the fact that, just before his departure, CSE was discussing the development of a "quick response team" for special situations.

"I believe that somewhere in a storage room at CSE is a quick-response package of equipment, sitting there crated and ready to be shipped anywhere at any time. If any explosion happens anywhere in the world, we can hop on a plane and are ready to go."

This is a very different situation from operating secretively out of an embassy in a country where no major trouble is brewing. For a quick operation you don't have to worry so much about having "Tempest-proof" equipment or about cover and getting caught — you just go in, get what you need, and leave. In fact, if peacekeepers are going as well, you may even be able to afford the luxury the Americans give themselves of bringing all the electronic gear by Hercules aircraft. If there were any special "Pilgrim" missions at the time of the Gulf War, that would be another good example. "No point worrying about all those things we used to torture our brains with," says Frost. "There was a war going on."

CSE had hired two people, an engineer and a computer expert, to look specifically at building a "quick-response" capability just before Frost's departure. NSA had developed such a team at College Park, and the Canadians wanted to follow suit. Frost remembers O'Brien telling him: "'Sooner or later, you're going to need it. . . .' We wanted to have not only equipment but people ready to go within a matter of a couple of hours. I believe CSE has achieved that capability now because everyone was adamant about it."

What has made that possible technologically, Frost assumes, is the certainty that CSE is now into digital recording, instead of using analogue magnetic tape. Digital is more reliable, has higher fidelity, and also turns out to be less expensive, more resistent, easier to carry. "You just stick it in an envelope and mail it. You don't even have to rewind the tape."

Hand in hand with those developments comes the improvement in the reporting capability of "Pilgrim". At first, as recounted in this book, it took several days and sometimes weeks of analysis to figure out if there was any useful intelligence emerging from a given intercept. Very early on the "Pilgrim" people realized that this was far too slow a response to justify the cost of their operation. They looked for ways to have their agents abroad communicate more effectively, directly and quickly with headquarters. They decided they needed more on-site analysis and better linguistic training for the operators. "The aim was really a mini-CSE lab on site that would increase not only our support for the ambassador locally, which was a good trade-off for getting him or her on side, but also the speed of our reporting back home."

Even more crucial are satellite communications from the sites back to CSE. There is in fact a huge Telesat satellite dish sitting on the roof of the Heron Road building. It wasn't there four years ago. Frost thinks it is only logical that CSE uses it to communicate with agents around the world, just like the Americans and the British. He assumes that Canadian agents in foreign lands now have the capacity to communicate directly with CSE without having to go through External Affairs when an urgent matter comes up. Perhaps they have even succeeded in doing what NSA does very well, "remote operation". Which would mean they no longer have to risk the lives of their agents by sending them into embassies, but can simply turn on the intercept equipment by satellite and expect the same results. CSE was working on that when he left.

The odds also are that CSE has what is known as "real-time reporting" back to base, via satellite. "Real-time" also means "on-line" — as opposed to "off-line" — encryption: an operator sits down at a keyboard and types up a message to send to the satellite; the message goes through a computer that automatically puts it in code; when the satellite downloads the message to its destination, the message again goes through a computer that decodes it and delivers it in plain language. This is a lot quicker than "off-line", where the operator had to give his text to a cryptographer who typed it up in code, which is also how it was received at the other end before being decoded.

Frost is also convinced that there are now "scrambled voice" communications from the "Pilgrim" sites at CSE. Instead of using teletype or Morse, agents can now just pick up the phone and use the satellite link to talk to headquarters, either to provide crucial intelligence or ask for directions. "It's probably done during normal business hours at the embassy, give or take half an hour or so either way." He doesn't believe that CSE has gone into "land-line" intercept. "Maybe — but I doubt it. Land lines are on the way out, anyway."

What CSE was feverishly working on back in the late eighties, though, was to find ways to deal with the up-and-coming "fibre optics", the wave of the future in communications. In radio communications you use a radiowave carrier, in UHF, VHF or whatever frequency, and modulate the carrier to pass the information. In fibre optics you use an optical device, either a laser diode (LD) or a light-emitting diode (LED — a diode between a semi-conductor with two terminals) to transmit information. Fibre-optic equipment is small, light and uses very little power. Its greatest advantage in general terms is that you can carry much more information over one line, which means increased capacity. In terms of the espionage world, it is also extremely secure because it is difficult to intercept. The initial costs of fibre optics may be high, but they are outweighed by low maintenance costs — another reason for their growing use.

"They are going to be used everywhere in everything," says Frost as he explains why agencies like CSE are so concerned. "With fibre optics you can replace six-inch-wide cables with something as small as an electrical wire and still pass the same amount of information." The problem with intercept is that what you are really trying to catch is a light beam travelling at 186,000 miles a second. So intercept involves cutting off the "light beam" from the receiver. The interceptor can always bounce it back into the line off a "mirror", but at the receiving end it is easy to notice that something has gone wrong since too much time has elapsed between the moment the signal was sent and the moment it arrived. In other words, it took a detour somewhere. What should be a straight line has become a triangle.

"Intercepting with a 'mirror', and then bouncing it back in with as short a time-delay as possible gets very complicated," says Frost. "The closer you can get the 'mirrors' to the beam, the less the time-delay. But that's not easy. There may be a way that they have developed at NSA to take the light beam, absorb the time-delay and somehow fool the receiver into thinking the signal was sent later than he thought. I don't know how they would do it, but I'm sure it can be done."

Another improvement CSE was working on was voice-recognition. Although they have been able for some time to identify a targeted individual's voice by the way he or she pronounces certain letters like "o" and "s" — just as easily as you would recognize a person's fingerprint — CSE wanted to go beyond that. They were looking to eliminate useless traffic. If, say, a "target" whose voice is being caught by intercept says the word "bomb", the magical "Oratory" box will automatically spit out whatever was said. But, as Frost points out, "The target could have been talking about a play that bombed on Broadway! We were looking at ways to refine that by 'key-word' groupings." In the early stages this seemed extremely complex to accomplish. In 1994, however, it was revealed in the press that CSE had contracted a Montreal computer firm to improve its "voice-recognition" capability. Maybe they have since found a way around the problem.

With all their possible or probable sites, with all their new technology, and with the "Cold War" having turned lukewarm, what are "Pilgrim" and its allies after these days?

Frost sees the list of priorities this way:

1. Anything to do with terrorism and drugs, often working in combination. "We were always looking for Carlos, and people like him."

2. Economic intelligence.

3. Immigration intelligence. The New Delhi operation had already shown how much of a concern this was for the Canadian government. In the mid-nineties, with a quota of 250,000 newcomers accepted every year, and the fear of criminals slipping through, it must be very high on CSE's target list.

4. For Canada, anything to do with Quebec separation. "That would be right up there. I wouldn't be surprised if it overshadowed economic or immigration priorities at the moment."

5. Anything to do with nuclear proliferation or military threat.

6. Human rights. "That's always a popular one with our politicians."

7. Anything to do with the environment. "That again always gains a lot of political points. If somebody is killing whales, that sort of thing."

Those would be the priorities of the permanent sites currently manned by "Pilgrim" operators on a daily basis. At any time, however, other issues — perhaps overfishing, a really big issue at the moment for Canada, Europe and the U.S. — might become special tasks for the "Pilgrim" operators. There is no doubt in Frost's mind, for instance, that it was CSE, with its overt intercept stations, that tracked down the two ships Canada impounded in 1994 for catching juvenile fish, although the vessels were outside the 200-mile territorial limit.

Renewed nationalism in Russia and the other republics of the former Soviet Union and the constant state of upheaval and unrest that seems to prevail in those former Communist countries also justifies CSE's continuing interest in what is going on behind what used to be the Iron Curtain. So does economic espionage, with the Russians being suspected — even accused — of "dumping" goods at low prices onto the world market, as they did in the case of nickel, which produced massive lay-offs in Canada's mining industry when the price of the precious metal plummeted.

It is worth remembering that the battle with the Soviet Union served as the principal training ground for most of the agents CSE has in the field at the present time. Although the end of the "Cold War" did douse the flames of enthusiasm of the spycatchers, there is little doubt that the Russian embassy and the agents from the former

U.S.S.R. are still very much the subject of surveillance and that neither the RCMP and CSIS nor their intercept specialists at CSE have any doubt that the KGB and the GRU are still operating in North America under a different name. And since counter-espionage people are trained to be suspicious, "the game" of catching them will go on for some time yet.

Has the staff of CSE increased? All Frost can do is extrapolate from the years of restraint in the eighties when "Pilgrim" never seemed to have a problem. "Some departments at CSE seemed to have budget restraints, but at 'Pilgrim' the problem of money was never raised. We just went out and bought what we needed, got the staff we needed, the extra PYS [Person Years]." When Frost looks at the parking lot of CSE today, he doesn't see an increase in cars. But that doesn't mean the number of employees has been reduced, because in his final years there access to the parking lot had been drastically reduced to senior personnel. There is also that huge new expansion in the back that looks like a gigantic cinder block. Somebody has to be working there. . . .

But Mike Frost is not supposed to brood about such things in retirement. For him, that world has gone forever. There are not supposed to be any worries on a Florida golf course. . . .

Mike slices his iron shot into the trees. Damn. It's always the smallest things that go wrong.

EPILOGUE

TO MIKE FROST'S GREAT SURPRISE, the writing of this book, the long and numerous talks we had, the arguments, the blow-ups and the laughter at sharing our experiences, the clash in our drastically different backgrounds, became an unexpected exercise in soul-searching and a cleansing of sorts. As we progressed, he began to realize that, for all the sacrifices he had made, perhaps the people who had paid the heaviest price were the members of his family, his wife Carole and his three sons, Tony, Danny and David.

This and other reflections brought him to the conclusion that certain things have to be improved, or even drastically changed, within the "Pilgrim" organization if it continues in the orientation it seems to have taken. Paramount to him is the necessity to provide some sort of professional counselling for the families of CSE employees, especially the people in the field. "I never realized how high a price I had asked my family to pay. I would ask Carole to lie, I would ask my kids to lie, I would ask them not to say where I was going when I was travelling abroad. . . . And I remember Dave asking me: 'Well, Dad, when *I* tell you I've been somewhere and it's not true, you punish me.' " Frost had no answer for that. But he does believe that CSE should have some form of counselling for children, especially as they become old enough to understand some of the things that are going on. He feels the same need for counselling applies to the spouses. "Carole knew where I was going, but she had to go through so many channels to get to me when I was overseas, it wasn't worth it. She didn't even know what hotel I was staying at."

Frost would also recommend regular psychiatric evaluations of "Pilgrim" agents to try to isolate the potential problems they may have. "In my case, I nearly lost it," he admits.

NSA does this. Whenever an agent returns from a special assignment he or she is assessed psychiatrically to see if there is anything that should be considered and handled with care. Mind you, NSA also imposes polygraph tests on its employees and it used to be one of their main complaints that Canadians could walk through the agency without having had to go through one. As history has shown, though, that didn't prevent NSA from being infiltrated by "moles" or betrayed by their own agents.

Frost is more concerned, however, about the welfare of the agents in the field. He knows of at least two suicides at CSE, and a lot of "strange deaths": people dying of heart attacks, sitting at their desks, or in a stairwell, or eating breakfast, none of them with a previous history of heart trouble. "I've seen so many deaths that to me it says something about the stress of the job and the lack of counselling that people get there. One reason why the stress was so intense was that you simply had no release for it, except by going to a gym and beating that shit out of a punching bag. You couldn't discuss things even with people in CSE itself, never mind with your friends and family."

Another result of such secrecy is what he describes as an "astronomical" number of marriage breakdowns that he believes would beat any national average anywhere, and a large number of love affairs going on between CSE employees. "If you work with a given person at a desk and you can share with her something you can't share with your spouse, you've already developed a bond with her that you don't have with your spouse."

Another improvement Frost would like to recommend is some way to provide extra pay for those who go beyond the call of duty, as the "Pilgrim" people did time and time again. "For all the stuff Frank Bowman and all those brave guys did, for all the sacrifices their families made, there wasn't a cent of extra pay."

Finally, there is the thorny question of whether embassy staff should be told that a potentially dangerous intercept operation is going on where they are being posted. Frost still believes you can't hold a general meeting of the staff and tell them what's going on. But perhaps Canadians posted abroad should be told that there is a chance that embassy collection is being done from their place of work, something American and British diplomats are fully aware of. At least they could then make a more enlightened decision about whether they want to take the risk or not. "I hope this book brings that out."

No one can attest to the impact of a spy's life on one of his children better than Frost's second son, Danny, who agreed to share his thoughts freely about his father's career and how it affected him. His testimony is both revealing and touching about what it's like to be the son of a spy or, as he likes to call his dad, "a spook — because a spook may be doing something wrong but for all the right reasons, whereas a spy does it for all the wrong ones."

Danny remembers how he couldn't tell anybody in school, including his teachers, what his father did for a living. "I would have to say that he worked for the government, but that I wasn't allowed to talk about it." Growing up as a child, to a certain extent he found it "somewhat neat, because it kind of set me apart from the other kids" to know that his father was doing something so secretive nobody could know about it but him. (Although he didn't know much, over the years Danny did piece the puzzle together quite accurately.) He remembers once when his older brother Tony wrote down on a school form that asked for the father's occupation: "Spy." "Dad got a call from a befuddled teacher and had to make up another of his stories."

As the three sons got older, their father handed them a set of answers that they were to give to any questions relating to their father's occupation. "First, we were simply to say that he was a civil servant. If they pressed further, we'd say he worked for the National Research Council or later, when CSE came under that umbrella, for the Defence Department. If they pressed any further, we'd say he was a communications officer for the Security Establishment. And if they asked more questions, we had to shut up and report it to Dad."

"Neat" as the deception may have been at first, Danny's attitude changed drastically at some point in his childhood. "I eventually developed a deep resentment toward Dad, very early on. Mostly because he was this man who would show up once in a while. . . . I had taken on the role fairly young that I was the man of the house when he wasn't around. So when he came home, he was taking over my job and I didn't really like that. I'd feel like: Who is this man?"

Then came the "bad boy" days of adolescence when he was told by "this man" that he couldn't do certain things or go out with a certain kind of people. "So, of course, I did everything that I wasn't supposed to do. You're not supposed to do drugs, get into crime or hang out with the kind of people I was hanging out with . . . I really felt, as I grew up, that I was very much a prisoner of Dad's regimen, so I did everything I could to break out of that confinement."

"I'm still resentful now," he says at the age of thirty. "But at least I know where the resentment is coming from. I had a lot of hostility and anger toward him, but I didn't really know why. I also know now that, all in all, he will never be different. His whole life was to know what was going on at any give time. . . . So I get a phone call now and he asks me: 'Who was it?' I tell him: 'The call wasn't for you, Dad!' "

He doesn't question the love his father has for him, or that his father's reasons for being interested in his activities are not good ones. "If I had had his upbringing, and had been pigeon-holed into a job where everything was regimented, everything had its little box. . . you can't just turn it off."

Danny admits he is very much a "Mama's boy", in that he takes his mother's side in any parental confrontation. "I know my father loves Mom very much, but the way he treated her, mostly because of his job, sometimes pisses me off. Like even today my mom likes to travel, but he won't do it because he's travelled too much."

His father was gone a lot. But, as Danny says, "Even when he was home, he was gone a lot. I remember him being around. . . . But I don't have memories of us playing football, throwing a ball around, stuff like normal kids do . . . only one memory of him once taking me out to teach me how to play baseball. We did go out on the boat, but there were mostly adults around and they'd leave us kids to do other things. . . . I don't remember ever going fishing with my dad. Most of this stuff I did with my uncles, on my mother's side. One taught me how to skeet-shoot and fish, another taught me carpentry. They were the ones who were always around. Dad was in Alert or somewhere else.

"I know he feels a lot of regret for not having been there as much as he thinks he should have been, but, all in all, I don't begrudge him for that. And I can tell him, and I know, that he did the best job he was capable of doing."

Danny is also grateful for the experiences he had that other kids didn't, like living in Inuvik for a while. But mostly Danny is thankful for the passion for reading about and following international politics that his father inspired in him. In an age when fewer and fewer people read, he is still an avid bookworm, and he attributes that largely to conversations he overheard his father have about how important certain world events were.

"I knew well before anybody else, for instance, that when the hostage crisis was going on in Iran, Canada had Americans in the Canadian embassy and we were trying to get them out. Now that's information that's hard to keep to yourself! Another thing I got from my father was a very strong sense of loyalty to this country. His loyalty is so great that when they brought over those Russian cars, Ladas, to Canada, Mom and Dad went out to try one. After they returned, he said: 'I just can't start sending money over to Russia after spending my entire life trying to fight communism!' "

For all his resentments, probably Danny's biggest complaint is about the way CSE treated his father in his final days there. "I knew when they sent somebody out to pick him up at the boat and bring him to Detox, they weren't doing it out of loyalty. They just didn't want one of their employees drunk and going through a nervous breakdown on the loose in Ottawa. It was to cover their own asses, not to help him."

Danny Frost feels that, when it comes to telling right from wrong — not in a basic sense, but as far as society sees it or writes it in books of laws and edicts — he lost his virginity at a very young age, and still has to live with the cynicism that created.

Acronyms and Abbreviations

BRLO	British Liaison Officer
BZ	Bravo Zulu
	• used for personal congratulations of the highest order — a job very well done
CANSLO	Canadian Senior Liaison Officer
CANUKUS	Canada, United Kingdom and United States (intelligence-sharing agreement)
CBNRC	Communications Branch of the National Research Council (Canada)
	• now CSE
CFSRS	Canadian Forces Supplementary Radio System
CIDA	Canadian International Development Agency
COMINT	Communications Intelligence
	• intelligence obtained by intercepting, processing and analysing electromagnetic communications transmissions from any source, e.g. plain-language teletype
COMSEC	Communications Security
	• the monitoring of a country's own communications to detect compromising or unwanted radiation
CSE	Communications Security Establishment (Canada)
	• located in Ottawa
	• formerly CBNRC
DF	Direction Finding
DSD	Defence Signals Division (Australia)
	• Australian SIGINT headquarters — sometimes called Defence Signals Directorate

ELINT	Electronic Intelligence
	•intelligence obtained by intercepting, processing and analysing electromagnetic non-communications transmissions from any source, e.g. radar
FDM	Frequency Division Multiplex
GCHQ	Government Communications Headquarters (U.K.)
	•located near Cheltenham, England
GRU	Chief Intelligence Directorate of the Soviet General Staff (U.S.S.R.)
	•*"Glavnoye Razvedyvatelnoye Upravleniye"*
KGB	Committee for State Security (U.S.S.R.)
	•*"Komitet Gosudarstvennoy Bezopasnosti"*
LRTS	Long Range Technical Search
	•now SIGDEV
MI5	British Domestic Intelligence Organization
MI6	British External Intelligence Organization
NACSI	NATO Advisory Committee for Special Intelligence
NSA	National Security Agency (U.S.)
	•located at Fort Meade, Maryland
OTP	One-Time-Pad
	•used to hand-encrypt and decrypt messages
PSAC	Public Service Alliance of Canada
PTT	Post, Telephone and Telegraph
RFI	Radio Frequency Interference
SIGDASYS	Signals Intelligence Data System
SIGDEV	Signals Development
	•was LRTS
SIGINT	Signals Intelligence
	•intelligence obtained by intercepting, processing and analysing radio transmissions of any type from any source
	•SIGINT includes COMINT, ELINT and TELINT (*q.v.*)
SUKLO	Senior United Kingdom Liaison Officer
SUSLO	Senior United States Liaison Officer

TDM	Time Division Multiplex
TELINT	Telemetry Intelligence
	•intelligence obtained by intercepting, processing and analysing electromagnetic telemetry transmissions from any source, usually satellites
TEXTA	Technical Extracts from Traffic Analysis
	•used to identify and catalogue intercepted signals

FREQUENCIES

ELF	Extra Low Frequency — below 3kHz
LF	Low Frequency — 3kHz to 300kHz
MF	Medium Frequency — 300kHz to 3MHz
HF	High Frequency — 3MHz to 30MHz
VHF	Very High Frequency — 30MHz to 300MHz
UHF	Ultra High Frequency — 300MHz to 3000MHz
SHF	Super High Frequency — 3000MHz to 3GHz

GLOSSARY

Amherst
GRU satellite system

Broadside
Code name for American intercept operation in Moscow

Capricorn
RCMP monitoring of CN-CP Telecommunications in/out of Soviet Embassy, Ottawa

Counter-espionage
Any and all operations aimed at penetrating foreign intelligence agencies or activities

Fibre Optics
Optic oscillators such as laser diodes and light-emitting diodes are used to carry information. Their advantages over radio communications include increased capacity, reliability and security. Initial costs are considered high but are compensated by low maintenance costs.

Gamma
Used in the classification caveat to indicate U.S.S.R. intercept considered to be of the utmost importance. Also used to indicate intercepted conversations of targeted American nationals.

Gorizont   Soviet Tropospheric Scatter Communications System

Guppy   Used in the classification caveat to indicate intercepted conversations of top U.S.S.R. officials, e.g. from car phones

Ionosphere   A section of the atmosphere 80-400 km above the earth's surface that bends or refracts radio waves back to earth

Keyhole   U.S. spy satellite

Kilderkin   CSE site used to monitor electronic emissions from Soviet Embassy, Ottawa

Mole   Infiltrator of an intelligence or espionage organization

Pilgrim   The interception, processing, analysis and reporting of intelligence obtained by the collection of electronic emissions at Canadian embassies and chancelleries abroad

PILGRIM CODE NAMES:

Artichoke Caracas, Venezuela

Badger Beijing, China

Cornflower Mexico City, Mexico

Daisy	New Delhi, India
Egret	Kingston, Jamaica
Hollyhock	Bucharest, Romania
Iris	Rabat, Morocco
Jasmine	Abidjan, Ivory Coast
Julie	Feasibility study for Project Pilgrim
Sphinx	Moscow, U.S.S.R.
Stephanie	First embassy collection, Moscow, U.S.S.R.

Reflection	The changing of a radio wave's direction, as from a polished surface
Refraction	The bending of radio waves from one direction to another
Spoke	Used with the classification "SECRET" to indicate a limited degree of sensitivity
Talent	U.S. spy satellite
Troposphere	A section of the atmosphere between the ionosphere and the earth's surface that reflects radio waves back to earth

Tryst   Code name for British intercept operation
                             in Moscow

Umbra   Used with the classification "TOP
                             SECRET" to indicate a high degree of sen-
                             sitivity

Yanina-Uranium   KGB satellite system

INDEX